PEACE WARRIOR

MERCER
UNIVERSITY PRESS

Endowed by
TOM WATSON BROWN
and
THE WATSON-BROWN FOUNDATION, INC.

PEACE WARRIOR

A Memoir from the Front

Daniel L. Buttry

MERCER UNIVERSITY PRESS
MACON, GEORGIA

MUP/ P455

© 2012 Mercer University Press
1400 Coleman Avenue
Macon, Georgia 31207

First Edition

Books published by Mercer University Press are printed on acid-free paper
that meets the requirements of the American National Standard for
Information Sciences—Permanence of Paper for Printed Library Materials.

Mercer University Press is a member of Green Press Initiative
(greenpressinitiative.org), a nonprofit organization working to help
publishers and printers increase their use of recycled paper and decrease
their use of fiber derived from endangered forests. This book is printed on
recycled paper.
ISBN   978-0-88146-400-9
Cataloging-in-Publication Data is available from the Library of Congress

This book is dedicated to

Sharon Buttry,
my true comrade in loving arms,

beside whom I have been honored
to struggle,
from whom I have learned,
and with whom I have dreamed.

CONTENTS

INTRODUCTION

The year 1998 was a significant year for my sense of identity. I was nearing my fifties and serving as the co-pastor of First Baptist Church in Dearborn, Michigan. I was also working part-time with the Baptist Peace Fellowship of North America doing global peacemaking. In that capacity I took my first trip to Nagaland in Northeast India, a key step in a journey of peacemaking that would last fifteen years (and counting). I was part of negotiations with Naga leaders that turned a potentially violent election into a massive nonviolent civil disobedience campaign. It was also the year that I saw *Saving Private Ryan*.

Why was I so deeply moved by *Saving Private Ryan*? I went to see it by myself as I knew my wife Sharon did not care for war movies. I was weeping and deeply shaken by this film, and long after I came home I reflected on my feelings and the roots from which they had come. I had lived two lives that had seemed contradictory to me: One growing up as a military child with warrior heroes, the other as a peace activist. While eschewing violence and its terrible toll, I was still attracted to something in military culture. There was a deep aspect to my identity in that culture that I could not deny despite my protests of war and my actions for peace. The shaking in my soul at the movie theater brought me to an identity crisis.

I felt the crisis on two levels. There was the public level of my nearly thirty years of peace activism, which seemed to deny my heritage growing up. There was also a family level to the crisis not framed in issues of violence or nonviolence but in terms of the value we put on individual human lives. I was experiencing the long-term stress of dealing with a loved one who was mentally ill and witnessing the tremendous price paid by everyone around that person. Just as the soldiers in the movie questioned the value of trying to save one person, I was forced to ask that same question. There is a moral math that doesn't calculate very well: Why risk the lives of eight soldiers to save one? Why risk damage to the lives around this one hurting—and hurtful—person to try to salvage that single, tormented soul?

As I followed the entwined strands of my feelings and reflected on what the movie had stimulated within me, I realized that I have the heart of a warrior. The warrior heart is not eager for violence nor does it glory in the struggle. The warrior in me and in many of my role models (and in the Tom Hanks character in the movie) have hearts willing to sacrifice their lives for the sake of others' lives. There is a greater love of life for others and for one's community that transcends love for one's own life. The warrior is committed to defend that life at the cost of one's own if necessary.

That struggle was in my heart and bones, both professionally and personally. I was living it out in my closest relationships and in my work around the world. I had turned from violence to embrace the tactics, the values, and the philosophy of nonviolence in response to a new commander in my life: Jesus Christ. These reflections ultimately brought me to a point of peace as I realized I was a *nonviolent warrior for peace*. The warrior in me was not inconsistent with nonviolence as the means and peace as the end. Instead the warrior was redeemed, transfigured, and released for renewed action. Each life was valuable, and I could spend my life in the nonviolent struggle for a future and a human community that valued each of those lives. The two parts of my past were melded together in a burst of joyous motivational energy for the next chapters of the story. That is the story of this book.

It seems presumptuous of me to write a book of memoirs. Why do I assume anyone would want to read about my life and work? Certainly there are people who have done far more significant work in the field of peacemaking, and I've written about many of them in *Blessed Are the Peacemakers* (Read the Spirit, 2011). In each aspect of my work—as a local activist, national religious staff person, mediator with armed groups, trainer in conflict transformation, nonviolent strategist, or interfaith bridge-builder—I have worked alongside people whom I felt were more important to the particular project and who acted with more courage or displayed greater creativity than I ever did. For each area of my work there were and continue to be people I admire and from whom I learn. I especially respect and honor those who work tirelessly within one particular country or conflict situation and go much deeper that I ever have gone or can go. I don't want to tell my story to try to overshadow their contributions to the cause of making peace and building justice. I hope that some of their stories will be told along with mine, for in many cases this might be the only opportunity that their noble and courageous efforts will be made known outside their own contexts.

At times I've felt like the fictional Forrest Gump (also played by Tom Hanks), a person who just happened to be at the right place at the right time when history was being made. I have touched many struggles, sometimes making just a minor contribution and at other times playing a more significant role. Even when my role was small, I witnessed important events and the acts of special people. In two cases, the negotiations in Burma and the peace efforts among the Nagas, there is historical value in telling what I have experienced. The whole story of those episodes cannot be told without a clear account from someone close to my vantage point.

As I have read articles or histories of events of which I was a part, I have often said, "That's not all that happened!" or "I wouldn't tell it with that slant." I'm sure that others with direct experience who read my version of these events will have similar thoughts. Sometimes I added up various elements in a certain context to arrive at a different sum than another person in that same context might have reached. I have sought to be as accurate as possible, neither downplaying nor expanding my role in any situation, and to be fair to those who had different perspectives and responsibilities. The full truth will need other stories added into the mix beyond my story.

So I offer this memoir humbly aware of and thankful for the community of people who produced me, the cloud of witnesses who inspired me, the comrades and companions along the way, and the rising generation that perhaps will correct the mistakes and build on our accomplishments. I thank my wife, Sharon, for her love, support, encouragement, critique, forgiveness, challenge, and grace. She has a large measure of that peace warrior spirit in her as well, and I can think of no better companion for this journey.

I thank Sharon, Harriet Buttry, Ken Sehested, Daniel Hunter, David Ortopan, Frank McAuley, Reid Trulson, and George Lakey for reading the manuscript and making suggestions. I thank my friends in the United Kingdom for their guidance and support. These friends have made this work better, though any remaining shortcomings are mine alone. For my colleagues and companions in work and in various struggles, I give thanks for your work, your witness, your dedication, and your faith. Where I have told a part of your story I hope I honored you well. You have bigger stories of which I am a small part. I thank those who have prayed for me over the years; certainly much of what has been accomplished could only have happened with God's anointing grace. I hope the telling of my tale will give blessing, guidance, and insight to any who read it.

1

MAKING OF A PEACE WARRIOR

Childhood: Onward, Christian Soldier

I grew up in a Christian military family. My father was a chaplain in the U.S. Air Force, which necessitated that our family move frequently. Dad followed Uncle Sam's call, and we tagged along with him to New York, Alabama, back to New York, Florida, England, Utah, Japan, and Ohio, where Dad retired from the military service. I grew up with military personnel as my Sunday school teachers, my Boy Scout leaders, the people I saw every day. I even knew the loss of life that could strike military families: The husband of one of my Sunday school teachers and the father of a classmate both went down in a cargo plane that disappeared over the Pacific when I was an eleven-year-old in Utah. I never met the father of the girl I took to the prom because he was flying missions over Vietnam.

That's what I wanted to do—fly those planes over enemy territory. My heroes were fighter pilots: Eddie Rickenbacker, the top U.S. ace in World War I who flew with his "Hat in the Ring" squadron; the Flying Tigers in China; "Pappy" Boyington and the Black Sheep Squadron; and Richard Bong, who flew his P-38 against the Japanese and notched forty kills. My dad served with a B-17 group flying out of England in World War II. We used to rush home from the base chapel on Sunday evenings to watch *Twelve O'clock High* on television, and I dreamed of flying with General Frank Savage on bombing runs against the dreaded Nazis.

As I learned to read I focused on books about the U.S. wars. I eventually owned more than a hundred books on World War II alone, reading that was amply supplemented by visits to the base library to get a book on this battle or that campaign. In high school I began writing my own multi-chaptered stories of heroic fighter pilots and American prisoners-of-war trying to escape. As I went through the existential anxieties of mid-teens my stories grew darker. I wrote about a wounded German soldier freezing to death behind Russian lines. Trying to impress her with my cool composition, I even showed that story to Sharon Crader the first time I was alone with her during my senior year in high school.

One of my best friends went to West Point. I had hoped to go to the Air Force Academy, but my eyes were too near-sighted for me to be accepted. By the time I reached the point of choosing my college and career direction, I had come to understand the role of other figures in the wars besides the men who flew the fighters, drove the tanks, and fired the guns. I began to understand politics. The gruff, cigar-smoking Winston Churchill who stood up to the Nazi onslaught during the Battle of Britain and offered his people "blood, toil, tears, and sweat" became a new kind of hero to me. It was the late '60s, and I could be a political warrior, noble in a field that was becoming tarnished as the Kennedy-era idealism was eroded by the war in Vietnam and by the "credibility gap" of the Johnson and Nixon administrations. When I was given a college scholarship by the Officers' Wives Club on our airbase, with all the embarrassing hubris of youth I told them I wanted to be a senator, "a statesman, not a politician."

Under the bluster of wartime exploits, hero-worship, and dreams of glory and grandeur, my warrior role models, both living and in books and movies, were establishing important foundational values in my heart. One of those foundational values was the importance of sacrifice. Anyone who joins the military knows that one's own life can be put on the line at any time. Soldiers know that if they are ordered into combat, many of them will die, and they bravely move into deadly situations. Perhaps the paradigmatic sacrifice was the soldier who threw himself on a grenade to save his comrades, the selfless act of a number of soldiers, which would inevitably be recognized with the Congressional Medal of Honor. Jesus said, "No one has greater love than this, to lay down one's life for one's friends" (John 15:13 NRSV). I grew up on the stories of people who practiced that love for their buddies beside them as well as for family and home far away.

I also learned the value of striving for a cause that was worth paying a high price to support. Every war I read about had the noble values of freedom and liberty woven through it. Good people and good nations like ours did not engage in violence for power or conquest; that was what the bad guys such as Hitler and Tojo did. We always had values that transcended the horrors of the war. We fought to set people free, whether blacks enslaved in the South, or the occupied countries in Europe and Asia, or Jewish victims in concentration camps. We don't live for crass selfishness, but rather we spend our time, our effort, and if need be, our blood, on a high cause.

I learned to value courage in myself and in others. I didn't need to be fearless. Many of my heroes were afraid, but acted through their fear to do what they believed needed to be done. A time comes to all of us when the struggle rolls our way, when it is our time to stand on the stage of history. People of courage respond to that moment so as to turn the tide, or, if they don't succeed, to be an inspiration for future generations by their courageous and noble sacrifice.

Besides these warrior values imbued from my military childhood, I also learned leadership. Whoever I might be, from private to general, I had to be responsible for myself, for my men, and for those depending on me to protect them. I couldn't step back from my responsibility; rather I had to seize it with commitment and competence. Perhaps I might feel overwhelmed by the challenge, perhaps I might be torn by uncertainties, but when the challenge is before me as a leader I must act as best as I can.

In war officers can get killed, requiring lower ranking soldiers to take the responsibilities of leadership suddenly thrust upon them. I experienced this sudden rise to leadership in Boy Scouts. When we lived in Utah I was in a large troop with many high-ranking scouts. I had reached the rank of Star, two ranks below Eagle. In that leader-laden Utah troop I was a mere assistant patrol leader. When we moved to the tiny air station at Wakkanai, Japan, suddenly I found myself the highest-ranking scout. I was named senior patrol leader, the top scout for the entire troop. Having had so little experience, I balked at such a high level of group leadership, but the encouragement and support of the young airmen who were our scoutmasters helped me step up to the task and discover and develop my own leadership gifts. They had been trained in responsibility and leadership, and they passed those values and skills on to me, evidenced first in scouting and then later throughout my peacemaking work.

A Child of the World

I was raised as a child of the world. I came by that global perspective almost genetically, as my parents were global people from two different perspectives: as mission-minded Christians and as a military family. While they were students at Wheaton College, my mother and father seriously considered becoming missionaries to Brazil, until they believed God was leading my father into military chaplaincy. That missionary passion never left them, informing the shape of ministry they had within the military.

One of my earliest memories was global in nature. When I was four years old, my father brought a missionary to visit our home in Florida. Dick Reed was a missionary to Liberia with radio station ELWA. My father provided hospitality at our house and had invited him to be a guest speaker for the base chapel. Somehow Dick Reed's visit made a lasting impression on my young mind. Maybe it was his descriptions of a place and people far from my limited experience. Whatever it was that seized my attention, the missionary, Liberia, and the radio station were etched into my memory. Years later the first country I visited in Africa was Liberia, where I witnessed the devastation of the civil war in which the ELWA station had been destroyed.

Twice we lived outside the U.S. When I was almost five years old, our family relocated to England where Dad was the chaplain at the small Chicksands Air Station. There was no base housing for families, so we rented a home in the village of Flitwick. I attended the local school where for two years I was the only American student (until my younger brother joined me). I sang "God Save the Queen" each morning, learned British history, and fought British boys over my boast that we had beaten them in a war. Like the colonial Yanks, I didn't fight "fair." The boys would square up with their fists in proper British fashion while I would get down and dirty, punching them straight in the nose. When we were hauled off to the headmaster's office, my view of history was vindicated, which didn't do much to stunt my American arrogance.

Our second overseas assignment, just as I entered my teenage years, was life changing. We were stationed in Wakkanai, Japan, a tiny radar outpost on the northern tip of the northern island of Hokkaido. On clear days, just across the straits we could see the Russian-held island of Sakhalin. I played on the beaches where, years later, the debris would wash ashore from Korean Air Flight 007, shot down by Russian fighter jets. The frantic radio transmissions of that tragedy were picked up by the Wakkanai station. Our base was on the front line of the Cold War.

In Japan I was introduced to a totally different culture. There were fewer than a thousand Americans on the base, including dependents, so we had easy access to the fishing town that was quite alien to everything I'd ever known. My friends and I could hop on a bus and go downtown to buy model airplane kits from Japanese stores, trying out our rudimentary Japanese phrases. There were only a handful of high school students—I had eight classmates in the ninth grade. Our senior class had one student the first year and two the second year we were there. Every year we went to visit Japanese students in school English clubs in other cities, staying overnight in the students' homes. I remember especially going to the city of Asahigawa in central Hokkaido, staying in a small wooden house with rice-straw mat floors, and rolling out the bedding each night. We walked to the bus stop on the hard-packed, snow-covered streets. I loved being in Japan.

I discovered the "ugly American" in Japan, which awakened my consciousness of cross-cultural issues and the ways we carry ourselves in a different country. On one of the train trips in which students from our school went on a major outing, some of my classmates procured some beer and became loud and obnoxious. The Japanese passengers in the train car were quiet and looked at us with disdain, but they were too polite to challenge their international guests about their rudeness. Though I looked like the classic bookwormish nerd, I stood up and exploded at my classmates. I excoriated them for their behavior, saying they were making me ashamed to be an American. We represented our country here and should carry ourselves with dignity, respecting the people whose land we were visiting. I almost never got angry, certainly not in public, and this outburst quieted everyone down for the rest of the trip. My awareness had transcended my own culture, allowed me to empathize to some degree with people from another culture, and to see with shame the domineering, arrogant, and crass way that so many of my fellow citizens treated people from other parts of the world.

My parents showed me a different example of cross-cultural behavior, beginning with how they dealt with diversity within our own national context. In the interracial mix of the U.S. military in the 1960s my parents modeled the celebration of diversity. We had people of different races in leadership in the base chapel programs and as guests in our home. One of my mother's proud moments was overhearing me argue over issues of race with my Mormon best friend while we lived in Utah. I was in fifth or sixth grade, but already I had learned from my parents the value of all people no matter our differences. I had also developed the courage to speak out and challenge forms of bigotry.

When we moved to Japan, my parents showed on an international stage their openness to all people. Before we moved Mom had us kids studying Japan and even learning a few Japanese phrases. When we arrived at our new assignment, my mother was involved in cross-cultural activities with U.S. and Japanese women, sometimes confronting the narrowness and superiority of her countrywomen in the face of the gracious and courteous actions of the Japanese women. Dad could make us laugh at some of his cross-cultural blunders, such as talking louder in English while trying to order food at a Japanese restaurant as if volume would solve the language problem. But Dad also built a deep partnership in mission with a Japanese Anglican pastor. They were like brothers in ministry, the Japanese pastor as the visionary and my dad as the nuts-and-bolts (or hammer-and-scrounged-building-supplies) guy who would turn the dreams into reality. They were a model of love, respect, and teamwork, building first a milk bar to serve high school students who had no place to hang out and then a girls' dormitory for students commuting from the rural areas. I helped in some of their building projects, which gave me the opportunity to witness up-close a cross-cultural partnership that was dynamic and made an impact in the world.

First Stirrings of Activism

The first stirrings of activism developed in my senior year of high school in Reynoldsburg, Ohio. Environmental concerns were being intensely discussed in the media and in our school. One of my friends, Scott Simeral, and I formed an ecology club we called Concerned Citizens for a Clean Environment. Beginning in early spring, we organized students to pick up litter around the town each Saturday morning.

Scott and I built a coffin in my garage to help educate the citizens of Reynoldsburg about what we were doing and why. Where the head would be in the coffin we cut out a hole and put in a mirror. We painted the coffin black, and in lurid red letters wrote: "For pollution or you?" While student cleanup crews were scouring the town with trash bags we had a small team with the coffin at the main shopping center passing out leaflets about environmental issues and identifying our school group (but hopefully not creating too much more trash!). We would also go into local businesses that were dumping trash behind their stores, such as the piles of burned-out florescent light tubes we found along one back alley. We confronted the owners with what we had found and demanded that they properly dispose of their trash. It created quite a stir when a number of determined students came into a store demanding to see the manager! Our efforts paid off as the back-lot dumps were quickly cleaned up.

Scott and I worked with our science teachers to sponsor after-school "teach-ins" on environmentalism. The main event that spring was the first-ever observance of Earth Day. We organized a delegation from our high school to go to the campus of Ohio State University to participate in their special education events. We felt we were on the cutting edge of a movement to make our world a better place.

The first demonstration I ever participated in was one I organized. Scott and I felt we had to end our weekly trash pick-ups with a special action. As seniors we would not be back at the school, but we wanted to be sure that the work of our ecology club would stick in people's memory and perhaps be continued the next year. We gathered at the high school on the last Saturday before graduation and marched about a mile to the town library on Main Street at the central shopping strip-mall. At the head of the march was a student carrying the American flag, followed by pallbearers carrying our coffin. The rest of us followed in single file in silence, carrying bags of trash. A local television news team taped the whole event.

When we got to the library we gave a few short speeches then took axes and chopped up the coffin. In our teenage minds, hacking up the coffin was a powerful symbol of our attack on pollution, though it sure made another mess! Then we solemnly picked up the pieces of the smashed coffin along with bags of trash we had gathered earlier in the morning and marched down the street to city hall. We deposited all the rubbish on the front steps with a call for a more serious commitment by our local government to environmental clean up and policing.

After graduation I left Reynoldsburg and lost touch with my high school friends. For me, however, the imprint of that initial teenage activism was lasting. The commitment to ecological responsibility has remained both in big and small ways; I frequently stop to pick up bits of litter wherever I walk, and I always recycle. More significantly, the combination of education, public witness, and nonviolent protest actions was to shape the work I would do in many other issues from hunger to nuclear war to racial violence. I knew from experience that I could organize people to take collective action about an issue of importance.

Conversions in College

During my freshman year at Wheaton College in Illinois I reached two turning points in my life. These conversions would become the polar stars guiding my course in the years ahead.

The first conversion was a commitment to Jesus Christ. I had been raised in a Christian family. I had been nurtured in a grace-filled context that made it easy to recognize the grace of God, and I knew plenty about the teachings of Christianity. But as a child of strong Christian parents, especially of parents involved in ministry, I needed to separate my own faith from the faith of my parents. During my last two years of high school I went through a typical adolescent time of soul-searching, not so much rejecting the faith of my parents as trying to find a faith that was truly my own. I was living in a nation in turmoil: The U.S. of the late 1960s, at war in Vietnam, with riots in our cities, demonstrations on our campuses, students shot down by National Guardsmen, and leaders being assassinated. I was very patriotic on the surface, even giving an address at graduation in 1970 that included the trite words, "America, love it or leave it!" Still, I was adrift and struggling, facing issues about death and the meaning of life in a confusing world. I chose to attend my parents' *alma mater*, Wheaton College, located just outside Chicago, specifically because it was a Christian school. I desperately wanted to find the answers to the questions that were plaguing me about faith, God, and living in a worthwhile way in the real world.

One autumn night following special chapel services, I committed myself to the living Christ, sitting with a friend on the chapel steps. From that point on my life was not to be my own but was to be given over to God. I was a follower of Jesus, whatever that might mean. I was soon to discover that such a commitment could shake up what I had once thought was nailed down and certain.

Shortly after I made my decision to follow Jesus, I joined a small group of friends who did everything together. We sat together at the dining hall. We got up before breakfast each morning to sing praise songs and pray. We worshipped together at a local Assembly of God church that would accept us as "Jesus freaks" with our long hair, patched-up blue jeans, and love of rock music. We went to Jesus rock festivals together. We would go to Chicago's O'Hare Airport to talk about Christ with passengers waiting in the terminal in those innocent days before tight airport security. We presented "The Four Spiritual Laws," an evangelistic booklet put out by Campus Crusade for Christ, urging people to "ask Jesus into their hearts" and put Jesus on the "throne of their lives." But I was the one about to discover what it really meant to let Jesus take control of the core of one's being.

Christie Colao was a central member of our gang of friends, and during dinner in the dining hall one evening we began to argue about the war in Vietnam. I argued that the Christian position about war was the "just war" position, hearkening to the long-established tradition of justifying wars fought for a "just cause" under "just authority" and by "just means." Furthermore, I said, the U.S. involvement in Vietnam was a just war because we were protecting the Vietnamese from atheistic Communists who were invading to take away their freedom. I was on the debate team in high school, and I could argue circles around her. But Christie had one simple question that pierced through all my reasoning: "What does Jesus say?" She said, "Dan, you've accepted Jesus Christ as your Lord and Savior. You've committed yourself to follow him. What does Jesus say?" I spewed verbose rationales for war like a squid venting a cloud of ink, but I couldn't hide from that penetrating question: "What does Jesus say?"

Our argument ended inconclusively, but I went back to my dorm room and grabbed my Bible. I poured through the Gospels, reading again and again what Jesus had to say about war and violence. I read, "Blessed are the peacemakers for they shall be called sons of God" (Matt. 5:9 RSV). I read, "Love your enemies and pray for those who persecute you" (Matt. 5:44 RSV). I read, "Would that even today you knew the things that make for peace! But now they are hid from your eyes" (Luke 19:42 RSV). I read from the lips of Jesus as he was being nailed to the cross, "Father, forgive them; for they know not what they do" (Luke 23:34 RSV) I read, "Greater love has no man than this, that a man lay down his life for his friends" (John 15:13 RSV), but this time I saw not the soldier giving his life to save his comrade-in-arms but the nonviolent Jesus sacrificing himself out of transforming love. I read what Jesus said and took it deep into my soul. In keeping with the commitment I had made to follow him I made a decision to follow the ways of peace. It was a one-night, 180-degree turn-around. I had no idea what it might mean. I had no idea of what to do next. I had no idea where this decision would lead.

However, I was still enrolled in ROTC (the Reserve Officer Training Corps). Wheaton College required all freshmen men who were not registered conscientious objectors (COs) to participate in ROTC. That was the only way they would maintain a high enough enrollment in the program to keep it on the campus. Major James Sangster was our professor of military science. He was an African-American officer who had served a tour of duty in Vietnam, and he volunteered to return to Vietnam immediately after our academic year concluded. Major Sangster, however, did some positive things that helped solidify my decision to become a conscientious objector. Beside teaching military science, he taught some of the realities we would be facing. One of our classmates dropped out of ROTC because he had become a CO, so Major Sangster gave him an entire class period to present his paper on conscientious objection. Major Sangster gave no rebuttal, merely introduced the topic saying, "This is another perspective. You need to know it."

Then Major Sangster showed us two films. One was about the beginning of World War I. It showed the political competition that ratcheted up the war preparations. As the war broke out the

11

soldiers from both sides cheerily boarded the troop trains to loving farewells as if they were going on a spring outing. The movie ended with scenes of the human meat-grinder that trench warfare became. Could anything be so utterly worthless and wasteful as this war? The second film was about the atomic bombings of Hiroshima and Nagasaki. It was a government film that focused more on the devastation wrought by the atomic bombs than on the glory of war. It showed horrific pictures of burned civilians with their skin peeling off and medical personnel delicately trying to care for their shredded bodies. I had wanted to fly those bombers, but this was the fruit they bore—gore, not glory; horror, not heroism.

At the end of my ROTC class in spring 1971 I made my decision. I would become a conscientious objector. I wrote in my class evaluation words of appreciation that Major Sangster had been a positive influence on me becoming a conscientious objector. I never had any personal relationship with him, and I doubt that he remembered me as more than a name in the attendance book. But I hope that Major Sangster appreciated my comments because he was a good teacher. I feel better having people like him in the military: people who think, who see complexities, and who are willing to listen to the other side, rather than those who are blind warriors for the cause of nation even if the nation is involved in what is perverse and oppressive. Major Sangster became a hero for me even as I took a path the exact opposite of his.

Before I could register as a conscientious objector, I had one last difficult conversation to hold. I needed to talk with my father. Dad retired from the Air Force in 1970 and took up a pastorate in Shenandoah, Iowa. Shenandoah was in the southwest corner of Iowa, a region that was politically conservative. The town of Glenwood, about twenty minutes away, had a strong chapter of the ultra-conservative John Birch Society that sponsored a large billboard outside of town with the message "Kill a Commie for Christ." Eventually, community uproar resulted in the billboard being changed to read "Win the War" at a time when the rest of the country was trying to find a way out of Vietnam. Southwest

Iowa was the region where my draft board was located and the context in which my Dad ministered.

When I came back from college that summer, Dad and I shut the door to his office for our man-to-man talk. My mother feared that her wonderful family life was about to be torn apart by this war that had torn apart so many other American families. But on the other side of the door a conversation far from what she imagined was unfolding. I told my Dad that I respected and valued his ministry. I said that if having a son register as a CO would harm his ministry, I was willing to register as 1-AO, available for military service but in a non-combatant status such as a medic. It was a cop-out compromise for me, not what I really believed was right but what might be smoother sailing in what I feared would be conflicted waters. Dad peered at me sternly and said, "Don't you ever give up what you believe in your conscience. Stand up for your beliefs, even if it is costly. Don't worry about what I might have to deal with; I can handle that." I knew he disagreed with me, but I also knew he was a person of deep conviction himself. He had counseled many people through issues of conscience. He was also a Baptist who knew what the historic Baptist commitment to "soul liberty" meant. Freedom of conscience was a value and responsibility that was highly cherished and won at a great cost to people who stood up for freedom of religion and conscience in the face of persecution from governments and from state-churches challenged by a prophetic witness and contrary perspectives. My Dad, the retired Air Force lieutenant colonel, gave me the courage, to stand up fully for what I believed in the depths of my being. He was a great father and an outstanding Baptist. We left his office closer than we had ever been in our lives, though we disagreed about the war and the Christian response to it. My old warrior dad demanded of me the guts to take my first concrete step as a peace warrior, and for that I am forever grateful.

I went ahead and applied for CO status as I registered for the draft. I expected difficulties such as those encountered by many who attempted to register as COs, but the draft board in

Southwest Iowa evidently had no trouble reaching their quotas. After just a couple weeks I received notification of my acceptance as a CO with no hearing being needed. That year when the Selective Service conducted the draft lottery to prioritize birthdates for selection in the military draft, the number for my date of birth, 26 September, came up as 344. Because all eighteen-year olds with 343 birthdates before mine would have to be drafted first, a totally unlikely occurrence, I could have simply slid through the rest of my college years confident of never going to Vietnam. However, I was glad that I had wrestled with my convictions, had that conversation with my father, and made a public commitment in the face of a national issue of war and peace.

Justice: Moving beyond Pacifism

I was a very quiet CO; the objections of my conscience didn't get much notice in the world. For me, pacifism was a rather private affair. I stayed out of war and dropped out of ROTC, but that was the end of what pacifism meant to me. I had not studied the rich and varied history of pacifism, so I accepted the stereotype of pacifism being passive, a negative definition of simply refusing to participate in war. Meanwhile I continued to grow in my Christian faith, becoming a Bible major and getting active in various campus Bible studies and ministries such as teaching Sunday school to handicapped children. I had always been a "good kid," and my pacifism became just another facet of that goodness.

After I married Sharon Crader and we graduated from Wheaton College in 1974, Sharon and I moved to Ipswich, Massachusetts, just north of Boston. I enrolled in Gordon-Conwell Theological Seminary. During the mid-1970s a terrible famine struck the sub-Saharan region of Africa known as the Sahel. Sharon and I began conducting hunger workshops for local churches and the community. In the process of preparing those workshops, I did a lot of research on hunger and discovered some facts that revolutionized my worldview and my ethics. I read U.S. Department of State documents that showed that U.S. foreign aid resulted in a net inflow of money into the United States. The aid was not directed to helping the destitute but was directed to opening up foreign markets for U.S. companies to do business. Page after page of statistics showed that our aid served to generate money out of the poor countries to enrich those already wealthy. Despite public pronouncements regarding U.S. generosity, the reality was that our government was not giving aid but making investments.

Furthermore, I discovered that the countries in the Sahel were net exporters of food during the famine. Large landowners were buying up the small farms in the more fertile southern regions of each country to create large agribusiness estates. The poor farmers were forced to move toward the north, toward the desert. That land was more arid and less productive. As more people were forced onto this marginal land, overgrazing by their cattle stimulated desertification. Throw in a drought, and you have a human catastrophe. We in the West saw the pictures of the parched land, the children with distended bellies, and the carcasses of the cattle. We dug deep into our pockets and gave to help the starving children. Meanwhile, the farms to the south were producing tons of vegetables to ship to the tables of Europe.

A friend attending the evening Christian fellowship group in our home gave me further education on the economic dynamics of global business and hunger. He was from Hawaii. Hawaii's pineapple industry was in decline. I remembered touring the pineapple fields on our way to Japan and smelling the fragrance of the plants. My Hawaiian friend told me about pineapple farmers going bankrupt, losing their lands, and going on welfare or trying to find jobs in Honolulu or on the mainland. Meanwhile, the pineapple companies like Del Monte had moved their operations to the Philippines. The corporations were buying land in the Philippines and then forcing peasants either to get off the land they had farmed for generations or to work for much lower wages than the laborers in Hawaii. The New People's Army was engaged in a violent war against the Marcos dictatorship that supported and was enriched by its corporate partnerships. Peasants who had nothing left to lose joined the rapidly growing NPA. Back in the U.S., I was going to the grocery store and delighted to find that I could afford pineapples now the price had come down. So as I reached for that can of Del Monte pineapple chunks, I became part of the network that saw some grow wealthy, others lose jobs, others lose land, others take up arms to fight back, and yet others get U.S. military aid to stay in power and continue the repression.

As I saw these dynamics I realized that hunger could not and should not be addressed merely by sending relief aid to give emergency food to those who were starving. The famine in Africa was aggravated by natural causes such as the drought, but it was created by human causes. This was a famine caused by greed, exploitation, and marginalization, taking care of those with a lot already and ignoring those with next to nothing. In a word, true famine relief demanded justice. Seeing this underlying problem opened my eyes to what was happening in many countries, including my own, where the poor were getting poorer and the rich getting richer. I began to hear the protests of those at the margins. I began to sense the anger and desperation that led to violent revolt such as in the Philippines. I began to understand how military aid and propping up dictators were directly connected both to my comfort and the discomfort and death of the dispossessed.

My earlier, simplistic understanding of pacifism as merely personal was no longer enough. Personal pacifism in the face of a hungry world was washing my hands of my responsibility for the injustice that plagued the world's majority while I continued to eat three good meals a day. I had to move beyond passivity in the name of pacifism to positive peacemaking. I had to get engaged in the creative struggle to bring peace to the world. Any serious examination of the need for peace exposed the injustice that lay at the base of wars. Peacemaking had to incorporate and be founded upon a struggle for justice. If the cries of the dispossessed were not taken seriously, if the marginalized were not welcomed as partners, leaders, and shapers of the peace, then peace would be stillborn no matter the process to attempt to bring it into being. A peacemaker had to incorporate some dimension of revolutionary struggle to establish justice where injustice reigned. Our means might be very different from the New People's Army and the rising revolutionaries in Latin America, but they were dealing with the questions I needed to deal with too. I couldn't criticize them until I came up with a better answer. I certainly couldn't judge them when I was benefiting from the system that was despoiling their people and their land, so my peacemaking transformed from personal pacifism to nonviolent activism in solidarity with those struggling in poor countries. I had a lot to learn about issues, actions, and opportunities, but I felt I had my bearings straight about the direction in which I should now travel.

Chaplain Lucas Buttry and Harriet Buttry with their first child, Danny.

Author (tallest in back row) with Boy Scouts in Japan.

Author in his English school uniform

Chaplain Lucas W. Buttry in Wakkanai, Japan

2

BAPTISMS OF FIRE

Community Peacemaking in the City

Following graduation from seminary in 1978, I accepted the call to pastor Dorchester Temple Baptist Church, an urban neighborhood church in Boston. The church straddled the dividing line between white Dorchester and black Dorchester. It was in the Codman Square neighborhood, one of the few places where the lack of neighborhood cohesion led to looting during the blizzard of 1978. The church was a dying congregation of mostly older white people, some black children from the neighborhood, and a few of the children's mothers. They worshiped in a huge, aging facility. Over the next few years the church experienced dynamic renewal and became a vibrant multi-cultural congregation, but that's another story that I wrote about in my first book, *Bringing Your Church to Life: Beyond Survival Mentality* (Judson Press, 1988).

In that Codman Square neighborhood I underwent my baptism of fire as a community peacemaker. Busing school children to try to achieve racial diversity in city schools had been an issue sparking controversy and violence in Boston for a few years before I came to Dorchester. Busing was still a hot topic that spilled out into other areas of racial interaction. Our community was plagued by periodic racial killings and other acts of violence. The congregation had seldom been active in community issues before, but at the interview stage of the pastoral search process I made it clear that such activism was and would continue to be an important element to my ministry. When I arrived that summer of 1978 I joined a local organization called Christians for Urban Justice (CUJ). Some of the CUJ folks ended up coming to Dorchester Temple. Meanwhile, when a local march was organized to protest racial violence, Sharon and I joined in, bringing members of the church with us.

As the church went through renewal and grew in numbers our involvement in the community increased. Some activists had joined our church through our partnership with CUJ, many coming initially as students in CUJ's summer intern program and then deciding to move to the city and become a part of our church community. Other people from the neighborhood were invited to church, became Christians, and got involved under the guidance of my teaching ministry which demonstrated that works of justice, peacemaking, and meeting community needs were part of Christian discipleship. Sharon and I modeled our commitments with action in the local community. I helped found the Codman Square Community Development Corporation and the Codman Square Housing Development Corporation. Sharon helped establish a battered women's shelter and a cooperative nursery school. In all those activities we eventually were joined by church members or had neighborhood activists come into the church through our contact with them in the community organizations.

One focal point of racial conflict was Wainwright Park. Wainwright Park was a short walk from our house, and we often took our children there to play. Wainwright Park had been "white turf," and all the homes around the park were owned and occupied by white families. One summer in the early 1980s, the city of Boston was doing repairs in one of the city-owned housing projects in a predominantly black area of Dorchester. They moved three black families into a triple-decker house that faced Wainwright Park. A few nights later a firebomb was thrown onto the porch of the house. It was extinguished quickly, but the neighborhood was put on alert that tension was beginning to escalate. Concerned people from the community, from our church, and from Our Savior's Lutheran Church organized an around-the-clock vigil on the porch of the home for the weekend.

Sharon and I took one of the shifts in the wee hours of the night. The family in the first floor opened their home to us, grateful for our presence, our welcome, and our solidarity with them. We rotated between the front porch and the kitchen of the first-floor apartment and drank coffee, Coca Cola, and tea to keep awake. Many of our friends and church members participated over the weekend. There were no more incidents as the protective uprising of the community blunted the efforts of those who used violence to intimidate. That Sunday our worship service at Dorchester Temple was infused with a special passion. Though many of us were physically worn out from lack of sleep, we were energized because of having had the opportunity to love our neighbors in such a dramatic way. We prayed for our neighbors with a new fervor, which bound us together with a determined joy.

The tensions continued around Wainwright Park. Some of our church members who lived in the immediate neighborhood joined in community patrols. They talked with local white teens, sifting through the angry taunts against white "liberals" who were siding with the "invading" blacks. We discovered that many of those white youth had moved before in the early 1970s. Their families had lived in the west side of Codman Square at one time. A special federal program gave low-income minority homeowners cut-rate mortgages in the northwest quadrant of the square. The mortgages were federally guaranteed. Realtors went into the predominantly white neighborhood spreading fear about declining property values because blacks were moving in and offered white families a last chance to sell at a decent price. Many white homeowners snapped up the offers. The realtors made a profit on the quick turn-around sales. Then banks "red-lined" the area, refusing to give the new low-income homeowners the loans they needed to repair roofs, fix furnaces, and do other major repairs to their aging homes. Without adequate support, many of the homes were abandoned. There were more foreclosures in that one section of our neighborhood than in the whole rest of Massachusetts during that period. The federal government paid off the banks. Decaying, abandoned houses were torched, leaving street after street looking like a war zone. The realtors and banks made a financial killing, white families moved out, black families lost their homes, a neighborhood was devastated, and the federal government and taxpayers paid the bill. The housing disaster of northwest Codman Square provided me a vivid local example of the interplay of institutions and economic injustice about which I'd initially learned when I studied the globalized trade of pineapples.

Now these young whites were afraid that neighborhood history from their childhood was repeating itself. Their parents had told them stories of how blacks moved into their old neighborhood west of Codman Square and then the neighborhood deteriorated, unaware of the institutions that deliberately encouraged those dynamics and profited from them. Blacks were coming in again, but this time these white families were determined not to flee. Their violence was unacceptable but understandable as the white youth thought they were fighting for their homes. It was a cry of the powerless who were desperate not to be forced to move yet again, but that violence was also threatening to shred the fragile fabric holding our community together.

We worked to organize the community, involving the local churches, block clubs, neighborhood patrol groups, the mayor's office, and police officials. The previous city administration had begun renovations of Wainwright Park only to halt them for supposed lack of funds after large portions of the park had been torn up. For more than a year the mounds of broken concrete and dirt made the park an eyesore and even a danger to children. The new mayor, Raymond Flynn, had come into office in 1984 with a commitment to strengthen the neighborhoods, and we told him that Wainwright Park was a key to restoring our neighborhood. He put the park repairs on the fast track, including a new basketball court and hockey area. We also had a new neighborhood relations officer at the local police station who came to our meetings with openness and creativity. He took our concerns back to the police department, and soon many of the officers were out of the patrol cars and walking the beat where they could get to know the people in the neighborhood, including the youth. The web of relationships between families and institutions, black and white, young and old, police and public were forged and strengthened as we listened to one another, shared, and worked on common concerns. We were all changing as we spent this time together and moved from confrontation to cooperation.

Within a year the repairs on the park were finished, and we celebrated with a big basketball game. Mayor Flynn, who had once been an All-American basketball player at Providence College, called retired Celtic Dave Cowens to join him on a team from the police department. They played an integrated neighborhood all-star team. The message was clear that the Wainwright Park neighborhood would be for everyone and that we would all work together to make it the kind of place in which we all wanted to live. If anyone wanted to get violent, the police would be there to keep the law and order, closely coordinating with the neighborhood organizations. But the assumption and the invitation was that everyone would be a positive part of our community. On my last visit to Wainwright Park before we left Boston in March 1987, I rejoiced as I watched black and white kids playing together, little ones on the playground equipment, youth over on the basketball court. Mothers, and some fathers, were out chatting with each other as they watched their children. Wainwright Park wasn't quite Martin Luther King's "beloved community," but it was moving in the right direction.

From Our Neighborhood to the World

Many of the members of Dorchester Temple who worked for peace on our streets were also concerned about the growing tensions in the world. When Ronald Reagan became president in 1980, the Cold War intensified. In order to respond as Christians to the moral challenge of the nuclear arms race, I invited people in our congregation concerned about peace issues to gather at the parsonage. Out of that meeting we formed a group to which we gave the default name "Peacemakers Group." We began studying the Bible on the topic of war and peace; we also studied about the particular issues of the arms race. I fed the group articles from

Sojourners, a magazine for socially and politically progressive Christians. We heard Helen Caldecott from Physicians for Social Responsibility describe what a nuclear blast would do to the city of Boston. As we looked at her map of the city's destruction, we saw that our neighborhood, which was further out from downtown, wouldn't be vaporized. We would just die rather quickly and miserably from radiation.

The call to establish a "nuclear freeze" was launched in New England, and we became supporters of that simple idea to just stop building weapons and then move from there toward nuclear disarmament. We studied the Bible in the weekday evenings. On weekends we marched in downtown Boston or joined in vigils at nuclear weapons engineering firms in Cambridge. We wrote our congressman and senators. We prayed for our enemies, whom we discovered weren't so much the Russians as Ronald Reagan and his associates. President Reagan aroused more anger in our hearts than anyone else with his talk of the "evil empire" and his nuclear saber rattling. As voters in the U.S. democratic system, we were more responsible for him being our leader than average Russians were for their leaders. So we prayed together in the group not merely to love the "easy" enemy that our nation had in its nuclear sights, but to love the "harder" enemy to whom we felt closer, our own president with whom we had profound disagreements.

As our church Peacemakers Group connected with other peace groups, I began to represent our group in gatherings of the various organizations, quickly entering into regional leadership. I joined a coordinating committee on a movement to halt the deployment of medium-range missiles to Europe, the so-called Euro-missiles. Through that organization I took my first trip in 1983 to Washington DC, to advocate for peace with U.S. legislators and policymakers. We met with various people, most notably Senator Paul Tsongas and Congressman Thomas "Tip" P. O'Neil, who was Speaker of the House. I remember enjoying the interaction with Senator Tsongas, who was not an ideologue but rather someone looking for workable solutions. With Tip O'Neill, rather than being awed by being in the office of one of the most powerful men in Washington, I was struck by all the dandruff on his dark blue suit coat. These wielders of power were just people after all. Tip's dandruff humanized for me all these figures who filled our nightly news broadcasts.

Many of our local efforts were far less glamorous than going to Washington to meet members of Congress. I worked with a Catholic priest, Father Robert Branconnier, to prepare a special Lenten service at a large church in downtown Boston as part of a citywide ecumenical campaign. We developed a wonderful program only to have six people show up. I was discouraged to have all our diligent preparation spent on so few people; it seemed a waste of time and effort. Father Bob, who was one of my peace mentors, set my perspective straight. He told me that all gathered with us were valuable in and of themselves. These were the ones God had gathered here. The validity of our peace ministry was not to be measured in numbers at any particular event but by our faithfulness to God's call. Father Bob didn't just talk the faithfulness line; he lived it. Years earlier when he was a parish priest in North Dakota he would hold prayer vigils at U.S. Air Force missile silos when test firings were conducted, sometimes as a solitary witness standing out on the vast prairie. Father Bob taught me not to count bodies, rather to weigh my own heart.

There were, though, exhilarating moments for counting. The highlight in the nuclear freeze days of our peacemakers group was going to New York on June 12, 1982 to join with nearly one million demonstrators in what might have been the largest political demonstration in U.S. history. We didn't travel as a group. Some of us rode in the huge bus caravan going from Boston. Some took the Amtrak train, and others drove. We hoped to meet, little realizing what a massive crowd was gathering. When Sharon and I emerged from the subway escalators into downtown Manhattan, we entered a mass of determined yet jubilant humanity. It was almost impossible to move, people were so tightly packed together. The march couldn't take place on just one street but spilled over onto three broad parallel avenues. We slowly inched our way along the route, singing, chanting, and enjoying the atmosphere of so many people calling for a different vision for our human future than one of perpetual conflict and possible nuclear conflagration. When we finally got to Central Park, we couldn't get anywhere near the stage where musicians and speakers continued the rally. We couldn't even see where the stage was as we looked out over a crowd larger than any we had ever seen. It was mind-boggling and delightful.

Even amid this sea of demonstrators, we were aware that our huge crowd was just one small part of a global movement of people concerned for peace. Similar marches were happening across the U.S. and Europe. People were rejecting the insane logic of nuclear deterrence and the spiraling arms race. The currently accepted public recollection of that time is that Reagan led the U.S. to victory in the Cold War. However, as one who lived through those days and was politically active, I remember it differently. The massive campaigns in the streets, town halls, and assemblies of North America and Europe pressured Reagan to engage in détente and arms reduction talks he did not want. The Cold War was winding down before the fall of Communism, and the pressure to end it was not just from within the Soviet Union but also from within the Western alliance countries. Administration leaders complained of "Hollanditis," a spreading "disease" of protest first seen in a million Dutch citizens marching for peace in the streets of Amsterdam. The massive and persistent protests had a political impact on the governments of Europe and even on the reluctant government of the U.S. When the Communist governments in Eastern Europe and then the Soviet Union collapsed, most of us in the peace movement rejoiced, for we saw them collapse in the face of people's movements much like our own. It wasn't Ronald Reagan who brought down Communism; it was the people who lived under those repressive regimes who seized the historic moments to claim their own freedom.

As the Cold War moved toward negotiations, summits, and Strategic Arms Reduction Talks (START), U.S. involvement in the wars in Central America in the 1980s heated up in what was blandly called "low-intensity conflict." The Sandinista revolution had succeeded in Nicaragua in July 1979, assisted by Jimmy Carter's critical decision to not help the Nicaraguan dictator Somoza because of his abysmal human rights record. Reagan reversed Carter's policies and began supplying remnants of Somoza's National Guard who reformed as the "Contras." U.S. National Guard troops visited Honduras to train the Contras and leave their equipment behind to be used against the Sandinista government. The war in El Salvador was getting worse. In 1980, three U.S. nuns and a laywoman had been murdered, and Archbishop Oscar Romero assassinated, the most visible among thousands being butchered in that country. Reagan dramatically increased military assistance to El Salvador, along with sending military advisers. The U.S.-supported military regime in Guatemala continued its brutality against the indigenous people and against agricultural workers who tried to organize unions. The region faced a bleak and bloody time.

Our peace group at Dorchester Temple, which had ebbed as the intensity of the freeze campaign ebbed, was re-energized in 1984 when Scott Walker, a schoolteacher in our church, visited Nicaragua with a group of Boston educators. Scott gave a moving report upon his return. I then presented the group with the "Pledge of Resistance," a commitment promoted by *Sojourners* magazine to engage in nonviolent action against any attempt by the U.S. to invade Nicaragua, of which there was much talk in the media. The "Pledge of Resistance" grew out of a retreat of religious-based peace organizations and activists and became a major focal point of the Central American peace actions. The Pledge organizers called for people across the U.S. to sign commitments to resist a U.S. invasion of Nicaragua by nonviolent civil disobedience or other support actions. Our peace group joined the campaign, some of us signing to commit acts of civil disobedience and others signing to stand in support of those involved in the civil disobedience.

Our church peacemakers group went to various demonstrations in downtown Boston and decried U.S. policies toward Nicaragua and El Salvador. Once our group took a bed sheet and wrote an excerpt from a pastoral letter by the Baptist Convention of Nicaragua, which said, "The government of the richest, most powerful nation in the world is blocking, attacking, and destroying the life aspirations of our people." That quote on the sheet was photographed and placed on the front page of the newspaper from the Evangelistic Association of New England, a paper distributed to every church in New England. We felt we were a megaphone for our sisters and brothers in Nicaragua, whose voices were both far away and unheard.

As it became clear that the Reagan administration would not launch an invasion of Nicaragua, but instead was asking Congress to send millions of dollars in military aid to the Contras, the strategies shifted for the Pledge of Resistance. A call for civil disobedience went out for May 7, 1985, the eve of a major congressional vote for Contra aid. Scott Walker and I were ready to commit civil disobedience with the support of the rest of the group—but I was not an ordinary citizen; I was pastor of a church and would carry that identity with me, especially if arrested. I decided to bring the matter before the Board of Deacons at the church. I told them that I believed the U.S. policy in Central America was wrong and that our brothers and sisters in Nicaragua were suffering from U.S. actions. I said I wanted to join in an action of civil disobedience against those actions, but I would submit to the will of the church leadership since I would be publicly recognized as their pastor. This felt very different to me than the conversation I'd had with my dad about become a C.O. I was trying authentically to engage the church leaders in a discussion about our moral responsibility and congregational relationships rather than avoid making and owning my own decision of conscience.

We had an amazing discussion that evening, during which one of our African-American members reminded us that we were meeting on April 4, the date Martin Luther King, Jr. was assassinated in 1968. We remembered his witness for justice and peace, sometimes at the price of going to jail to make clear a legally perpetrated evil. One World War II veteran who had landed at Omaha Beach on D-Day said he disagreed with me but that he wanted his pastor to be a man of conscience. He would back me whatever I decided to do. Two other veterans spoke about the importance of action on our conscience. The decision was unanimous for me to go ahead as I felt I should do with the support of the church leaders. I felt an incredible infusion of joy and strength from my congregation as I prepared for my first illegal peace witness.

This was the first national call to action by the Pledge of Resistance. Actions were held all across the U.S. on May 7, 1985. In Boston we gathered at the John F. Kennedy Federal Building, which was on the plaza across from city hall. This had been the site of most of our demonstrations, and thousands were gathered again to protest the upcoming vote in Congress. At 4 p.m. Scott and I bade farewell to the members of our peacemakers group and made our way toward the Federal Building door. We entered the lobby of the building and sat down along with 584 other activists who had decided to commit civil disobedience. We completely jammed the lobby, the space between the elevators and any other place into which a body could be crammed. The security personnel were peeved and taken aback. They had dealt with a dozen demonstrators the previous week and had thought there would be a similar small number. Instead they were overwhelmed and flustered once they realized that none of us planned to leave. The building was shut down at 5 p.m., with workers exiting elevators and gingerly stepping over demonstrators to get out. Police began to arrive, looked at the size of the gathered protesters, and waited for reinforcements. Soon state troopers began to arrive to supplement the city police, and later federal marshals joined the state troopers and city police.

At around six o'clock when no one obeyed the order to leave the building the arrests began. The police tied the protesters' hands behind their backs with plastic cinch-ties and yanked them to their feet. If protesters wouldn't get up and walk voluntarily, they were painfully dragged by their bound arms. Those arrested were shoved into elevators and taken downstairs. Scott and I were further back in the crowd, pressed against a plate-glass window. Our friends from our peacemakers group were on the other side of the window, encouraging us with their presence while we waited our turn to be arrested. Scott and I were arrested almost two hours after the arrests initially started. We rose to our feet, were bound, and led to the bank of elevators. Some of the protesters jokingly baah-ed like sheep as we were "herded" by the police officers into the elevator and then down basement corridors.

Because of the large number of arrests, by the time Scott and I were arrested there was no place to put us. The jails had been filled as had the gymnasium at a local prison, so we were locked in chicken-wire cages in the basement of the federal building. The cages were used to store boxes of forms and other paper goods. There were about sixty people crammed into the cage with us, so most of us had to stand. Next to us was a large empty space, another cage that they evidently didn't need for detainees. Some of our group pulled out the chicken wire separating the two storage spaces, and, relieved to be able to sit or lie down, we spilled into the larger cage.

By now it was 10 p.m. Nobody had been to the bathroom since we entered the Federal Building at 4 p.m. to begin our occupation. Many of the police were angry because they had been called in from their off-duty activities to deal with us, but we finally negotiated with them about going to the restrooms. They escorted us in small groups down the hall. We weren't hardened criminals; we were mostly church folks from affinity groups like Dorchester Temple's peacemakers group. When we returned from the restrooms, many people started to get ready to spend the night in the cages. Somebody broke into a big carton that held paper human outlines, targets for police shooting practice. I fitfully dozed that night on the concrete floor, barely cushioned by paper targets of human forms and keenly aware of the irony of being a peace demonstrator trying to stop the killing of people, only to find myself on this strange bed.

The processing of the demonstrators was bogged down by the sheer numbers and aggravated by many of us identifying ourselves as "Mary Sandino" or "Joe Sandino" in solidarity with the Nicaraguans suffering under our nation's policies. Late the next morning we were fingerprinted, then brought through the court for arraignment in groups, giving our name whether real or Sandino-ized. The "Sandinos" were detained longer, but the rest of us were released on our own recognizance. When Scott and I returned from the subway station to our neighborhood, we were greeted like heroes with shouts, laughter, and embraces. In our context it was a relatively daring thing to do, but now as I look back I realize that so many other demonstrators around the world have suffered far more at the hands of police or those who imprison them. Our civil disobedience action was a relative lark, whereas for so many it is an action that puts at risk one's health, one's future, even one's life.

The U.S. government did not stop their assistance to the Contras, even when Congress would not authorize aid. Scandalous deals were arranged to procure arms through back channels by Oliver North and others. Our protests continued. The Boston police decided not to arrest the demonstrators, no matter what we did. Arresting 586 people generates a huge amount of publicity, so the police increased their use of physical intimidation and force instead of arresting us. At a peaceful sit-in, a member of our church was hit on the head by police by the crosspiece for a wooden police barricade. Police dragged another woman from our group by her hair, backward through horse manure. We were all intimidated by mounted police officers bringing their horses right into the mass of seated demonstrators. A horse looks terrifyingly huge and powerful when you are sitting cross-legged on the ground and it is tramping right over you.

We also learned a lesson about media coverage when hundreds of us shut down a major bank building in downtown Boston for a whole day because that was the location of the regional office for the Central Intelligence Agency. Throughout the day thousands of people walked past us or dealt with the inconvenience of the closure of the bank and all the offices in the building. But that night the news was filled with the U.S. bombing of Libya, and our story was not even covered in the local news. It seemed as though deliberate decisions had been made to minimize the news coverage of our actions. We would have to find our own ways to tell the story about peacemaking rather than trusting others to tell it for us.

Police and the IRS

Peace activists engaged in street demonstrations and protests inevitably will encounter the police. In the 1960s police were viewed as the enemy by anti-war protesters and were frequently called "pigs." In demonstrations I had the opportunity to observe many different police officers. Some of them were fine examples of self-disciplined public servants. Others allowed their desires to dominate and control or allowed their fears get the best of them.

One anti-nuclear demonstration offered a stark contrast between two officers standing in front of me, separated by only a couple of other policemen. To set the scene, Vice President George H. W. Bush, had earlier in the 1979 presidential campaign spoken about a "winnable nuclear war," a concept that many U.S. citizens viewed as both abhorrent and dangerous. So when Vice President Bush came to Cambridge to speak at the Massachusetts Institute of Technology, many of us showed up to protest. The nasty, angry spirit among the demonstrators was contrary to what I had experienced at most public protests. I thought if these people were in power we would have some of the same problems we were complaining about with the Reagan administration.

The police were lined up down the middle of Massachusetts Avenue with wooden barricades in front of them. We protesters were massed on the other half of the street and spilled onto the sidewalk and down the side streets. A young policeman was clearly tense, with a grim, hard look on his face. One demonstrator came running wildly down the line in the small space between the demonstrators and the barricades. He was acting erratically, perhaps high on drugs. When he got to the young cop, the policeman suddenly shoved him in a very rough, forceful way into the crowd. The demonstrator lost his balance and was held up only by the bodies of demonstrators against whom he slammed.

Immediately the tension in the crowd skyrocketed. Curses were hurled, and I sensed the anger flaring in the crowd.

Just a few steps away was an older police officer, perhaps in his fifties. He evidently had been sitting too much at a desk; his paunch guaranteed he would not be chasing many demonstrators down the street. But this older, out-of-shape officer was keeping the peace. He talked continually to the demonstrators: "Where do you go to school? What are you studying? Oh yeah, well, you might think about getting into computers. That's where the future is going—you know that, right?" Surrounded by simmering rage and shouted chants, this policeman had carved out a little circle of calm and even a community of mutually-recognized humanity spanning a barricade. Whether this officer was conscious of what he was doing (I think he was intentional), he was practicing creative nonviolence in maintaining public order. He was doing his job far better than the young cop looking for a head to bash.

When I was arrested in the Pledge of Resistance occupation of the Federal Building in Boston, my observations of police officers became personal. I spotted a federal marshal from our congregation among the arresting officers. He was one of the rougher police with the demonstrators. He would wrench handcuffed people to their feet and slam them down hard on the marble floor where they were to wait for elevators. As I waited to get arrested myself I stared at him with a grim face, hoping to catch his eye, but to no avail. When Scott and I were arrested and taken over to the elevators, the marshal from our church finally spotted us. He simply smiled and shook his head, but I noticed he changed his behavior immediately. He became much more gentle in how he handled people. His use of excessive force evaporated.

Later in the evening while we were locked up in the cages in the basement of the building the marshal from our church came down. We chatted for a few minutes through the chicken wire. He told me the previous week he had been one of the arresting officers called in to deal with a handful of demonstrators. One of them was Father Bob Branconnier. This marshal was actually a member of Father Bob's parish; he also attended Dorchester

Temple because his wife was Baptist. As he approached Father Bob, he told his fellow marshals, "I can't arrest him; he's my priest!" To then see his pastor getting arrested the next week was amusing to him. He never lost respect for us, continuing as an active parishioner in both churches, but I think his understanding of people being arrested was changed by seeing both his spiritual guides in handcuffs.

Many of the police officers that night were rather curt toward us, but one officer stood out to me for his combination of courtesy, fairness, and maintaining a clear sense of what the legal and practical rules would be in that situation. He overrode unreasonably harsh decisions lower-ranking officers had made about our accommodations. After things had settled down for the night and people were quietly chatting, I listened to the conversations among the police. Many had been called out of personal activities to come in and deal with the unexpected size of the demonstration. This particular officer had tickets to the Red Sox game that night—a big game, too, if I recall correctly—but he had the professionalism not to allow his entertainment (and financial) loss to translate into treating his prisoners improperly. When we were released I told him how much I appreciated how he handled himself as a police officer. He was not "the enemy," and he didn't treat us like enemies either.

A very different type of enforcement took place through the Internal Revenue Service. From the time when Henry David Thoreau, a favorite son of Massachusetts, had refused to pay the poll tax to finance the war with Mexico to the present, there are people who have resisted paying taxes as a part of their peace witness. During the height of the Cold War with the threat of planetary annihilation hanging over us, tax resistance was another way to enter into the struggle to bring peace. Sharon and I decided that we would withhold 50 percent of our federal income tax, a rough approximation of how much of the federal budget was directed to paying for past, present, or future wars. Our action launched a five-year financial and accounting guerilla war between us and the IRS that at times became absurdly humorous.

From 1979 to 1984 Sharon and I felt we were at a particularly strategic place in our lives to make a tax witness. Dorchester Temple provided us with a parsonage, so whatever the IRS might do to us we would still have a roof over our heads, an important issue as we began to have children. For the first two or three years we sent in our taxes with 50 percent withheld. We enclosed a cover letter with our 1040 form explaining why we were not paying our full taxes. We were willing to pay our taxes in full if there was a fund for national needs that excluded war since we in good conscience could not contribute to war or war preparation. (Each year during that time legislation was introduced in Congress to create a National Peace Tax Fund for conscientious tax resisters, but it never garnered more than a handful of congressional sponsors.)

At first we received many form letters from the IRS demanding that we pay our full tax amount and threatening us with various penalties. When we never responded, the IRS assigned us to a hearing in Washington DC. There was no way we could afford to go down to Washington, and I knew what the outcome would be. There was no legal basis at all for our withholding the taxes, and the IRS courts had never found in favor of tax resisters. Then one day our bank notified us that a huge withdrawal had been made from our accounts by the government, amounting to the withheld taxes, interest, and penalties. By this time Ronald Reagan had become president. Tax resistance was a growing movement, and Reagan dramatically increased the interest rates and penalties for failure to pay taxes. As I read the notice from my bank and the new mail from the IRS, I realized that the funds ending up in the federal treasury from my pocket were now far greater than when we started our tax resistance.

So we changed our strategy. Instead of withholding 50 percent of our income taxes, we withheld $25 as a symbolic protest. Again we sent a cover letter with our tax return explaining what we were doing and why. Later that year I was called into the IRS offices in downtown Boston, a procedure that was becoming very familiar. I explained our position, reiterating what was in the cover letter with our tax forms. The auditor had clearly dealt with tax resisters before and knew that this was not a situation that would be resolved by simply trying to convince us to change our behavior. Then the auditor noticed that the amount withheld was $25. "Why were you notified to come in here?" she asked. "We can only do an audit if the amount is $50 or more," and she dismissed me. The next year I raised our symbolic protest to $50, resulting in another visit to the IRS.

Somewhere along the way I got a notice from the IRS about our first two years of withholding which had been seized from our bank. The IRS had the money, but they wanted us to sign that we agreed to their finding that we had owed that money along with the assessed interest and penalties. I refused to sign, and for months correspondence at taxpayer expense went back and forth, not for any money to be gained but merely to get a signature for consent. They wouldn't close the file without my signature, and I refused to give it. Finally, that was one battle I won; the case was closed without my signature.

One year when I had begun withholding the smaller symbolic amounts the IRS sent me a refund check for half of my taxes. I did not cash the refund check because I knew eventually the IRS would realize their mistake and demand the taxes be paid in full, with interest. I held the check for a few months until the notice arrived. I simply enclosed their own check for the amount owed, stating that I owed them no interest since the funds had never been in my possession. What a mess that simple action made since I didn't follow standard operating procedures! Again it was months of correspondence, phone calls, and an office visit to straighten the mess out. I wasn't sure whether anyone in the IRS spoke to their own colleagues because the levels of miscommunication were so bad.

It is easy to question oneself about the value of such actions. Withholding $25 or even 50 percent of my taxes, knowing that the money will be seized in time, can seem like a pointless action. Why bother? Why protest in the streets if nobody will pay attention and the government will do whatever it planned to do anyway? In trying to answer these questions for myself I discovered a Hasidic tale that resonated deeply with me. The Hasidic rabbis told about a prophet who went into the city every week to speak out against injustice, evil, and oppression. Week after week, month after month, year after year the exploitation continued despite his prophetic calls for people to mend their ways. Friends and disciples of the prophet begged him to cease his futile attempts to call the people to righteousness. The prophet replied, "I must continue. I speak out so that I do not become one of them." My actions and the actions of my friends as we struggled for peace were for the sake of our own moral integrity. Maybe we could change the course of action by our government, and if so, that would be wonderful. But if not, we were still responsible to be voices for justice and peace. If nobody else raised such voices it was still incumbent upon us to speak and to act. Through our speaking and acting we fought the quiet complicity that allowed low-intensity conflict to rage with ferocity a long way off. We refused to bow at the altar of a national security gained by threats of nuclear annihilation. I cannot take responsibility for the actions of others, but I am responsible for myself.

Author preaching in the early years at Dorchester Temple

Author and Sharon Buttry as they began their time in Dorchester

3

THE BURMA PEACE INITIATIVE

A National Peacemaking Job

In March 1987 I left the pastorate at Dorchester Temple to become the manager of the Peace Program for National Ministries (NM), the home mission agency for the American Baptist Churches (ABC). That necessitated a move from our urban neighborhood in Boston to suburban Philadelphia. I experienced culture shock going from a workplace with no computers, a hand-cranked mimeograph, black rotary telephones, and chronic money shortages to an office with a computer, a phone with buttons, and a word-processing pool to quickly handle our various writing tasks. I went from seeing travel to Washington DC as an expensive trip that we could somehow make with enough sacrifice to hopping on the train to DC or New York whenever needed. I was flying around the country and even starting to plan international trips. I felt like a rookie being called up to the major leagues, standing in awe of the new surroundings and perhaps looking a little foolish in the process.

Dissatisfaction had been growing within me at Dorchester Temple, not because I didn't like the church or love the people. I would have stayed there if I could, but there was a growing pressure within me to do peacemaking and church renewal work on a larger scale. I was frequently called upon to do workshops on either topic at various conferences in New England. I had seen Larry Pullen, the first person to manage NM's Peace Program, when he did some workshops in the Boston area. When Larry resigned and NM announced that applications could be sent in, Sharon urged me to apply. I thought my chances for the job were nil, but I went ahead and sent in a resume. Their call to invite me for an interview caught me off guard; surely, they couldn't be serious in wanting me—I was small potatoes. I thought of canceling the interview and dropping out, but then I figured that this was a great opportunity to go to our national American Baptist headquarters both to see the place and also to give them a piece of my mind. I had many passionately held ideas about peace and church renewal. This would give me an opportunity to speak to a new audience, to national figures in our denomination's life. I thought I had nothing to lose; I would just lay it all on the line like I believed and thought.

The interview went very well. No sooner had I returned to Boston than I got a call from Emmett Johnson, the head of NM's Personal and Public Witness Unit. Emmett offered me the job, and after much prayer and further discussion with Sharon, I accepted.

Leaving Boston was hard. After a life of moving around as we followed my father's shifting assignments in the Air Force, Boston had become the first place that was "home" to me. I thought of my departure in terms of Abraham being called from his home to follow God into the unknown. I was leaving the wonderful community of our church, our peacemakers group, the closest friends I'd ever known, and an urban neighborhood that I'd come to know like the back of my hand. I had been deeply and thoroughly immersed in a particular locality, even though we would engage in national and global issues from that local base. Now I would be working at a national level and dealing regularly in international affairs. My own rootedness locally would be relatively shallow. Instead of being at "home" in one place, I would often be gone from where my family was and would have to find "home" on the road. I couldn't comprehend what all that would mean, but I knew responding to God's call meant not only meeting a need in my own heart but also acknowledging the loss of our Boston community. While the loss of that home in Dorchester has never fully dissipated, I have discovered other ways to have rich relationships and to put down roots even when I'm frequently on the move. Like Abraham and other sojourners, I have learned to lean toward the future that we can't quite see clearly. I wasn't just leaving home, but I was going toward a better home that still might be a long way off. We will have to create that home in the community of those journeying toward the same goal.

For the next nine years I directed the Peace Program for American Baptists. I conducted workshops on peace issues around the country. Each year I developed worship and educational resources related to the ABC observance of Peace Sunday. I traveled to Washington DC to engage in advocacy with those in Congress. I wrote newsletters to inform and mobilize a growing network of Baptist peace activists. I helped plan national conferences on social issues. I represented American Baptist Churches at the United Nations, traveling to New York six times a year to participate in U.N. briefings for non-governmental organization (NGOs) representatives. There were many wonderful experiences working with wonderful people over those years. But one strand of my work with an innocuous beginning proved to have a lifelong impact for me.

A Second Judson

One day in September 1987 an Asian man popped unannounced into my office. He introduced himself as Saboi Jum, a Kachin Baptist leader from Burma. I knew a bit about Burma. Adoniram and Ann Judson, the first Baptist foreign missionaries from the U.S., had gone there to proclaim the gospel. In seminary our missions class had visited the Salem, Massachusetts, docks from which the Judsons had sailed in 1812. As an avid reader about World War II, I also knew about General "Vinegar Joe" Stilwell and the Burma Road built from India to China with many ferocious battles to push the Japanese out of Burma. Saboi told me about war going on right then. I thought I was well read and knew a lot about what was happening in the world, but I had no idea that a war was going on in Burma.

Saboi explained how the Karens, an ethnic minority group, had struggled since 1948 against the majority Burmans. The Karen leaders felt there was no place for them or recognition of their people's rights in the newly independent Burma. They launched their own war for independence. Other ethnic minority groups including the Kachins eventually took up arms as well. When

General Ne Win overthrew the democratic government of Burma in 1962 and extended programs of Burman hegemonization, including actions to make Buddhism the state religion and eliminate the use of minority languages, the Kachins felt their culture was being destroyed. Protests were met with violence. Missionaries were expelled. The Kachins asked the departing missionaries what they should do, but the answers the missionaries gave about prayer and patient suffering seemed inadequate for the daunting oppression the Kachins faced. As a result, many Kachins, most of them Baptists who were the fruit of long-term American Baptist missionary endeavors, took to the jungles to join the insurgents.

Saboi was concerned that a way be found to peace. His people were suffering, and it seemed that no end to the fighting was in sight. He told me, "If the church won't work for peace, who will?" In 1980, as the leader of the Kachin Baptists, Saboi personally launched a peace initiative. He traveled to the jungle headquarters of the Kachin Independence Organization (KIO) and its army (KIA), then back for meetings with the government. Through this itinerant mediation he eventually secured a cease-fire agreement between Ne Win's government and the KIO. After a few months, attacks and accusations by the Burmese Communist insurgents undercut the cease-fire and brought about its collapse. Saboi had to lie low as waves of anger and renewed violence from both sides made any witness for peace too dangerous.

Now Saboi was sitting in my office asking for help to bring peace to his country. I hadn't a clue what to do. I gave him a few books off my bookshelf, knowing as I did what a futile gesture it was. The verses from James echoed through my head: "If a brother or sister is naked and lacks daily food, and one of you says to them, 'Go in peace; keep warm and eat your fill,' and yet you do not supply their daily needs, what is the good of that?" (James 2:15-16 NRSV) I told Saboi to go in peace and that I would pray for him, feeling utterly useless and helpless even as I sat at a national peace desk. However, after he left I did not forget about him.

Meanwhile, the Baptist Peace Fellowship of North America (BPFNA) and the Peace Program of National Ministries joined the European Baptist Federation to convene the first global Baptist peace conference, to be held in Sweden in August 1988. Ken Sehested, the BPFNA executive director, and I were working on program plans from the North American side. We both wanted to assure a Third World presence at the conference and not allow the East-West conflict to blind us to the conflicts devastating the poor countries of the planet. I immediately thought of Saboi and said we had to find a way to get him there. We invited Saboi to be one of the participants from Asia, Africa, and Latin America who would not only attend but would speak at a special forum regarding various conflicts around the world with their challenges and opportunities for peace.

The conference was held at a folk school in the central Swedish town of Sjövik in August 1988. Participants gathered from twenty-seven countries on five continents, from black-suit-and-tie-clad Russians going off to the lake with fishing poles over their shoulders to playful Latin Americans who took a collection so the bare-footed president of the BPFNA, George Williamson, could get some shoes. There were many presentations about Baptist history, peace in the Bible, human rights, and the current East-West conflict, but when presenters from South Africa, Sri Lanka, and Nicaragua told of the travails of their countries the conference moved to a more emotionally intense level. Then Saboi Jum spoke. He told stories of the suffering of his people, about villages burned down and people massacred, about young women raped and then murdered in front of their families, of villagers being taken out of their homes to be used as human minesweepers detonating booby-traps in the jungle. As he closed his presentation Saboi made an appeal to the gathered Baptists: "I believe, and I have a conviction, that it is the responsibility of the church to make peace in our country. And I need suggestions and help from the outside world." His comments came against the backdrop of daily news about the democracy uprising going on during those very days in Burma. The August 1988 uprising was met with ferocious violence by the military in which hundreds (later to be thousands) of demonstrators were gunned down in the streets.

After Saboi's presentation George Williamson and I embraced and wept. I said, "There aren't enough tears for what we are hearing." John Howard Yoder, the Mennonite scholar, was with us representing our Anabaptist cousins in the faith. He challenged George, Ken, and me about what Saboi had said, that we couldn't just put it off as a moving conference presentation. We had to do something substantial in response to this appeal to Baptists from one of our Baptist brothers. He told us about Mennonite involvement in the peace process in Nicaragua and that the Mennonites would be delighted to consult with us and work with us on some ideas of how to proceed.

Saboi continued the challenge himself, saying, "You sent Judson to bring us the gospel. Send us a second Judson to bring us peace." I was later to get into friendly arguments with Saboi over that statement. From my perspective the second Judson could not be an outsider. Just like Gandhi had to be an Indian and Martin Luther King Jr. had to be an African-American, the "second Judson" who would bring peace to Burma had to be from Burma. I could not be that second Judson; it had to be Saboi. However, just as Judson had Luther Rice support him by forming a missionary society to raise funds for his mission work, we in the BPFNA needed to find ways to effectively support Saboi.

As we left Sweden the news continued to unfold in Burma. The uprising continued throughout August and into September. Ne Win was officially retired, but most people believed he pulled the strings behind the scenes. He put forward two different generals to head the government. The first general had overseen a massacre of protesting students earlier in the year. This appointment increased the intensity of the protests, resulting in that general's removal. When the second general couldn't contain the demonstrators, the military retreated to their bases. For a few brief weeks there was a semi-peaceful anarchy in the streets of Burma's cities as people wondered what would be next. Suddenly on 18 September the Burmese Army launched a final crackdown against the demonstrators. Students and unarmed civilians were gunned down throughout the capital and in other cities of Burma. The army hauled off the dead for secret disposal, claiming casualties far lower than other witnesses reported. In a few days the democracy uprising had been crushed. A new junta was established, the State Law and Order Restoration Committee, more commonly known by the repulsive-sounding acronym SLORC, with General Saw Maung at the head. A grim calm gripped the country while thousands of surviving student demonstrators fled into the jungles toward the sanctuary of Thailand or the areas held by ethnic insurgent groups.

Against this backdrop, on 1 January 1989 Saboi flew into Philadelphia to consult with me for four days. He spent one intense day giving me a crash course on Burmese modern history, including a who's who list of all the political figures and their organizations. We visited the Fellowship of Reconciliation in Nyack, New York, to talk about peacemaking strategies with Doug Hostetter and Richard Deats, who had done nonviolence training to help lay the foundations for the People Power movement in the Philippines that overthrew the Marcos dictatorship. We hammered out a three-point plan: to reopen negotiations between the government and ethnic insurgents, to provide nonviolence training to democratic and ethnic opposition leaders, and to raise international awareness of what was going on in Burma.

In February we contacted John Paul Lederach of the Mennonite Central Committee for advice and counsel. John Paul gave us a realistic perspective for what we faced through his own experience during the peace process in Nicaragua. We traveled to Atlanta, Georgia, to the Carter Center, first to meet with Dayle Spencer of the Carter Center's International Negotiation Network, then with President Carter himself. Carter agreed to participate in the mediation process if we could get both sides to invite him. Carter's condition ended up blocking his participation as the government never agreed to it. However, President Carter did give us a letter of support for a mediation process, which proved instrumental in opening the doors for Saboi to get a hearing with the government.

Off to Asia

Saboi returned to Burma using his contacts within the Burmese Army's military intelligence to try to reach Khin Nyunt, a key general in the SLORC military junta. Saboi also worked to get messages to Brang Seng, chairman of the KIO, somewhere deep in the jungles of Burma. For a while it seemed that nobody was interested in talking; every response to Saboi involved conditions to which no government or armed group would ever agree.

Then in January 1990 I got a call at my office to come down to the National Ministries communications center to receive an incoming international fax. The cover page had finished, and the second page was slowly churning out. I read what I could see and was immediately filled with excitement. Saboi had met with Khin Nyunt who had agreed to talks with the KIO under certain conditions. I could read the first two conditions, and they were both reasonable. As the third and fourth conditions were slowly lined out on the fax machine my adrenaline shot up for they were conditions within the realm of negotiable possibility. We were now in this process with parties who were ready to be serious!

Furthermore, Saboi wanted me to come to Hong Kong within two weeks to meet with Brang Seng to talk about the conditions and try to set up talks. After quick consultations with the leadership of National Ministries and International Ministries to gain their blessing, I was off for Hong Kong and a journey dealing with an actual peace process. I felt like I was in completely over my head, so I devoured as much material as I could about Burma and spoke to as many people as I could who had any expertise in the region.

The flight over the Pacific to Hong Kong was highlighted by spy thriller movie *The Package* starring Gene Hackman. This was not the kind of entertainment I needed to calm my edgy nerves! When Saboi and I arrived in Hong Kong, we seemed caught in our own thriller. We checked into the hotel on Nathan Road in Kowloon and then received a phone call with our instructions. We were told simply to stand in front of the hotel; someone would get us and take us to "the chairman." Sure enough, after a few minutes a man emerged from the crowd on the street, greeted us, and said, "Follow me." We followed him to a waiting vehicle and were driven to a restaurant where we met Brang Seng.

Over the next few years I grew in my respect for Brang Seng. He was one of the few people in the process who transcended his own context. Everyone else I met was a fierce partisan for his or her own people, vested interests, or political position. Brang Seng, however, was able to rise above the context of the Kachin struggle, desperate as it had been. He could see the larger picture, including the needs and concerns of the majority Burmans. He never dehumanized those against whom he struggled, referring to the general who had ruled Burma, Ne Win, as "our older brother." Brang Seng had been the headmaster of a major Kachin school before leaving for the jungle to fight the Burmese Army. His Christian faith, though expressed at times in forms with which I could not agree, compelled him to take political risks to try to find a peaceful solution to the conflicts behind the war. He acted as a tribal chief, which in essence he was, clearly the center of attention and a gracious and gregarious host.

During that initial trip to Hong Kong in February 1990 to meet Brang Seng, Saboi and I secured his agreement to seriously consider the conditions Khin Nyunt had insisted upon for talks. It took a few more rounds of shuttle visits by Saboi to SLORC officials in the capital and Brang Seng in various locations inside or outside Burma to get complete agreement on the conditions. I accompanied Saboi to some of the meetings with Brang Seng at various locations in Hong Kong, Thailand, and Canada. However, the SLORC refused to let me meet with them, claiming that the conflict was an internal affair and thus outsiders should not be included in the peace talks. I participated as the only non-Burmese citizen on the Burma Peace Committee that Saboi formed. I consulted with the committee, mainly through Saboi, and shared with them in the work related to the ethnic insurgents.

Finally, the two sides agreed to the wording of all the conditions for talks, which they then each formally accepted. Face-to-face talks between the government and the KIO were held in Pangsai, Burma, in October 1990. Most of the discussions focused on beginning a larger negotiation process involving all the ethnic insurgents. The KIO was a member of the Democratic Alliance of Burma (DAB), which included most of the ethnic insurgents as well as student groups made up of those who had fled the brutal military crackdown on the 1988 democracy uprising. Brang Seng used the government's willingness to talk to him to broaden the discussions to include the entire DAB. Because of the ferocious fighting skills of the Kachin insurgents, the Burmese military was especially concerned to bring about an end to the combat with them. The generals in the junta were far less willing to consider an accord with other ethnic groups, and especially not with the students or other democratic activists. No agreement was reached at Pangsai other than to keep the process rolling.

Meanwhile, on 27 May 1990 elections were held in Burma to establish a new parliament in the wake of the changes of government that resulted from the '88 uprising. The ruling generals had assured the Burmese public and world community that the SLORC was only an interim body to run the country until a new constitution and government could be established. An election was held to set up a new parliament to draft the constitution and move toward a regular government. The entire electoral process was carefully controlled with all non-military candidates being denied access to media and severely restricted in what they could do during the campaign. Meetings of more than a few people were banned, making traditional political campaigns all but impossible. The National League for Democracy (NLD) was the main opposition party led by Aung San Suu Kyi, the daughter of Burmese independence leader Aung San. Aung San Suu Kyi rose to prominence during the 1988 demonstrations, and she became the national figure of hope for the restoration of democracy. In July 1989, she and NLD Chairman Tin U were put under house arrest. With the top opposition leadership under arrest and many other NLD candidates in prison, the military was certain that they would maintain complete control over the process and the outcome of the election. A few days before the elections, the generals opened the country to the global media to show the world their "free" election.

The military was stunned when the heavy voter turnout supported the NLD and Aung San Suu Kyi with more than 60 percent of the vote, giving the NLD 392 out of 485 seats in the parliamentary assembly, including in districts with heavy populations of military personnel. Almost immediately the generals began to give various security reasons why they would not turn over power to those who had been elected, even in a process they had designed and controlled with a heavy hand. Aung San Suu Kyi and Tin U remained under arrest. Scores of elected parliamentarians were arrested. Many others fled to the border areas. Eight elected NLD members of parliament who reached the Thai border established the National Coalition Government of the Union of Burma (NCGUB) under the leadership of Sein Win, Aung San Suu Kyi's cousin. The hopes that flourished briefly around the election were never allowed to materialize.

The High-water Mark for the Peace Process

Meanwhile, cracks were developing between the KIO's Brang Seng and the rest of the Democratic Alliance of Burma over the pursuit of the negotiations with the military government. Cease-fire agreements had been signed between some of the smaller ethnic insurgencies and the military. The leaders of the Karen National Union, the largest ethnic insurgent group who had been fighting since 1948, feared that Brang Seng would settle separately with the military. After one of his many trips to Asia to meet with leaders on both sides, Saboi called me up and said the peace process was unraveling. I was getting frustrated because it was becoming apparent that Brang Seng, while making progress with the military, was not able to convince his counterparts in the other ethnic insurgencies of the DAB that he was acting on behalf of all of them. Working the process with Saboi and Brang Seng at the center alone was not sufficient. So I told Saboi that we needed to get all the key players together for a major meeting to hash out a common strategy related to peace negotiations.

Along the way I had also discovered other international people and organizations who were working on the conflict in Burma. There was Michael Baumann, a German government official who was connected with a group of various German diplomats and NGOs (Non-Governmental Organizations) looking for a negotiated solution in Burma that would also improve the human rights situation. John McConnell with Quaker Peace and Service was bringing his experience of mediation in Sri Lanka to the opening opportunity in Burma. Pracha Hutanuwatra was a leader in the Thai democracy movement linked with the nonviolent Buddhist monk Sulak Sivaraska. Canadians Richard Weeks from Moral ReArmament and Murray Thompson from Canadian Friends of Burma had been in contact with Saboi about ways to engage constructively in peace efforts. We ended up forming a loose network for which I became the informal coordinator.

In June 1991 this loose unnamed international team was able to convene a meeting in Chiang Mai, Thailand, that involved top leaders from most of the main opposition groups including armed insurgencies: The Karen National Union, the Kachin Independence Organization, the New Mon State Party, Karenni insurgent leaders, the All-Burma Student Democratic Front, and the National Coalition Government of the Union of Burma. Saboi Jum was unable to attend because issues related to his U.S. visa made a return to the U.S. problematic at that point.

Because most of us on the international team had been working primarily with the Kachins, Saboi Jum and Brang Seng, we decided to meet individually with each group's leaders in order to hear the particulars of their stories and interests in the conflict. I was taken aback when Mon insurgent leader Nai Shwe Chin began his story, "Three thousand years ago...." Such a deep historical sense of entitlement and injury was beyond my short-focused, American timeframe. It was this abiding and deep-rooted identity with its often related litany of injustices suffered that made the forty-year insurgency seem like a short-term matter that called for patience and persistence. The Mons and the Karens were not about to give up their struggle, and the students were itching for a fight, still burning with anger from the massacres of their classmates and friends in the '88 uprising.

Our international team met repeatedly in separate groups and plenary sessions, informally and formally. At times we sat at a conference table at a Thai military resort, opening sessions with a formal statement by General Bo Mya of the KNU followed by my formal statement in which I called participants to find the ways to peace. Then we would get down to long discussions of the specific strategies for approaching the government, the differences of opinion within the opposition groups, the areas of mistrust about the SLORC's sincerity, and how to hold them accountable.

Off on the side, however, we began forming relationships. We traveled to a butterfly zoo together, acting as tourists for a few moments. As we ate dinner one night, a Thai musician entertained us using a karaoke songbook with his keyboard. Soon we had a fun rivalry going between the tables when several of us went up to sing with the musician. I took up the challenge for my table, selecting peace movement songs from the 60s such as "If I Had a Hammer" and sharing the story of these songs from my culture and history. These sidebar activities strengthened the relationships and allowed us to tackle thornier matters in our discussions.

Eventually we arrived at a consensus to support a unified peace process. The Kachin Independence Organization with the Burma Peace Committee would utilize their open channel with the SLORC to demand that the entire DAB be brought to the negotiating table. No separate concessions would be made as the opposition's greatest strength would lie in their unity and cohesion. We would press for good-faith measures being taken by the military, such as the release of political prisoners, to go along with any proposed cease-fires. The Karens especially remained skeptical about the feasibility of this approach, but they were willing to give it a try. A message was to be sent to SLORC about pressing on with peace negotiations involving the entire DAB and urging the release of some key political prisoners as a positive trust-building gesture.

We left Chiang Mai feeling that the opposition groups had addressed the strains within them regarding the strategy for peace talks. When Dr. Tu Ja of the KIO took me back to the airport he said, "When we first met only the Kachins wanted to try for peace, but then they saw your face and knew they could trust you." This humbling statement from Tu Ja showed me the importance of relationships in trying to make peace, which would prove to be both a useful insight and the point upon which the process would break down.

Collapse, Fragmentation, and Despair

In July 1991 Saboi Jum had worked out his visa problems and flew to Thailand to follow up on the Chiang Mai meeting. In just those few weeks the distrust between the Karen and Kachin leaders began to unravel the consensus we had achieved. The Kachins were eager to push forward in negotiations while the Karens feared that Brang Seng would cut a deal advantageous for himself that would leave the Karens in trouble. Though their fears were initially misguided, they became self-fulfilling. The consensus about a peace strategy unraveled as much from the inability of the opposition groups to work together as from the divide-and-conquer strategy of the military regime. When Saboi tried to patch the rapidly growing cracks in the DAB, he found that the Karens distrusted him because he was Kachin. Saboi called me with the discouraging news that the plan to move toward peace was disintegrating.

Meanwhile we heard nothing from Generals Saw Maung or Khin Nyunt on the SLORC side. The DAB letter that the Peace Committee carried to the government seemed to have fallen on deaf ears. A few months went by, and the international team members began discussing via fax what next steps we might take to spur the process forward. We decided John McConnell and I would send Saw Maung a letter. We offered to meet him and other members of the SLORC in person at anytime, anywhere simply to begin the relationships and explore together what negotiation processes might be like and what they could accomplish. We introduced the members of the international team, inviting the SLORC to select the people whom they felt would be best to meet. I drafted the letter and began floating the draft to the team, to Saboi, and to various people within National Ministries and International Ministries of the ABC for their input. After the letter was revised and the international team members gave their approval, I sent it to Saboi Jum to deliver to Saw Maung.

While we were seeking to keep the process moving forward in Burma, internal shifts were developing within the mission agency that had allowed me to engage in this work. Those shifts would produce a dramatic change in my relationship to the peace process in Burma as well as in my own life work. The leadership of National Ministries had undergone major changes in both top personnel and structure. The leaders who had approved my initial involvement in the Burma peace process were gone. Paul Nichols, the Executive Director of NM, died suddenly of an aneurism. My immediate supervisor, Emmett Johnson, retired. When I sent the letter to SLORC for comment by the new leaders at National Ministries, I initially received no response. Once I sent the letter on to Burma, however, there was a flurry of questions not only about the letter but also about my very involvement in the peace process.

I was called to meet with the management council of National Ministries to discuss what I was doing and why, as a staff person for a mission society focused on the United States, I was spending so much time on Burma. I reiterated the history of the creation of the Peace Program. It was established by the denomination at the same time as a program on hunger. There was an awareness that hunger and peace had both global and national dimensions, transcending the American Baptist mission agency divisions of focus as "national" and "international" ministries. For personnel and bureaucratic reasons the Peace Program fell under National Ministries, and the hunger program under International Ministries—with an understanding that they often would need to move beyond those limitations. Throughout the Burma process I had consulted with IM staff, including former missionaries to Burma, and had received their blessing for my work. The new leadership of National Ministries felt that my involvement in Burma was taking me away from activities they considered to be higher priorities within the United States (and the primary focus of National Ministries): urban violence, post-cold war conflicts, and the U.S. military budget. They decided I had to stop my work in Burma. I could not follow through on the letter I'd sent to SLORC. In order not to put Saboi at risk while he was in Burma, I was told to wait until he had come out of Burma to tell him of NM's decision to halt my involvement in the peace process.

I was upset about the decision, feeling that nobody from NM had entered into the situation to see what was going on in the peace process and how critical my presence was. The decision was made on the basis of organizational vision and program priorities that could not be bent for what I perceived as an exception that was rooted in our mission history and mandate. My salary and program funds were governed by NM's leadership, so I had no base to establish myself separately to continue my engagement in Burma.

I bided my time until July 1992, when we had the second International Baptist Peace Conference, this time held in Nicaragua at a simple resort in La Boquita on the Pacific coast. Saboi was coming to Nicaragua straight from Burma. He had major news. There had been a shake-up in the military, and Saw Maung had been deposed. General Than Shwe became the new chairman and told Saboi that the request the international team made in the letter was no longer necessary because the government was going to move rapidly to negotiations and cease-fires. However, the opposition groups had split over their approaches to negotiations with the military. The Karen and Mon insurgents decided not to negotiate. The KIO quickly agreed to a separate cease-fire along with some of the other ethnic insurgents. The DAB expelled the KIO, organizationally expressing the major rift that had torn apart the ethnic insurgents. Saboi was happy to have a cease-fire almost in place; it would be finalized later in the year. But then I had to tell him my news.

Saboi was stunned when I told him I could no longer work on the peace process. During one of the sessions about mediation at which Saboi was a speaker, he informed all the conferees that the American Baptists had pulled me off the mediation initiative in Burma. There were about thirty American Baptist peace activists at the conference including the BPFNA president George Williamson, a pastor from Ohio. George wanted to see what he and the other ABC folks at the conference could do to get me back on the process, but I told him that I could not be a part of any of their efforts. I had to submit to the priorities and parameters established by my boss. A letter was drafted asking for me to be returned to the peace process, which George later conveyed to National Ministries. George had a follow-up meeting with the executive director of National Ministries to discuss the matter, but the decision held. I was done with the Burma mediation effort.

I tried to get John McConnell to take the role I had in the process. He was experienced and savvy, and I viewed him as a role model. The delicate web of relationships, though, was such that John could not just move in. Aside from the matter of personalities and personal history in the process, for Christians in Burma I represented as an American Baptist the long tradition of Christian missionaries who went back to Adoniram Judson in the early 1800s. That heritage in which I stood gave me extra clout and prestige in the eyes of many of the participants in the conflict. Now the message received by the Baptists in Burma was that the American Baptists had pulled out and left them alone, whatever the rationale might have been in the National Ministries leadership. The international team, which was not formally organized, disintegrated although many of the individuals and organizations continued in various initiatives related to Burma. Between the disagreements among the ethnic insurgent groups and the disintegration of the international support for the mediation process, Saboi and the Burma Peace Committee were left with little support or leverage.

Once the SLORC made separate cease-fires with the Kachin insurgents and some of the other northern insurgent groups, they could throw all their military might at the Karens and Mons. The army attacked Manerplaw, the remote mountainous headquarters of the Karen National Union and the center for armed opposition including the students and other survivors of the democracy movement. Manerplaw had been untouched by the government for decades but fell under the new assault. Other KNU and Mon positions fell, and the insurgent forces were driven into tenuous positions with heavy losses. The international resolve against the military regime after the '88 crackdown and the '90 election was eroding as the SLORC continued to hold Aung San Suu Kyi and other NLD leaders under house arrest or in prison. Japan eased the financial burden of the government's debt. China sent military aid. U.S. and European corporations signed business deals for oil development, soft drink production, and other enterprises. The junta, which had been close to financial collapse, got the reprieve it needed to reassert itself.

All this news of the growing strength of the Burmese military and the setbacks for the ethnic and democratic opposition groups fell like a huge weight on my spirit. I questioned whether I should have gotten involved. My support of the peace efforts had encouraged the Kachin insurgents to hope for peace, but because I couldn't finish what I started, the plight of ethnic minorities and democracy activists was worse than before. That was a harsh assessment, but one I felt deeply. Sure, there was now a cease-fire for the Kachins, but for the whole of Burma the war dragged on and the military had a stronger grasp on power than ever.

With a smoldering gloom in my spirit, I attended a board meeting for the Baptist Peace Fellowship. After the board meeting was over we went to see Steven Spielberg's Holocaust movie, *Schindler's List*. At the end of the movie when the war is over, Schindler is overcome with remorse for what he could have done; perhaps if he had sold the ring on his finger he could have saved one more Jew. I was with Schindler emotionally, living in that anguish. If I had argued my case better at Management Council so

NM would have let me stay on the project, if I had resigned and found other financial support to continue, if I'd done something so I could stay involved, maybe the opposition groups wouldn't have fragmented. Maybe they would have forced comprehensive negotiations. Maybe Manerplaw wouldn't have fallen. Maybe, maybe, maybe. Schindler's Jewish manager expressed the gratitude of the Jews he had saved and consoled Schindler with this rabbinic saying: "Whoever saves one soul saves the whole world." That wise word brought comfort to me and released the tears and anger I had pent up. I could not live with the imaginary scenarios of what might have been. I was responsible to do what I could, to act for peace in the context I faced. I could not be responsible for the decisions others might make, whether NM, the KIO, the KNU, the SLORC, corporations, or governments. I was responsible to be as faithful as I knew how to be to the work God had before me. Maybe I could have done better, but I had done the best I could with all my heart. Somehow in God's gracious economy, that was sufficient and would be blessed.

New Direction out of the Ashes

At the very conference in La Boquita, Nicaragua, in July 1992 where I told Saboi that I could no longer participate in the Burma peace initiative, a new dream was born that would give direction for my peacemaking for many years to come. Participants had gathered from more than thirty countries, and we discovered that Baptists were playing key roles in many conflicts—but with little or no support from mission structures. Gustavo Parajon had been on the mediation team in Nicaragua that led to the peace process that ended the war in his country. He was currently serving on the national Reconciliation Commission. Eleazar Ziherembere from Rwanda was working with a Catholic bishop to mediate between the Hutu government and Tutsi rebels in a process that brought about a cease-fire and the introduction of United Nations peacekeepers. Albert Ndandu was a leader in the nonviolent campaign to oust the Mobutu regime and bring democracy to Zaire. Salvadoran church leaders including Edgar Palacios headed up the National Debate for Peace in El Salvador that pressured the government and insurgents to engage in peace talks and end that war. South African church leaders working to dismantle the apartheid system had led the way in the Standing for the Truth Campaign. That sustained nonviolent effort gave the final push that led to the release of Nelson Mandela. Then there was Saboi Jum mediating between the military government and ethnic insurgents in Burma. Church leaders were meditating between armed groups or leading nonviolent movements for justice, peace, and freedom. They were engaged in these struggles with little help from Baptist mission agencies, armed only with their courage, their creativity, their pastoral passion, and the power of the Holy Spirit. What could we in North America do to stand with them and help them in their causes?

After hearing in a conference plenary session about Saboi's work and his disappointment about my being pulled off the peace process, four of us gathered to talk and dream around a table under a thatched *rancho* that overlooked a Pacific beach. With me were Eleazar Ziherembere from Rwanda, Albert Ndandu from Zaire, and George Williamson. We talked about all the stories we had heard. Eleazar and Albert shared ideas of what they would find helpful from the international community. George and I discussed frustrations and possibilities from the North American side. As we continued our conversation a dream began to emerge about forming a project under the Baptist Peace Fellowship that would relate directly to indigenous church leaders involved in strategic peace and justice struggles around the world. We would shape what we offered to the needs of the particular situation, not leaving it to the indigenous leaders to figure out how to fit into our criteria and frameworks, but rather having us make the adjustments to see how we could best serve in any particular setting. George and I left that conversation determined to move the idea toward action.

It took us a few years to have the dream grow from conception to birth. The BPFNA board discussed the idea thoroughly, working through issues of the vision, structure, staff, criteria for involvement, and so on. Throughout the process one big issue haunted us: we had no money to launch a fund with a globetrotting staff. Then in 1994 we received a poignant surprise. Victor Gavel had been one of the founding members of the American Baptist Pacifist Fellowship, one of the antecedents of the BPFNA. When Victor died, he left a bequest to the BPFNA. The board decided to use $30,000 from the bequest as an endowment to launch the new global peace partnership initiative. We called it the Gavel Memorial Peace Fund, a non-descript name in some ways in that it kept "Baptist" out of the title, which might help in some contexts. Having two names to use—Baptist Peace Fellowship or Gavel Fund—gave us options regarding our public front in any situation. Naming the fund after Victor Gavel and his late wife, Eileen Gavel, allowed us to honor our history and the "saints" upon whose shoulders we stand, a value that the BPFNA had expressed regularly through the telling of stories from earlier generations of Baptist peace activists.

I was the volunteer administrator of the fund, which initially meant working with the board to refine the criteria for its use and beginning to publicize the fund and raise money for our projects. In January 1995 we gave the first grant from the Gavel Fund. The BPFNA sponsored a "Friendship Tour" to Burma, now formally called Myanmar. Twelve of us traveled to Burma to visit the Baptist leaders and churches as well as to see first-hand what was going on in that country. We presented Saboi Jum with the first grant from the fund conceived out of the ashes of my being pulled out of the peace process. Saboi was still involved in peacemaking initiatives, and this was one small way we could begin to reconnect to his vision and work. As I handed the small amount of money to Saboi, I had no idea how the model of partnership peacemaking would grow and where it would lead me. I just felt the relief of once again doing something positive in a country and with a friend who meant so much to me.

I received a blessed postscript to this story while teaching with my wife at the Shalom Baptist Seminary in Nagaland, India, in 2007. A Kachin student from Burma was studying there, and he approached me to thank me for my work in bringing about the cease-fire between the Kachin insurgents and the government. He had lived for six years as a refugee in China, and the cease-fire agreement allowed him and his family to return home. Their village, which had been completely destroyed, had to be rebuilt. In spite of the ongoing struggles under the military regime, their living situation was much better than it had been while they were refugees. His words of appreciation were an unexpected balm to an old wound in my heart.

(Left) Planting a Peace Pole with Thelma Mitchell at the Mission Center of the American Baptist Churches while serving as Manager of the Peace Program; (right) Rev. Saboi Jum with a child soldier in one of the ethnic insurgent armies in Burma

Saboi Jum and author meeting with former President Jimmy Carter

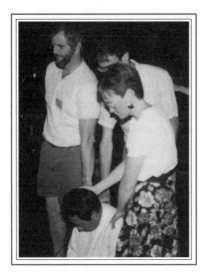 

(Left) Author (center, obscured), Ken Sehested and Sharon Buttry pray for Saboi Jum at a BPFNA conference to commission him for his peacemaking ministry; (right) Author presents Saboi Jum with the first grant from the Gavel Memorial Peace Fund

Saboi Jum and author meeting with Brang Seng, chairman (far right) and other leaders of the Kachin Independence Organization in a hotel room in Hong Kong

Brang Seng greets Saboi Jum for talks in the KIO remote jungle headquarters in Burma

Author making a formal opening statement at talks between international mediators and leaders of the ethnic insurgent organizations and democracy leaders from Burma

Author with former Nicaraguan President Daniel Ortega and Gustavo Parajon at the International Baptist Peace Conference in Nicaragua where the idea of the Gavel Fund was conceived

Author and seminary students in front of the peace mural at Myanmar Institute of Theology

4

THE NAGA PEACE INITIATIVE

Naga Background

Nagaland—I'd never heard of it until I came to Valley Forge to direct the Peace Program. I learned that a Naga named Kijungluba Ao was the second person to receive the Dalhberg Peace Award, the highest peace honor for the American Baptist Churches. The first recipient was Martin Luther King, Jr. in 1963. I looked further into the story of Kijungluba Ao while doing research for my book *Christian Peacemaking* (Judson Press, 1994) and discovered an incredible story about missionary outreach, suffering people, and courageous peacemakers. I dug out the biography of Longri Ao from International Ministries' library and learned of his involvement in mediation efforts in the 1960s and 1970s that culminated in the Shillong Accord peace agreement. (Longri was no relation to Kijungluba as Ao is a common tribal name for Ao Nagas, one of the larger Naga sub-tribes.) The story of Longri Ao so moved me that it became a major section in my book. Before long the Nagas moved from a fascinating topic of research and writing to a major portion of my life work.

My active involvement with the Nagas began in August 1993 when Ken Sehested, executive director of the BPFNA, took an advance copy of *Christian Peacemaking* with him to a meeting in Zimbabwe of the Human Rights Commission of the Baptist World Alliance. Ken shared stories of Baptist peacemakers from the book, including the story of Longri Ao. After the session Dr. Wati Aier asked Ken if he would like to know what had happened since that story. Wati, principal and founder of Oriental Theological Seminary, the premier Naga seminary, proceeded to tell Ken about the failure of the Shillong Accord, the fracturing of Naga unity, the on-going war between India and Naga insurgents, the suffering of the Naga people, and his desire to find a way toward peace. Wati invited Ken to come to Nagaland and see what was going on for himself.

In February 1994, Ken flew to Calcutta to meet Wati. They had planned to fly to Nagaland, but Nagaland had been under martial law for many years, occupied by the Indian Army. The Indian government did not give Ken the required "restricted areas" permit, so Wati arranged for some Naga leaders to meet secretly with Ken in Calcutta. Ken met with Yaopey, a human rights lawyer later assassinated as he was investigating Indian Army human rights violations. Ken also met with General Atem, commander of the forces of the National Socialist Council of Nagaland—Isak and Muivah faction (NSCN-IM). Ken learned the Naga story, a story he and I were to hear countless times over the following years as it is the Naga custom to tell the full story even if a listener knows it already.

This is the story we repeatedly heard: the Nagas are a tribal people of Mongolian racial origin, perhaps via Southeast Asia, who historically have had no ties— religious, political, linguistic, or otherwise—with the people of India. They lived in villages scattered in the rugged hills running southward from the Himalayas along today's India-Burma border. About 3 million Nagas are divided into thirty-nine tribal groups of various sizes and with different languages. They were headhunters, resulting in a terrifying reputation that left them isolated from the formation of various kingdoms in neighboring areas. When the British came as the colonizers in the 19th century, they incorporated the Naga Hills into the administrative area of Assam, India.

American Baptist missionaries first arrived in the Naga areas in 1872, and the Nagas responded positively to their presentation of the Christian message. Today an estimated 90 percent of Nagas are Christian; about 80 percent are Baptist. Nagas talk about the gospel turning them from being headhunters into "soul winners," and the main Naga slogan, even in their political literature, is "Nagaland for Christ!" They picture themselves as a beleaguered outpost of Christianity, surrounded by Hindus to the east (India),

Muslims to the south (Bangladesh), Buddhists to the west (Burma or Myanmar), and Communist atheists to the north (China). Their response to the surrounding cultures is religious missionary endeavor and political strivings for independence.

Nagas joined with Gandhi in the nonviolent campaign to throw the British colonizers out of India. They formed the Naga National Council (NNC) as their main political organization. When it was clear that the British were finally withdrawing, an NNC delegation met with Gandhi in 1947 to express the Naga aspirations for independence. Gandhi told the delegation, "Nagas have every right to be independent. We did not want to live under the domination of the British, and they are now leaving us. I want you to feel that India is yours. I feel that the Naga Hills are mine just as much they are yours, but if you say, 'it is mine' then the matter must stop there. I believe in the brotherhood of man, but I do not believe in force or forced unions. If you do not wish to join the Union of India nobody will force you to do that." The NNC declared independence for Nagaland on 15 August 1947, one day before India's independence. However, after Gandhi was assassinated on 30 January 1948, Indian President Jawaharlal Nehru, faced with the war in which India disintegrated into the two countries of India and Pakistan, refused to recognize Naga independence.

After a series of negotiations and failed agreements, the NNC sponsored a plebiscite, or referendum, in May 1951 in which the Naga public overwhelmingly voted for independence. The government of India sent the army to the region, and following arrests of key leaders in 1955, the NNC abandoned its policy of nonviolence and began armed resistance. The war rapidly escalated in brutality. The Indian Army forcibly relocated villages, razed many villages, and engaged in widespread destruction and killing. Naga families fled into the jungle where many died of starvation and disease. American Baptist missionaries were expelled because the Indian government suspected they were stirring up the independence sentiment. Reporters were also kept out of the region, sealing off an already-remote region from the attention of the world. The violence went unchecked for many years. Naga human rights groups claim that more than 200,000 people died during the conflict, most in the late 1950s and early 1960s when the war was almost genocidal, though the government of India claims that such figures are grossly inflated. Nobody can provide accurate casualty figures.

Beginning in 1964 there were a series of peace negotiations and various agreements spurred on by Naga Baptist leaders such as Longri Ao as well as international supporters led by Rev. Michael Scott of Great Britain. In one agreement the current Indian state of Nagaland was carved out of Assam, but many Nagas complained that this isolated Nagas in the surrounding states rather than brought all Nagas into one political entity. In 1975 the Shillong Accord was signed by various NNC leaders, but the peace agreement was fatally flawed. Key Naga resistance leaders were left out of the process, and the accord agreed to incorporation of the Naga areas into the Indian union (excluding those on the Burma side of the border). The Nagas, who had the NNC as their sole political organization up to that point, split into factions supporting or opposing the Shillong Accord. The new opposition faction was the National Socialist Council of Nagaland (NSCN). The two factions began fighting each other, and before long as many Nagas were dying at the hand of other Nagas as were being killed by Indian military forces. Later both the NSCN and NNC splintered further, sometimes with ferocious violence, over issues of leadership, distrust, and fears of secret agreements with India. By the time Ken and Wati met there were four groups: NSCN-IM (led by Isak and Muivah), NSCN-K (led by Khaplang), NNC (Adino faction, which mildly supported the Shillong Accord—nobody wanted to fully accept it), and the NNC (non-Accordist faction). The leadership conflicts among the Nagas produced a steady spiral of violence and an inability to provide a unified basis from which to challenge the policies of the government of India and advocate for Naga rights and aspirations.

Ken returned from India to meet with the BPFNA board and tell the Naga story. We were unsure how to engage in such a tangled conflict so far away and so removed from the world's attention. Because of the Baptist missionary heritage and the fact that all the political leaders were Baptists, we felt this was a unique opportunity for Baptist peacemakers to play a constructive role. In 1996 we had the opportunity to take the next step.

The Beginnings of a New Naga Peace Dream

I left National Ministries in June 1996, following Sharon to Detroit, Michigan, where she had taken the position of executive director at Friendship House, an American Baptist urban neighborhood center. I planned to work quarter-time with the Baptist Peace Fellowship directing the fledgling Gavel Fund. I tried to put together other jobs that would be flexible enough to allow me to continue the peace work. God led me to the First Baptist Church of Dearborn. Dearborn is a near west-side suburb of Detroit. I was called as co-pastor along with Rev. Jay Martin. The church gave me up to four weeks a year for my international peacemaking travels since Jay was there to provide pastoral care while I traveled. It was an ideal situation for that time in my life. I could still devote time to my family while keeping my hand in the creative development of the international peacemaking partnerships with indigenous peacemakers. The Naga peace initiative became the major project for that period of my work.

In November 1996, Ken and I were leaders in the Intensive Training Conference on Conflict Resolution sponsored by the Asian Baptist Federation in Chiang Mai, Thailand. The BPFNA was one of the co-sponsoring bodies. Ken and I were joined by Glenda Fontenot, the current BPFNA board president and a trainer in conflict resolution in both church and corporate circles. Amid the conference program with its plenary sessions and workshops, two unplanned events led to the conception of a new peace initiative among the Nagas.

Wati Aier spoke about the Naga situation at a plenary session. In the months prior to the conference, extensive violence had broken out between Nagas and Kukis in the Indian state of Manipur, just to the south of Nagaland. Both Naga and Kuki leaders were present at the conference, and Wati invited them all

63

to the front at the end of his presentation. Wati had told about the violence from both sides and expressed his own sorrow and repentance for the attitudes that had led to the conflict. Nagas and Kukis gathered in a circle and held hands while Ken Sehested led a prayer for peace and reconciliation.

One night after a plenary session Wati and Dr. V. K. Nuh asked Glenda, Ken, and me to meet with them to talk in more detail about the Naga situation, especially about the internal divisions among the Nagas that were leading to so much bloodshed. We began to think about where we might get access to the key leaders and what might be necessary to start a dialog toward peace. Glenda, Ken, and I offered all the help of the BPFNA, but when we left Chiang Mai we had no idea of the journey we would take because of that pledge of assistance.

Wati left Chiang Mai and immediately got to work. He contacted representatives of the various factions and introduced the idea of a face-to-face meeting to explore peace and reconciliation. He formed a group of supportive church and business people to be the respected group of community elders convening and hosting the talks. However, the main Baptist body among the Nagas, the Nagaland Baptist Church Council (NBCC) refused to get involved. V. K. Nuh was head of the Council of Naga Baptist Churches (CNBC), an overlapping body that included Nagas from all the states in India as well as Nagaland state proper. Dr. Nuh had worked for years on peace among the Nagas, and he passionately supported Wati in this new process. Eventually they secured tentative agreements from all the parties and from various political and social leaders to come to the U.S. for peace talks.

Wati contacted Ken and me about the developments, so we quickly needed to come up with a venue and the money to support a major gathering of Nagas, including insurgent leaders, in the U.S. We left it up to the Nagas to figure out how to handle the documentation to get into the U.S. given that some were operating under pseudonyms and with false passports. Because of the strong missionary history with the Nagas, Wati wanted a site that would give a Baptist pastoral and prophetic message in support of peace to the Nagas attending the talks. We tried to find a location near the American Baptist mission center in Valley Forge, but we decided on Emory University in Atlanta near the Carter Center. President Carter's peacemaking vision and being a Baptist would be our connection. We also invited Dr. John Sundquist, executive director of International Ministries for the ABC to attend as a missionary advocate for reconciliation.

Everything seemed in place for historic talks with all the factions, including delicate housing arrangements to keep warring factions separate from each other. Then political gamesmanship sabotaged the gathering. The chief minister of Nagaland, S. C. Jamir, insisted on coming, even though he was viewed by all the Naga factional leaders as a collaborator with the government of India. Isak and Muivah refused to come if Jamir would be there. Jamir ended up not coming; ironically, the government of India refused him permission to attend. Even though Jamir did not come, neither did Isak and Muivah, and we were left waiting to receive them at the airport the day everyone was flying into Atlanta.

We pressed forward with the talks, gathering at Emory from 28 July to 3 August 1997. Our peace team had two parts. The Naga team included Wati Aier, V. K. Nuh, and Bonny Resu of the Asian Baptist Federation. The U.S. team included Ken and me from the BPFNA, John Sundquist from International Ministries (we had some confusion between the two IMs—the American Baptist mission agency and the Naga insurgent organization!), and Ron Kraybill, a Mennonite conflict transformation activist who came to advise us in the process. Representatives from NSCN-K and the two NNC factions came, as did leaders from the Naga Hoho, a traditional tribal council, and a retired former chief minister of Nagaland representing the state politicians. While we gathered in Atlanta, large street demonstrations for peace were organized by local pastors back in Nagaland.

We began with a joint worship service and a sermon on reconciliation by Dr. Sundquist. Then the peace team met with each group separately to hear their particular views on the Naga story and struggle, including their concerns about what was necessary for peace. Eventually we got people together for plenary dialog sessions. One of the most poignant moments came when Dolly Mongro of the Khaplang faction, speaking for all sides said with grief, "We have killed so many of our own people." Without Isak and Muivah present it was impossible to make a peace agreement, but as the discussions continued we began to see the outlines of a possible joint statement emerge.

In the middle of our process, stunning news jolted us. Isak and Muivah had agreed with the government of India to a three-month cease-fire. Participants wondered how could they make such an agreement while refusing to talk with their own Naga brothers. Dolly Mongro was furious, feeling both insulted by Isak and Muivah and ignored by the Indian government. He telephoned India calling for attacks to be launched against Indian Army units to show that the NSCN-K was a force to be reckoned with as much as NSCN-IM. Ken, Wati, and I pleaded with him to no avail to hold back in keeping with the spirit of the Atlanta talks. We later heard reports that India quickly agreed by telephone to the cease-fire that had been under sporadic discussion with NSCN-IM for a long time. The reports suggested that this strange way to make a cease-fire was prompted by the Atlanta talks and India's desire not to see a united Naga front emerge.

Even with this sobering reminder of the seriousness of the conflict, the participants pushed ahead to agree upon a statement that we titled "The Atlanta Appeal." At the conclusion of the talks, the Naga participants joined in a worship service at the Oakhurst Baptist Church in Decatur where the appeal was read publicly and prayers for peace were raised. The participants pledged "to earnestly work for a new future for our people." The joint statement went on to say, "With this appeal, we call on our Naga people to follow suit by relinquishing old antagonisms, by giving up old grudges. Old memories of injury and insult have controlled our relations for too long. With this appeal, we urge all our leaders, in every sector of society, to take significant steps to bring reconciliation, building upon the best of our heritage" (*Baptist Peacemaker*, Fall, 1997). The appeal was signed by representatives of three of the four Naga political factions, leaders from the Naga Hoho, and members of the convening group.

With the excitement about the progress in the Atlanta talks and the public celebration of the appeal, there was still anxiety about the failure to draw Isak and Muivah into the talks. That anxiety would prove to be realistic, for shortly after the Atlanta talks concluded the levels of violence in Nagaland increased. Even with the cease-fire in place between India and NSCN-IM, the violence between Khaplang's forces and Isak and Muivah's soldiers escalated. During the months after the Atlanta talks, almost every time Wati drove the rough roads on the forty-five-minute trip from Dimapur to his seminary, he had to pass through opposing checkpoints every few kilometers: one set up by the Indian Army, the next by Khaplang's men, and then another by IM's cadres. Wati often saw bodies in the road, and once firing broke out immediately after he passed through an insurgent checkpoint. Isak and Muivah publicly condemned the Atlanta talks, labeling all who participated in them as "puppets" and "traitors," including specifically V. K. Nuh and Wati Aier. At the end of the Atlanta talks all the participants urged the BPFNA and the Naga peacemakers to increase their efforts to bring Isak and Muivah into the process. Without their involvement nothing would succeed. So in spite of the denunciations made against him, Wati continued to make contact with NSCN-IM representatives calling for a meeting between him and the two leaders. The BPFNA also sent messages urging such a meeting.

After much prompting, Isak and Muivah agreed to meet with Wati and me in Bangkok in early November 1997. However, Wati's flight out of Nagaland was delayed for a day, leaving me to meet with the two insurgent leaders alone in my hotel. It was a tough meeting. For four hours Muivah, and occasionally Isak, railed angrily about all the injustices suffered by the Nagas and the betrayals visited on them by other Nagas, especially Khaplang, the Naga Baptist church leaders, and even people working for peace. In their view all these leaders in one way or another were abandoning the Naga cause. Muivah told about the coup by Khaplang that led to the split in the NSCN, an attack in which a couple hundred Naga soldiers and leaders were gunned down in a large assembly area. Isak and Muivah crawled on their hands and knees over their fallen comrades to escape with a few others into the jungle. It was obvious that their feelings of bitterness were very deep. I was particularly stunned by their anger toward the church leaders, whom they perceived as having backed policies that amounted to surrender to India. After four hours of this intense venting of anger I was drained and discouraged.

That evening I went to the Bangkok airport to pick up Wati. Isak and Muivah had agreed to meet with us the next day out of courtesy to Dr. Wati. When Wati inquired about how things had gone, I told him I thought the peace efforts were dead; there was no way these guys were going to change. I turned out to be wrong. The four of us met for eight hours. Most of the time Wati and I listened while Muivah spilled out his angry denunciations again, pounding the table and stabbing the air with his finger to make his points. As the day wore on, however, Muivah's intensity waned a bit. By the end of the session, Wati and I were pushing back and challenging him on some points. They agreed to meet with us one more day.

On the final day of our Bangkok meeting, Wati and I urged them to agree to a cease-fire with the other Naga groups. If they could make a three-month cease-fire with the ultimate enemy, India, which had now been renewed once, surely they could make a cease-fire with their Naga brothers. Isak and Muivah refused to agree to that, but we did finally get them to agree to a four-day cease-fire at the end of November. Those four days were for the 125th anniversary celebration of the coming of Christianity to the Naga people. The Naga Baptist churches had planned a huge observance. Isak and Muivah, both Baptists, agreed to engage in no offensive military actions during the period of the anniversary. It seemed so little to Wati and me, a mere four days when we had hoped for at least a cease-fire of three months, yet it was the first cease-fire among the Nagas since the Shillong Accords were signed in 1975. The cease-fire was informal, with no signed document and no face-to-face encounters of the antagonists, bound merely by the word of the leaders. We had done our best; now we were to be outdone by the working of God.

The Naga Baptists convened a great gathering to celebrate the coming of the first Baptist missionaries with the gospel message. John Sundquist of International Ministries, who had been at the Atlanta talks, represented the sending body of those first missionaries. During his stay in Nagaland, many of the underground insurgent leaders visited with him late at night in his hotel room. Everyone kept telling John that God was going to move in a powerful way and that he was to articulate clearly the national consensus. That was quite a burden to put on a preacher!

For the climactic service on Sunday morning, approximately 130,000 Nagas filled a stadium in Kohima, the Nagaland capital, and spilled out into the surrounding streets. John, building on the themes of peace and reconciliation that had been raised throughout the gathering, preached on reconciliation with Wati translating for him. Second-level leaders from all four of the underground groups and the state politicians aligned with the Indian government were present, all professing Christians. (The top underground leaders were either in exile outside the country or in their remote headquarters in the jungle.) When John came to the end of his sermon, he spontaneously spoke directly to the underground leaders, calling on them in the name of Christ to stop the killing now, to ask for forgiveness, and to extend forgiveness to one another. Then he asked the leaders present if they were willing to stand in front of the people to witness that now was the time for peace. Leaders from all four groups rose. Then Wati invited all the Nagas present to rise and pray in "mass prayer" for peace. Everyone in the stadium stood and raised their voices aloud in passionate prayers for peace and reconciliation.

The spiritual power and expression of communal consensus in that moment created a social force that extended the four-day informal cease-fire for years. The killings stopped immediately.

Later there would be crises of one sort or another, a skirmish between patrols, or even the assassination of various individuals, but the demand for peace powered out of the fervent prayers of the people kept these flare-ups from reigniting new rounds of all-out war. The dream of peace had become a demand. Moving from a cease-fire to peace, however, would prove to be much more difficult than getting that first cease-fire.

Next Steps: Success and Frustration

In January 1998 I made my first visit to Nagaland in response to an invitation by Wati to lecture at Oriental Theological Seminary (OTS). I was following in Ken Sehested's footsteps as an OTS lecturer. Ken's visit in 1994 was before any of the cease-fires. Within an hour of checking into his hotel in Dimapur Ken was greeted by six armed, masked Indian Army soldiers who searched his room and questioned him. By January the cease-fires with India had been in place for six months, and the informal cease-fire between the Naga factions had held for more than a month. On the road between Dimapur and OTS the Khaplang faction's roadblock had disappeared, and the soldiers at the Indian Army and the NSCN-IM roadblocks were no longer stopping traffic. I was never stopped, searched, or interrogated.

Beside teaching the seminary students, I met with many of the leaders of various Naga civic organizations to discuss peace efforts. The upcoming Indian parliamentary elections were the main concern people voiced. Placards were plastered around Dimapur proclaiming "Nagas Want Solution, Not Election." To participate in the Indian vote for parliament was to acknowledge the incorporation of the Nagas into the Indian union, the but refusing to be part of the Indian union was at the base of their fifty-year struggle whether by violent or nonviolent means. Most of the community leaders were against participating in the election. Furthermore, they were fearful that the elections would spark violence from the insurgent groups. Muivah was quoted in the *Nagaland Post* threatening to kill people who took part in the polling. The cease-fires seemed to be headed for the garbage can. We discussed how to organize a boycott of the elections and whether we could persuade the insurgent groups to refrain from violence in favor of a nonviolent protest. Those of us working for peace had to move quickly if we were going to forestall the threatened violence as the elections were scheduled for late February, barely a month away.

Wati and the BPFNA had set up a meeting the first of February in Bangkok with insurgent leaders to try to press on with peace and reconciliation talks. Wati and I flew together from Nagaland to Bangkok where we met with Ken, John Sundquist, and Ron Kraybill. The effort to bring the Naga factions together fell apart, but Muivah agreed to join us. We were also joined by Dr. Pongsing Konyak, the general secretary of the Nagaland Baptist Church Council (NBCC). To bring the NBCC into the peace effort was a huge step forward as they had earlier stood aside from the Atlanta talks. The NBCC gave visibility and credibility to the peace initiatives as well as a broad network through their local churches to mobilize people for peace. Muivah had been scathingly critical of Pongsing and the NBCC. Pongsing was a Konyak Naga, as was Khaplang, so he was intimately acquainted with some of the devastation wrought within parts of Naga society by Muivah's actions. Bringing this political-insurgent leader face-to-face with the top Naga church leader proved to be an important step as they spoke directly to each other about their concerns.

The focal points of our discussions were the elections and the various types of responses that could speak about the long-term Naga political aspirations. After much discussion on current political issues, historic parallels, and opportunities to bring together Naga society, we came to a consensus on "A Peace Agenda for Nagalim," a statement we released in the Naga press. (*Nagalim* is the term in Nagamese for "the areas inhabited by Nagas," parallel to *Nagaland* in English, but without the political limitations resulting from India naming the Nagaland state, which only incorporated a portion of the Naga-inhabited areas.) The Peace Agenda called for continuing the cease-fires, urging substantive political talks between India and the Naga leaders, a boycott of the scheduled elections, and that everyone would refrain from violence in support of or against the election. It also called for the Sunday before the election to be a mass demonstration for peace through public prayer services in churches and the flying of white flags on buildings and vehicles. Pongsing agreed to the Peace Agenda, putting the NBCC behind the boycott and the prayer services for peace. Muivah signed the Agenda, committing himself to hold back from violence and allow a nonviolent witness to be made that would mobilize the broad Naga society.

I had argued with Muivah that the sporadic violence of the Naga insurgents was so mundane and forgotten by the world that his actions would garner little attention. On the other hand, a massive boycott and nonviolent witness would be of interest to a major global media outlet like the *New York Times*, which was running frequent articles on the Indian parliamentary elections. I was wrong. In spite of the fact that I sent press kits with background and contact information to the *New York Times*, BBC, CNN, and many other press organizations, nobody picked up the story of the Naga protest.

On Sunday, 22 February 1998, white flags sprouted all across Naga communities. Almost every Naga church prayed for peace and reconciliation. Then on the parliamentary election day 85 percent of the electorate boycotted the election. Those who participated were mostly non-Nagas, government functionaries, or even people who had been paid to vote, and according to some reports, to vote repeatedly. One poll reported only seven votes being cast. Some of the political candidates even stepped down, refusing to run against the overwhelming public rejection of the process. One Indian news magazine called the entire voting process a farce because of the breadth of the boycott. A clear public statement was made about a broad consensus among the Naga public for a political solution to the Indo-Naga conflict that recognized Naga political aspirations. The Naga politicians who participated in the Indian governmental structures at the state or parliamentary level were exposed as having no legitimacy among those who were governed. It also was an action that awakened broad sections of the Naga public to the influence they could have on the direction of the political process.

Following the boycott campaign, Ken and I kept working with Wati as we tried to get the Naga factional leaders together for face-to-face talks. Communications went back and forth from Naga peacemakers to Muivah in exile and to Khaplang in the jungle. Nothing was achieved. Occasional skirmishes would threaten the cease-fires and generate a flood of local newspaper accounts and denunciations, but the public pressure to move away from war held together the tenuous suspension of hostilities. As the months passed nothing changed. The public became more at ease with the lessened levels of violence, but there was still the unease of knowing that no solutions for either the intra-Naga conflicts or the political conflict with India were in sight. The activists in the churches and some of the social sector groups were growing frustrated. We seemed stuck.

The Birth of a People's Movement for Peace

In 1999 Wati and I decided the most helpful course of action would be to bring together and train the leaders in the various Naga organizations that had some sort of concern or program for peace. So in February we held a four-day conflict transformation training and planning workshop in Calcutta. Holding such an event in Nagaland was considered risky at that time because everyone would know it was going on, including officials who might be opposed to such a gathering. In Calcutta we could disappear into the mass of the city.

We had an amazing gathering of twenty-four Naga church and activist leaders. On the church side we had leaders from the NBCC, various educational institutions, and church associations. The top leaders came from the Naga People's Movement for Human Rights (NPMHR), the Naga Mothers' Association, the Naga Student Federation, the Naga Council (a civic organization), the United Naga Council of Manipur, and the Naga Women's Union of Manipur, as well as some key individuals respected broadly for their social wisdom. It was the first gathering of the social sector organizations to strategize for peace in the fifty-year history of the conflict. Until that point the main players had been the political organizations and their military wings with occasional efforts for peace made by small *ad hoc* groups sometimes under church sponsorship.

For half of the program I facilitated an intense training with a special focus on relationships and team building. Small groups were formed for the participants to process what they were learning and to build trust with each other. We studied the Bible about peacemaking and nonviolence and engaged in dramatic activities to stimulate learning and discovery.

The other half of the program was spent sharing stories and concerns, then plunging into planning. Tensions surfaced between official church leaders and the grassroots activists. Each side shared their hopes and frustrations, and together they recognized the value each had in the process and how they needed each other. Through the discussions a statement was drawn up that examined the divisions within the Nagas and called for unity. The statement urged Naga leaders "to refrain and stop their accusations and the shedding of anyone's blood in all areas of the Naga homeland" ("The Moment of Truth," Naga Peoples' Movement for Human Rights). United action beyond the statement was still beyond the reach of this group, but the participants were hoping to get further in the days ahead.

To maintain the momentum developed in February we gathered most of the same participants together in Calcutta for another three days in November. I led additional training exercises, especially moving toward issues of developing strategy. We had long discussions of mapping out the complex dimensions of the conflict and sharing ideas to address different aspects of the struggle. As we neared the halfway point of the final day I despaired that we would achieve anything of substance. Discussions had gone around and around, and not a single action idea seemed to be close to falling into place.

Then in the last couple of hours of our time together I witnessed an amazing convergence of thought. Inspiration erupted within the group, igniting an idea with high energy that seemed to effortlessly unfold into a concrete plan. Drawing upon the historical models of Gandhi's Salt March and the Freedom Rides of the U.S. civil rights movement, these Naga social sector leaders decided to launch "The Journey of Conscience." The Journey of Conscience would be a journey from "the heart of Nagaland to the soul of India," taking shape in a physical journey of a large delegation from Nagaland to Delhi. They would travel to arrive in Delhi on 30 January, the anniversary of Gandhi's death. That date would be used to remind Nagas and the Indian public that Gandhi had endorsed Naga independence and that the Naga hopes had been gunned down with him. They would have a service at Gandhi's tomb, a forum with Indian human rights groups and other concerned people, and a public nonviolent demonstration. The delegation would include activists, educators, journalists, and choirs. All would be committed to maintain a strict nonviolent discipline throughout the journey.

The Journey of Conscience, carried out in January 2000, was a huge success. A conference was held in Delhi where Indian human rights activists, journalists, scholars, and retired politicians listened to the presentation of the Naga story and concerns for a just peace. At Gandhi's tomb the Naga choir sang and prayers were held for Nagas killed by Indians, for Nagas killed by other Nagas, for Indians killed by Nagas, and for Naga and Indian families hurt by the conflict. Then as the Nagas took to the streets in a demonstration for justice and peace, the Journey of Conscience ranks were swelled by the Naga students studying in Delhi's universities.

The success of the Journey of Conscience propelled it into an ongoing focus for the movement rather than a one-time event. A trip to Nagaland was organized for Indians to see what was going on within the borders of their own country and to learn directly from the Naga people about their plight instead of hearing everything through the filters of the Indian media. In succeeding years, cultural and activist traveling groups were organized to present the Naga story in other parts of India and Asia, even producing CDs and videos to reach wider audiences. The people's organizations were breaking through the isolation that had kept their suffering and their struggle out of the world's awareness.

They were also changing the political context in which the government of India and the Naga political and insurgent factions were operating. These people's organizations, through their coordinated efforts, were raising a public demand for an end to the violence and a genuine negotiated settlement. That pressure not only provided more glue to preserve the fragile negotiating process between the NSCN-IM and the government of India but also achieved successes in getting various Indian groups to acknowledge the legitimacy of Naga rights and concerns, something that impressed even Muivah, the experienced insurgent leader.

The Long, Slow Journey Forward

After the Journey of Conscience, the efforts to bring peace to the region slowly moved forward with many stumbles and steps back. Over the next few years the Naga factions were unable to make any formal agreement that might move the parties toward reconciliation, but the intra-Naga violence was sporadic at worst. In December 2002, the government of India lifted the bans against the NSCN-IM and NSCN-K, allowing political discussions to proceed openly, including open public consultations between the insurgent leaders and Naga community leaders. Formal talks continued with regularity between the NSCN-IM and the Indian prime minister's office. The cease-fires were periodically renewed, and after many years of delay political discussions finally began.

The progress of the peace process between the Nagas and India caused other conflicts to escalate as vested interests in the status quo were challenged by possibilities being considered in the India-Naga talks. The state of Manipur saw increasing hostilities as large portions of Manipur's land were claimed as part of the "greater Nagaland" that Nagas would like to see formed. In Manipur the Nagas live in most of the hill country, but the political process of the state is dominated by the Meiteis, who live mostly on the plains. Northeast India is rife with ethnic insurgencies, of which the Naga insurgency has been the longest running. While the Naga conflict seemed to be working its way slowly toward a conclusion, other conflicts were very volatile. Furthermore, there was no movement at all toward peace with the Nagas living on the other side of the border in Burma or Myanmar. The Naga areas in Burma are even more remote than the areas within India, and the political process in Burma is tightly controlled by the Burmese Army.

After the Journey of Conscience I continued to stay in close contact with the Naga people's organizations. Daniel Hunter, a young activist and BPFNA board member, and I visited Nagaland in 2000 to do training with the seminary students at OTS and consult with the NPMHR activists. When we returned in late 2002 to facilitate a three-day advanced strategy workshop and planning sessions for the people's organizations, it was exciting to see the growth of their movement. Many of the activists were getting extensive leadership training in conflict transformation and experiential education. They were organizing their own grassroots training and needed us less for training and more as an expression of international solidarity.

My relationship with Isak and Muivah grew during those years. A breakthrough happened when Muivah spent a year in prison in Bangkok for traveling on a false passport. Following our 2000 Nagaland trip, Daniel Hunter and I had met in Bangkok with the younger NSCN-IM leaders and talked especially about asking for forgiveness. Confession and forgiveness had been major themes of the efforts for reconciliation among the Nagas, themes addressed in the Atlanta Appeal and the statement coming out of the 1999 people's organizations meeting in Calcutta. Muivah had offered to extend forgiveness to those who had "betrayed the Naga cause" if they would disavow the Shillong Accord and support NSCN-IM's efforts to find a solution through negotiations with India. I had long argued with him that his side had also done harmful things during the course of the conflict and that many people had legitimate grievances against him and his cadres. Over the years I had received from the NSCN-K and NNC groups many detailed accounts of mass killings and assassinations attributed to NSCN-IM. The responsibility for bloodshed and bitterness was on all sides. As Daniel and I discussed this issue with the second-level leaders of the NSCN-IM, we were impressed by how quickly they understood that they had enough political capital and respect to lead the way to healing of the Naga divisions by confessing wrongs done even as they continued to give political leadership.

Muivah had been held in prison for a few months and was only allowed the normal daily fifteen-minute visits with a Plexiglas window between the prisoner and visitor. Daniel and I were allowed to meet for an hour with Muivah in a prison office. Besides talking about the various current issues in the peace process, I met with him as a pastor to a brother going through a difficult situation. My care for him seemed to be deeply appreciated. I talked also about confessing the wrongs done by his side as a way to open doors of trust with alienated portions of Naga society. Muivah said nothing at the time, but the next day— for the first time in a formal statement—the NSCN-IM leadership acknowledged that in their zeal for the Naga cause excesses in violence had resulted in needless deaths and injury. Later, following a murder of a Chakesang Naga leader by NSCN-IM cadres in December 2004, Isak issued a statement of responsibility and regret from NSCN-IM, a statement that in earlier years would have been full of only accusations and justification.

Akum Longchari was one of the young activists who came up through the ranks of the Naga Student Federation, then into the Naga People's Movement for Human Rights. He attended the Calcutta trainings as well as the two-year-long Conflict Transformation Program at Eastern Mennonite University in Virginia. Akum had been leading many workshops on conflict transformation among the Naga grassroots for NPMHR. Because of the growing strength and success of the Journey of Conscience movement, Muivah invited us to come and train the NSCN-IM leadership in negotiation and conflict resolution. They had continued to extend the cease-fires with the government of India, but if they were to engage in more substantive political talks they would need to develop their skills in how to work at the negotiation table. The skills to be successful political bargainers are very different from the skills to run a successful guerilla war. Akum and I met in Bangkok with Isak, Muivah, and seven of the second-tier leaders for a three-day training program.

As Akum and I facilitated the various learning simulations and exercises, I was intrigued by the level of engagement by these battle-toughened insurgents. It seemed as if new horizons were constantly opening up in their thinking. At one point, in response to a question, one of the second-tier leaders began to reel off the former standard party line, something I'd seen him do *ad nauseam* in another context. Muivah bluntly cut him off, saying, "We've got to start thinking in new ways!" To be a part of reshaping in a positive way the ideological mindset of a major insurgent group was exciting and humbling. Following the training Muivah issued a press release about the peace talks with India in which he said, "I believe that the Nagas and India can come to a win/win solution to our conflict." I was glad he had learned the language of conflict resolution, but how deep would the spirit of such a transformative effort go?

For the next few years, peacemaking efforts continued with no clear breakthroughs but no major steps backward. Many other trips to India, meetings in Thailand or the U.S., and trainings in Nagaland took place. The global media began covering a bit more about what was happening with the Nagas, although there still was scant attention paid to their struggle on the whole. Their isolation has broken down considerably, for even though Nagaland remained under martial law and with restricted access for foreigners, Nagas were getting out into the wider world in a more visible way. Isak and Muivah were able to come above ground and speak regularly in the Indian press as well as in some global media channels. Leaders of the Naga people's organizations traveled outside of India to speak in various forums and to study and train in settings with other international activists. Their newfound access raised their visibility among people concerned with struggles for justice and peace. Solidarity organizations were established in the U.S. and Europe, some with a slant toward one or another of the Naga factions. Through the NSCN-IM faction the Nagas joined the Unrepresented Nations and Peoples Organization, a global group of indigenous people and occupied nations to advocate for their rights and nonviolent resolution of their conflicts in international forums such as the United Nations. Since Ken Sehested's first contact with Wati Aier the conflict has been dramatically transformed and moved in a direction in which a solution became imaginable and in which grassroots people were growing in the power and hope to shape their own destiny. But the breakthrough for reconciliation among the Nagas remained frustratingly elusive.

Naga factional soldiers display a banner in appreciation of the Baptist Peace Fellowship's work in the Naga peace initiative

Demonstration in Dimapur, Nagaland in support of the Atlanta talks

Wati Aier (center), Muivah (far left), Pongsing (center right), Ron Kraybill (far right), and Ken Sehested (right, facing away) at peace talks in Bangkok

(Left) Wati Aier speaks during the Calcutta meetings that gave birth to the Journey of Conscience; (right) Author with pro-peace posters in a Naga community

5

AROUND THE WORLD

A New Commission

While serving as pastor in Dearborn, Michigan, and working quarter-time with the BPFNA I was involved in projects beside the Naga peace initiative. I traveled to Myanmar, Indonesia, the Philippines, and Cameroon during that period, mostly to facilitate conflict transformation training. Sometimes I traveled and trained solo, sometimes with a BPFNA colleague.

Through all these international activities I stayed in close contact with the staff of International Ministries (IM) of the American Baptists. I consulted with IM missionaries and area directors about some of the issues to be faced, especially with Ben Chan, who was responsible for mission partnerships in much of Asia including the Naga churches. As a pastor I attended IM's World Mission Conference a couple of times and had a number of conversations with John Sundquist, IM's Executive Director. Because of the success of our Naga peacemaking efforts and perhaps the Mennonite involvement in peace efforts in places like Nicaragua, International Ministries incorporated the phrase "conflict transformation" into one of the forms of "Christ-like" mission in their new "Go Global" mission statement. The expanded mission statement also set a goal of hiring "global service missionaries" who would work around the world in areas of special expertise, including conflict transformation. I began talking to John about whether I was the person to respond to that aspect of the "Go Global" vision, and he encouraged me to begin the missionary application process.

Timing was an important issue for me. I intentionally had limited my involvement in the Gavel Fund to quarter-time because of not wanting to travel too much while my children were still in school. My youngest child, Janelle, would graduate from high school in 2003, so that would be a time when I could make a transition from the pastorate to a full-time international peacemaking position. Sharon and I both entered into the missionary application process with IM, but it became clear to all of us that God's call for her to urban mission in Detroit and Hamtramck was still very strong. To be a global service missionary, I mainly needed an international airport; where I lived mattered little. IM agreed to call me to international service while being based in Detroit. At the World Mission Conference in summer 2003, I was commissioned as a missionary and began my full-time service with IM.

As an IM missionary I've visited many countries to do short-term training programs and consultations. The best involvements are ones in which I return repeatedly to build upon what we had done in earlier visits. I get to understand better the particular context of the place, and the leaders with whom I partner get to work with the concepts and practices of conflict transformation at deeper and more thorough levels. In some cases I've been able to build off of work I had done earlier with National Ministries and the BPFNA, but in many cases new doors were opened through the network of mission partnerships IM has established over the years. In this chapter I will tell some of the stories in which my involvement was smaller in scope than the initiatives in Burma and with the Nagas yet still significant. My involvement sometimes spanned different chapters of my work life.

Liberia

Rev. Napoleon Divine was introduced to me at a Baptist gathering in Philadelphia. Napoleon was pastor of the Christ International Baptist Church, a congregation mostly of Liberians who had fled to the United States. Napoleon had left during the turmoil following the 1980 coup by Sergeant Samuel Doe who seized power and executed President William Tolbert and many cabinet ministers. Napoleon had been a radio announcer at the time. He was seized by a group of soldiers and taken to a field to be shot. He muttered a prayer offering his life into God's hands when a luxury car drove down the road. The soldiers immediately left Napoleon to chase after the bigger prize. Napoleon fled Liberia, eventually making his way to the U.S.

Napoleon shared with me his dream of organizing a delegation of American Baptists to go to Liberia to learn about the situation and to monitor the post-civil war elections scheduled for May 1997. I liked the idea, so we laid plans that eventually developed into a joint delegation between National Ministries of the ABC and the Baptist Peace Fellowship. National Ministries was resettling many Liberian refugees as well as housing the Peace Program. Six of us from the two organizations ended up going in addition to Napoleon.

The rule of Samuel Doe had been very chaotic, and eventually a civil war erupted with a number of opposition factions led by various warlords. Charles Taylor was the most prominent rebel leader, and his invasion from neighboring Ivory Coast began the civil war. Doe was captured and executed when another rebel faction seized part of Monrovia. Eventually a peace accord was reached with the various factions. An interim government was established with representatives for the various groups. The election was scheduled to determine the president of Liberia who would lead the country out of the period of war. There was hope for healing, restoration, and reconciliation.

We quickly discovered that what was hoped for was not to be. The fighting had stopped, and the cease-fire was monitored by the troops of various West African nations. But the struggle for power was far from over. The elections were pushed back to July, too late for us to change our plans for the May trip. We dropped the plans to be election monitors. Napoleon suggested that we do training on forgiveness and reconciliation, so we worked two days of training into our program.

The destruction of Monrovia and the surrounding countryside was pathetic to behold. The city Liberians liked to call the Paris of West Africa was in ruins. Most major buildings were gutted. One five-story government ministry building was a concrete skeleton that had been turned into a displaced persons' camp with blue plastic sheets from the United Nations dividing family living space for the 5,000 residents. We visited churches and ministry sites, hearing tale after tale of woe. The Baptist seminary was in its third site after the previous two had been destroyed. A high school was not only ransacked, but their entire collection of library books were scattered in the rain and ruined. We worshipped in a church pock-marked with bullet holes and with a drummer who was missing a leg.

The Baptists were going through a profound soul-searching. Liberia was founded in 1821 by freed American slaves who returned to Africa as colonizers. One of the colonizers was the first Baptist missionary from the U.S. to Africa, Lott Cary. Cary established Providence Baptist Church, which became the premier religious institution in the land. The main hill in Monrovia has three buildings around a square: The original Legislative Building, the old Presidential Mansion, and Providence Baptist Church. President Tolbert, a leading member of Providence, had been president of the Baptist World Alliance as well as of his country. To the world Liberia's leaders presented a strong, sophisticated image, but within the country it was a different story. The bigotry of the Americo-Liberians (the descendants of the colonizing former slaves) was stunning. Some caricatures of the indigenous people by the Americo-Liberians were as vile as the worst racist depictions in the Jim Crow American South. Americo-Liberians blocked indigenous people from education to keep them locked into a class of cheap labor.

This intense and institutionalized bigotry stirred up the resistance that culminated in Samuel Doe's coup. After Doe succeeded in seizing power, he joined Providence Baptist Church because of its national religious status. To have the unrepentant murderer of the most prominent member of the church now join that congregation must have been unbearable to most of the members. But in the context of fear following the coup everyone kept silent. Charles Taylor, the third major national figure after Tolbert and Doe, was educated in Baptist schools. As he fought his way across the Liberian countryside, he engaged in acts of notorious brutality and left a swath of death and destruction. As Baptist leaders reflected on the legacy of Tolbert, Doe, and Taylor, they sadly wondered how they had gone so wrong to produce such a crop of political leaders for their country.

We came face-to-face with this warped legacy during the most chilling moment of the trip, when we visited the nation's finance minister. The finance minister was a henchman of Charles Taylor, presented by Taylor for the interim government as part of the peace agreement. As we came into his office, he and Napoleon warmly embraced, having been school mates together back in the old days. Then when he sat down behind his desk I beheld one of the weirdest transformations I've ever seen. It was as if I was watching special effects in a Hollywood production: The man's faced changed from that of a cordial host to one that exuded absolute evil. I was looking at a killer, someone who could and probably had committed mass murder without a qualm. We talked about policy matters and the future of Liberia, but I was more shaken by the encounter with this man than by any experience in my life. I've seen many tough people over the years, but I never saw a face that looked so completely given over to the power of evil.

We later discovered what was really going on at the finance ministry. We visited Ruth Foster, the acting president of the interim coalition government. She had received no funds from the national treasury to run her office. She gave us two Liberian secret service agents to be our bodyguards. They had not been paid for nine months, so we tipped them for the services they provided to us. Instead of money going to government services, all the national funds were being channeled into Taylor's political campaign. His party headquarters along the main road was open twenty-four hours a day, provided free food, and ran a continual party with blaring live music. His campaign was based on buying votes from a hungry populace and threatening them with war if he was not put into power. One person we interviewed said he would vote for Taylor though he despised the man; otherwise Taylor would continue the war.

Our Baptist hosts took us to visit the displaced persons camp centered around the gutted government building. As we were about to enter the camp, a group of men from the camp confronted us with anger and hostility. They demanded with pride and anguish, "Have you come to behold our suffering?" The camp residents had organized themselves and selected their own leaders. These leaders were not about to let their families be displayed on a tour of human misery. For about half an hour we talked with these community leaders in the center of a gathering crowd. We told them about our mission to seek healing and reconciliation in Liberia. We told them of our desire to learn about what had happened and what was going on, most especially from those who were suffering the most. We invited the leaders to attend our training program and offered to provide them travel money for the taxis to downtown. Finally, the community leaders felt they could trust us, and they led us on a tour of their camp. We heard the stories of those who had lost everything in the war, including loved ones, homes, dignity, and hope.

Three of our delegation members from National Ministries had to return early, leaving just Napoleon, Bill and Jean Moore, and me. The four of us moved out of the expensive hotel near the U.S. embassy—there had been hardly any other public accommodations left standing in the city—to the home of Napoleon's brother located in the bush beyond the outskirts of Monrovia. The next day I began the training at Providence Baptist Church. Around 125 people gathered, including the leaders from the displaced persons camp. These Liberians were desperate to learn the skills of peace-building and reconciliation. Many came hungry, so we hastily organized a way to feed any who needed breakfast and lunch. Many came sick, some with malaria or typhus, yet they pushed their tormented bodies to come for the training because of their longing for an end to their national nightmare. I've never had such a needy yet deeply committed group of people attend a training.

On the first day I taught on the dynamics of conflict and conflict resolution, focusing especially on the Liberian experience of faulty peace processes (see the Red/Blue Game in ch. 7). At the end of the day the delegation from the displaced persons camp told us they did not need taxi money for the next day. The training was exactly what they needed, and they would pay their own way rather than take assistance. I was deeply moved by their dignity and their affirmation that what I was offering them was of great help and value.

I was troubled by the plans for the second day of training. Napoleon and I had initially planned to deal with the themes of forgiveness and reconciliation. What I'd seen and heard, though, made those topics seem premature. It was a foregone conclusion that Taylor would win the election. Our experience with the finance minister and conversations with people from various walks of life indicated that one nightmare would be replaced by another. Taylor might win an election, but he was not democratic. No prophet was needed to predict the brutality that would characterize his authoritarian rule. So what should I do?

Napoleon had the same questions. While I was leading the training, he had visited the election commission. Their assessment was the same as ours, and they were all discouraged and dismayed at the prospect of the future with Taylor as president. I suggested to Napoleon that maybe we needed to teach about nonviolent struggle. The war was over, but the struggle for justice, human rights, and genuine peace was just entering a different phase. Napoleon agreed, but I was full of fear. I had seen the face of the finance minister. Napoleon and I had been interviewed on the radio. The training was in the center of the city in a public place where we could not monitor who was attending. Taylor's thugs were still active, dealing with opponents through threats and physical intimidation. And where we were staying was isolated in the bush, at the end of long, lonely roads where it would be easy for someone to disappear and never be seen again. Perhaps these were fantasies of my fears rather than real possibilities, but I spent the night in prayer for wisdom and courage about what to do with the Liberians in the training, who were so desperate and hungry for what we were offering. The words of Jesus about a loving father giving a child bread and not a stone came to me. I had been sent to give bread, something to nourish the passion for peace that would bring hungry and sick people out for training. I could not play it safe; I had to teach what I believed was right and best. The next day I taught about nonviolent action, based on Jesus' Sermon on the Mount. The response was enthusiastic. "This is what we need," many said to me. "Thank you!"

Some of the participants in the training were young pastors who had seen the failures of the older generation of Baptists and been abandoned by the better-off church leaders who had fled the country. They knew that working for peace and justice was the only way that Liberia could have any hope. Because we came from the Baptist Peace Fellowship of North America they questioned us extensively about the vision and structure of our organization. While we were still there they organized a meeting to launch their own Liberian Baptist Peace Fellowship.

Rev. Solomon Ernst was chosen as their first president. He had been one of the leading figures in Christians United for Peace, a group of church leaders who demonstrated for peace and held church conferences about the restoration of Liberia. After we returned to the U.S., we continued working with the Liberian Baptist Peace Fellowship, sending Gavel Fund grants for peacemaking training sessions led by Solomon and other group leaders in Monrovia and throughout the Liberian countryside. Later during a protest over human rights abuses, a local police officer severely beat Solomon. He had to flee the country to avoid becoming another casualty at the hands of Taylor's newly installed government.

Solomon's departure from Liberia left the Liberian Baptist Peace Fellowship in suspension, and for a while I was cut off from what was happening in the country. Then in May 2001, the All-Africa Baptist Fellowship (AABF) sponsored a continent-wide conference on peace and development in Buea, Cameroon. I arranged with the AABF to conduct a two-day intensive training on conflict transformation prior to the conference. I informed my contacts in Africa about the AABF conference and the training program, including Rev. Jimmy Diggs, one of the young Liberian pastors I had met on the 1996 trip. Jimmy was trying to revive the Liberian Baptist Peace Fellowship and was eager for training and connecting to the international peacemaking network. New rebel groups were on the move against Charles Taylor's government, and the growing civil war created new waves of suffering and new challenges for peacemakers.

One night after the conference activities in Cameroon, Jimmy wanted to talk about the situation in Liberia and strategize about how to advance the peace agenda. The power was off in Buea that evening, so Jimmy and I talked by candlelight over a table in the hotel restaurant. Jimmy brought me up to date about both the political developments in the civil war and the state of the Christian community's peace efforts. He wanted to be a part of ecumenical mediation initiatives as well as strengthening the Baptist participation in peacemaking from the diplomatic to the grassroots levels. We worked on various approaches he could take, and I committed the Gavel Fund to provide some assistance for his efforts.

When Jimmy returned to Liberia, he was named the representative of the Baptist Convention to the ecumenical peace coalition that later played an intermediary and advocacy role at peace talks in Ghana and Nigeria. He worked alongside the women of WIPNET, the Women in Peace-building Network, who would later be featured in the documentary *Pray the Devil Back to Hell* and my book *Blessed Are the Peacemakers* (Read the Spirit, 2011). The Gavel Fund provided transportation assistance for Jimmy's trips to Sierra Leone and Ghana to facilitate communication between the warring parties and look for openings for peace discussions. Jimmy also organized some conflict transformation training programs, including in some of the refugee camps.

While the peace talks were going outside the country, rebel offensives brought the war into Monrovia and seized Jimmy's home and church in Caldwell (on the outskirts of the city). Jimmy and his family fled to a displaced person's encampment in the center of the city, but even with this personal dislocation Jimmy was also working feverishly to continue the witness of the Baptist Convention for the negotiations. When the rebels withdrew Jimmy found his home stripped bare and his church severely vandalized. Anything of value was stolen by the rebels, even down to forks and spoons. Windows were pulled out of the church walls, leaving gaping ragged holes in the concrete. I was impressed by Jimmy's tireless pursuit of peace when he and his family were suffering so much directly. His courage and determination compelled me to pray daily for him.

When rebel pressure and the resulting peace accord in 2003 led to the ouster of Charles Taylor and the installation of another interim government, an opportunity opened for me to return to Liberia. I had been scheduled to speak at another AABF peace conference in September 2004, this time in Ghana. The conference was postponed after I had purchased the air tickets, so I arranged to go to Liberia instead. Jimmy pulled together many Baptists pastors, youth leaders and women's leaders for a three-day intensive conflict transformation training program. The participants were highly engaged in the training activities and Bible studies as we explored the traumas experienced in the war, their hopes for the future, and ways to move forward in achieving those dreams.

After the training Jimmy took me to his home. As we drove the pot-holed dirt road to Caldwell he showed me the tree line from which rebels had fired on fleeing refugees. Jimmy had found a small boy, lost, alone, and terrified. As he held the boy close to his body, running low under the bullets and mortar fire, Jimmy had whispered the Twenty-third Psalm and told the boy to keep saying, "The Lord is my Shepherd." I was in tears imagining the hellish terror of that day. I spent the night as a guest in the Diggs's home. They had been able to repair much of the damage and replace some of what was stolen, but the scars of war were still evident. Betty Diggs presented me with two beautiful quilts with the Baptist Peace Fellowship logo hand-stitched in each one. The gift was a thank you for all the assistance and prayers of the BPFNA during the war.

That Sunday I preached at the Caldwell Baptist Church. The congregation had been buying new windows, one by one, to replace the ones stolen by the rebels. They were dedicating a new window covered in protective newspaper and leaning at the front of the church. We sang in a joyous processional, tearing off bits of the newspaper until the entire window was revealed. There were still many gaping holes in the walls of the sanctuary. The wounds of war are slow to heal, in people's hearts even slower than the ransacked buildings.

Ethiopia and Eritrea

Imagine your enemy on hands and knees weeping tears of sorrow before you, asking forgiveness, and praying to God with overwhelming grief. Or perhaps imagine yourself kneeling in sorrowful and repentant prayer before your enemy. That was the scene I was privileged to witness during the Ethiopian-Eritrean Peace Conference I helped organize outside Detroit in 2000. I worked with Pastor Tibebu Alemayehu to bring together Ethiopian and Eritrean Christians living in North America for three days of prayer and peacemaking training, sponsored in part by the BPFNA.

While I lived in Boston our church welcomed four Ethiopian men who had fled the brutalities of the Marxist regime of Mengistu Haile Miriam, which overthrew and murdered Emperor Haile Selasse. Famine also drove many Ethiopians, desperately clinging to life, to camps in Sudan and Kenya. Eritreans seeking independence had been fighting Ethiopia for many years, propelling yet more refugees to flee the war zones. The stories of our four refugee friends brought the plight of Ethiopia and the Horn of Africa into my heart, though at the time I could do little more than give money for famine relief and provide hospitality to lonely, suffering men seeking to start their lives anew.

Years later while I was serving as pastor in Dearborn, Tibebu walked into my office. He was an Ethiopian evangelist and church planter with a small congregation that met in a spare room at a

91

local hospital. What had brought him to my office was the vision he had for a reconciliation ministry between Ethiopians and Eritreans, who were still at war. The civil war had come to an end in 1991 with a peace agreement that gave independence to Eritrea, but after a few short years of peace, war reignited over a border dispute. Tens of thousands were dying over the question of which country owned a small town in the desolate wilderness boundary area. Tibebu was a student at Ashland Theological Seminary's Detroit campus, and the dean had attended our worship services and knew of my concerns for peace. When the dean heard Tibebu's dreams he referred Tibebu to me. As I listened I knew this man was a kindred spirit. The energy and excitement grew between us. Our congregation invited Tibebu's small fellowship to use our chapel for their services, but meanwhile Tibebu and I began a collaboration that would last for years.

Tibebu pulled together a planning team of Ethiopian and Eritrean evangelical pastors. (Outside the U.S. the term "evangelical" usually simply refers to Protestant Christians.) We developed the plans for a weekend retreat that would be part training and part peace-revival with prayer and worship focused on reconciliation. Seventy people, divided almost evenly between Ethiopians and Eritreans, gathered from six cities in the U.S. and three cities in Canada at a retreat center in Brighton, Michigan. Eleazar Ziherembere, my peacemaking friend from Rwanda who had now come to the U.S., joined us to share his own struggles for peace and to lead some of the training exercises with me.

I led training sessions and Bible studies on conflict transformation, but the drama erupted in the context of worship. Rev. Takei Bebrahtu, an Eritrean pastor from Columbus, Ohio, preached a message on reconciliation. The Ethiopian Christians present spontaneously responded by kneeling in a circle at the front of the room praying out their grief for all the wrongs done by Ethiopians to Eritreans. As they wailed and wept, Takei led the Eritreans in forming a circle around the kneeling Ethiopians, holding up hands over them in blessing, and praying words of forgiveness. I had never seen anything like this, especially taking place at a time when Ethiopians and Eritreans were killing each other on the battlefield.

Then as the Ethiopians rose and wiped away their tears, the Eritreans knelt down and wept out their sorrow for all the wrongs done to Ethiopians at the hands of Eritreans. The Ethiopians offered the grace that they had just received. They encircled the Eritreans with raised hands of forgiveness and blessing. While blood was being shed in the Horn of Africa, tears were being shed for mutual repentance and forgiveness at a Michigan retreat center.

Later Eleazar and I led the two groups first separately, then jointly in an exercise based on Psalm 85:10 in which we explored the issues of truth, mercy, justice, and peace related to the conflict. From the exercise we were able to develop a joint agenda for transformative action. We concluded with a service of communion within the congregation of a local Baptist church, with Eritrean and Ethiopian pastors serving a mixed congregation. Our oneness around the Lord's Table was a prophetic witness for a hope to bring an end to the distant war that was tearing apart their homelands.

That conference was followed up by another one in Toronto and then a third in Washington DC. In Washington Daniel Hunter joined me to facilitate the conflict transformation training, but this time we added an advocacy component to the program. We had a prayer breakfast to which we invited Alabama congressman Earl Hilliard of the House Sub-Committee on Africa. We asked Congressman Hilliard to address the group about U.S. policy related to Ethiopia and Eritrea and ways we could effectively engage in advocacy for peace in the region. Then I took the conference participants to the U.S. Capitol where we met with staff of the House Sub-Committee on Africa to learn further about the legislative processes and the most effective points where legislation and policy could be influenced by advocacy groups.

Following the visits on Capitol Hill we took our advocacy for peace to the streets. We held prayer vigils at both the Ethiopian Embassy and the Eritrean Chancery. Together Ethiopians and

Eritreans prayed for peace outside their respective embassies. Tibebu went into the Ethiopian Embassy with a letter from the group calling for peace and urging that both countries take steps of good faith to bring healing to the two nations. Then Takei took an identical letter to the Eritrean ambassador. While we were praying outside the Ethiopian Embassy, the deputy ambassador came out to speak with our group. When we introduced ourselves as a group of Ethiopians and Eritreans together, he was physically taken aback. Such a gathering in and of itself was a powerful witness to him. After we concluded our vigils the participants were giddy with joy at having made their witness for peace. In their home countries such a public peace action would not be tolerated, and none had ever participated before in a public demonstration of any kind.

Further conferences were held in other cities, but I lessened my involvement. In part this was due to other demands on my time, but I was also intentionally forcing the leaders of the movement to not be so dependent upon me for planning and program leadership. This had to be their movement, led by their vision and supported by their sacrifice and money. I stayed in touch through Tibebu but kept my distance as they continued to meet together and express their witness for peace toward the evangelical churches back in Ethiopia and Eritrea. Tibebu and I would occasionally get together to hammer out proposals to go to East Africa for training and dialog sessions, but the funding never came through for any of our plans.

Then in 2006 the opportunity came for me to accompany Tibebu to Ethiopia to do some conflict training with the Evangelical Churches Fellowship of Ethiopia (ECFE). We could not deal directly with the issue of Ethiopian/Eritrean reconciliation because the Eritrean churches were experiencing persecution and contacts with them were not working out well. So we turned our attention to some of the internal peacemaking concerns for Ethiopia in partnership with the ECFE. The ECFE is the best-organized and most vigorous council of churches I've encountered. During the persecutions of the Mengistu regime in the 1970s and 1980s, the churches turned to each other for strength and support in common mission. A unity was forged in those difficult years that continued when Mengistu fell and Ethiopian society opened. Tibebu and I led a conflict transformation training workshop for two days with around seventy participants from many ECFE member denominations.

January 2006 was a time of increasing political turmoil. An election had been held in November 2005, and when opposition leaders challenged the validity of the election, the capital and many provincial towns erupted with protests. More than forty people were killed, and more than a thousand opposition leaders were imprisoned. When the students launched their own demonstrations, government soldiers fired on demonstrators and killed a number of students. Many evangelicals had been part of the political opposition because of the lack of religious freedoms for those who were neither members of the Ethiopian Orthodox Church nor Muslims.

The response to the conflict transformation training with the ECFE was so positive, one of the ECFE leaders said, "We have to get you onto the campus." He arranged for me to meet with the Evangelical Student Christian Fellowship at Addis Ababa University. Nearly 400 students gathered for a Friday night Bible study. I led them through Jesus' teachings on the Sermon on the Mount, exploring nonviolence and the Ethiopian context. Many of the students had never had biblical teaching that directly addressed political and social turmoil in a way that reflected faithful Christian discipleship. They were electrified and excited to link their passionate spirituality in a positive way with the smoldering tensions on the streets.

As I was doing the training with ECFE and the students and preaching in local churches, I saw the tensions boiling over around me. While walking near my hotel I saw a large crowd running and yelling, but everything calmed down in a minute. Students had been stoning a government bus just a block away. My companion said such behavior was common because the buses were an easy target for those dissatisfied with the government. Later while driving by a soccer match in the main stadium, I noticed the streets lined with police in riot gear. One section of the stands was empty; at that point I noticed police moving through that section clubbing people with their batons. People were streaming out of the stadium exits. I asked the university professor with me if this was soccer hooliganism or political turmoil. He told me it was all political. My contribution seemed so small in that moment, like flicking water from one's fingers onto a roaring bonfire, but the seeds of peace need to be planted somehow. I returned two more times to Ethiopia, once accompanied by Sharon, to do follow-up peacemaking work with the ECFE and the Baptist churches as well as working with leaders of student ministries.

The Republic of Georgia

My first visit to the Republic of Georgia opened one of the deepest heart-connections for me in my journey as a Christian and as a peace activist. In February 2004 I visited Georgia, part of the former Soviet Union, when the Global Consultants for International Ministries were brought together by our area director, Reid Trulson, for meetings and a discovery visit with the Georgian Baptists.

Georgia had just come through the "Rose Revolution," a nonviolent movement that overthrew the government of Eduard Shevardnadze in November 2003. During the visit of our missionary team we had a one-day conference with the Georgian Baptists in which I led a workshop on conflict transformation and peace-building. Because our group was conducting five simultaneous workshops, we exhausted the small pool of competent translators, and I realized communication was going to be a big issue with my workshop. I quickly shifted my plans and formed the participants into small groups to prepare wordless skits that would express the experience and meaning of the Rose Revolution for them. This exercise gave the Georgians an opportunity to re-enact what had so recently happened as well as to begin reflecting on the significance of the events. With high energy the groups conveyed demonstrating in the streets with joy, power, and persistence, storming the presidential office building armed with roses, and breaking the grip of systemic corruption to bring to power a government that would serve the people.

As a follow-up to their skits, I asked them to describe what had been achieved in the revolution and what had either not been achieved or had fallen short of their expectations and dreams. I wept as I heard them speak about their experience of the birth of hope and the realization they could change their own reality. There were still major issues ahead of them; corruption was more stubborn than they had realized, and human rights abuses were continuing. Minorities continued to experience discrimination. The Rose Revolution was a major triumph, but the struggles for genuine justice and peace were a long way from being over.

The Georgian Baptists appreciated deeply the opportunity to reflect on what they had experienced. They had been so intimately involved in the flow of these historic events that they had not taken the time to step back and assess what they had accomplished and what remained to be done. Lela Kartvelishvili had been one of the leading revolutionaries as well as a leader in the Central Baptist Church of Tbilisi. She was a close associate of the new president Mikhail Saakashvili who had led the rose-wielding occupation of the presidential office building. She had carried the Georgian Baptist flag into Shevardnadze's office in the front line of demonstrators. Lela appreciated my help in facilitating this reflective process, so she gave me a tiny gift: a piece of Shevardnadze's chair in a small frame. She told me the demonstrators had smashed the chair in a fit of symbolic passion, but she rescued a few pieces to remember the moment.

I returned to Georgia seven times over the next few years. I facilitated trainings in conflict transformation and in using experiential education for social change. One of the major issues we worked on was the discrimination against religious minorities. The International Center for Conflict and Negotiation (ICCN), a Georgian NGO, sponsored most of the trainings. One three-day training on religious tolerance saw participants from an amazing array of religious communities: Baptist, Orthodox, Roman Catholic, Armenian Apostolic, Assemblies of God, Salvation

Army, Seventh Day Adventist, Baha'i, Krishna (the term the Georgians used for this branch of Hinduism), and Iezid. I had never heard of Iezids, but discovered that this is an ancient Kurdish religion of about a million adherents that traces itself back to the time of Abraham in ancient Ur. They believe in one God who is manifested in the sun. We explored the human rights concerns they faced and ways they could work together to counter persistent discrimination.

Though I facilitated trainings and consulted with various church and community activists, my primary experience in Georgia was as a witness. Georgia has been going through some amazing revolutions, and one of the key figures is a Baptist bishop named Malkhaz Songulashvili. Malkhaz's work and experiences are worth a complete book for themselves. I listened to his stories, worshipped alongside him, feasted and drank Georgian wine with him, hiked with him in his beloved Georgian hills and mountains, and hoped to encourage him through my solidarity and willingness to offer whatever I could for the Georgian people. As Malkhaz reflected on the Rose Revolution, he said, "Now we realize that we may raise our voice against injustice without violence. We experienced the power of non-violent opposition, and for the people of the Caucasus this is something entirely new." Malkhaz became an activist for nonviolent action against injustice and oppression in Georgia and throughout the republics of the former Soviet Union.

The Rose Revolution ignited hope for change in Ajaria, the predominately-Muslim autonomous republic in the southwest corner of Georgia along the Black Sea. Aslan Abashidze, a Soviet-era politician, had run the affairs of Ajaria with almost total control. (I hated to see the name Aslan, which I associated with the beloved Christ-figure lion in C. S. Lewis's *Chronicles of Narnia*, attached to a nasty, thuggish dictator.) Abashidze's rule was notorious for corruption and human rights abuses. He supported Russian policies against the Georgian national government. During the presidential campaign in the first election in January, 2004 after the Revolution of the Roses, Mikhail Saakashvili said that Abashidze's "dance would have to come to an end." Saakashvili's willingness to stand up to Abashidze ignited hope among Ajarians, and they mobilized to vote for Saakashvili against the call of Abashidze. Their slogans were "Everyone minus one" and "Everyone against one." The Ajarian democracy activists organized a broad-based network, including shadow leaders ready to replace movement leaders who were arrested in Abashidze's crackdowns. Abashidze was certain of his control, so he was shocked when the vast majority of his region voted for Saakashvili.

Then when Saakashvili sought to unify his fractured country, Abashidze refused to allow the president to visit his region. Abashidze had the bridges connecting Ajaria with the rest of the country blown up. Saakashvili ordered an economic blockade of Ajaria. Georgia seemed on an inevitable path toward civil war. Opposition arose primarily among students and teachers in the Ajarian provincial capital of Batumi. They spray-painted the slogan "Aslan must go" on walls. When the police painted over the slogans, activists painted slogans on the streets just before rush hour to get the most visibility. They released balloons with "Aslan must go" to get caught in trees. When Abashidze declared a state of emergency and closed the universities, approximately three thousand people protested in the streets. Abashidze's forces met them with water cannons, iron rods, and batons. More than sixty people were injured, some critically.

Crowds of nearly 15,000 came out to the streets of Batumi. Peace activists from Tbilisi tried to cross into Ajaria to join the demonstrators, but they were turned back by Abashidze's troops. Some of these activists sent me desperate e-mails detailing their frustration and fears that civil war would erupt. Meanwhile Bishop Malkhaz donned his purple clerical robes and went to the Ajarian border alone. He climbed over the rubble of one of the blown-up bridges. Soldiers warned him they would shoot, but Malkhaz said he was going to stand with the people. He passed through the soldiers who chose not to fire on this unarmed, robed churchman who would not be stopped by their threats. Malkhaz went into Batumi and spoke to the crowds, affirming their vision of democracy and calling for disciplined nonviolence. No other religious leaders were visibly present in the demonstrations. It became clear that Abashidze's support was rapidly evaporating. By the end of the day on May 6, 2004 the dictator had flown to Moscow for refuge while demonstrators embraced, cheered, cried, and laughed. "That was one of the most moving days I have ever had," Malkhaz said.

Malkhaz later traveled to Ukraine to join the demonstrators in the so-called "Orange Revolution," named for the orange flags the demonstrators flew. Malkhaz spoke to the crowds, urging them to press their cause with a commitment to nonviolence. He was joined by two friendly Orthodox priests. Their Georgian flags were a sign of solidarity with the Ukrainians and a witness of hope for what could be achieved.

In March 2006, Malkhaz headed into the center of a democratic uprising, this time in Belarus. When he and his Orthodox priest and journalist companions unfurled the Georgian flag among the demonstrators, it didn't take long for the Belarus police to seize them and whisk them off to an interrogation center. They were questioned by KGB officers and held overnight. The next day they were escorted to the train station and put on a train to Ukraine. Their passports were stamped with a five-year ban from entering Belarus under the accusation of being international terrorists.

Rather than perpetrators, Malkhaz and the Baptists of Georgia have been the targets of persecution and violence. Following the collapse of Communism, the Orthodox Church in Georgia has sought to recapture the place of prominence and dominance it had during the time of the czars. Protestant expressions of Christianity were labeled as "sects." One extremist priest, Father Basil Mkalavishvili, gathered followers with a call to put down these sects. A number of Baptist churches were burned, and I stood in the charred ruins of one sanctuary. Later I laid hands in prayer to ordain a woman who was pastor to one of those churches. Tears streamed down my face as I prayed for her and her ministry amid such hate and violence. I led a series of workshops on how to deal with persecution nonviolently and facilitated thinking through strategies to turn the situation around.

In February 2002 the Bible Society warehouse, in a Baptist facility in Tbilisi, was torched. Many times I have celebrated the Eucharist early on Sunday mornings in the small chapel in Malkhaz's home. Malkhaz had placed a burnt Bible salvaged from the Bible Society warehouse on the altar, where he says it will remain until religious liberty comes for all the people of Georgia, whatever their faith.

At one Eucharistic service in his home chapel, Malkhaz gave us prayer candles with another story. The British Broadcasting System interviewed Metropolitan Athanasios of Rustavi, the second hierarch of the Georgian Orthodox Church, about the destruction of the Bible Society warehouse. Athanasios said as far as he was concerned it would be fine if all Baptists were dead. In response to this public statement, Bishop Malkhaz wrote personally and publicly of his love for the Metropolitan, of their shared faith and their shared desires for the well being of Georgia. After a few months, the Metropolitan knocked on Malkhaz's door, saying he was there to repent, ask forgiveness, and do penance. His voluntary penance was to offer the Baptists gifts of food, candles, wine, and vodka! I held one of those candles around the altar with the burnt Bible as we prayed for peace among the people who claim to follow Christ.

A year before I first visited Georgia, on 24 January 2003, the radical Orthodox priest Father Basil Mkalavishivili had led a group of his followers on a violent attack of an ecumenical Christian service, including Orthodox representatives, held at the Central Baptist Church to observe the Week of Prayer for Christian Unity. The organizers of the service told the worshippers to disperse before the service began, lessening the number of victims beaten in the attack. In the wake of the Rose Revolution, the renegade priest was finally arrested for his violent acts in March 2004. That November he went on trial with nine of his followers, the week after one of my training sessions. If I'd known what was about to happen I would have gladly extended my visit! Bishop Malkhaz was called to testify. For three hours he spoke about the attack on his church, the values of Christianity, the ecumenical movement, and religious liberty. The judge and prosecutor asked many questions about differences among Christians and about the distinctive features of the Georgian Baptist Church. At the end of his presentation the judge asked Malkhaz, "What do you wish for them?" Malkhaz replied, "I demand that these people are pardoned and released from the prison." Everyone in court was aghast at his statement. Defense lawyers quickly asked for clarification. Malkhaz said his absolution was without condition, explaining that this was the nature of Christian love and forgiveness. Finally, since nobody could accept what he has said, Malkhaz added, "I do not demand anything from them except the red wine which we will drink together when they are set free." The courtroom erupted in laughter. Malkhaz then ignored the rules of the court and walked over to the cage where the prisoners where held to shake their hands, including the hand of Father Basil. As he left the court a boy tugged on his sleeve and said, "Thank you, Bishop." It was Basil's grandson, whom Malkhaz then blessed. That evening he received a message from the prisoners: "Even if we are not released from here, we will be ever grateful to you."

A few days later Malkhaz wrote to President Saakashvili calling for the release of those who had persecuted him and the Baptists. The next Sunday was the tenth anniversary of Malkhaz's ordination as bishop. Among the gifts and well-wishes were two small icons of Christ and the incarnation and a huge cake from Father Basil and his followers. Malkhaz concluded the day saying, "In the past we were praying that Mkalavishvili was arrested; now we are praying that he is released from jail." Despite Malkhaz's call for a pardon, Basil Mkalavishvili was sentenced to six years in prison with his associates receiving lesser punishments.

Amid all the foment and action of democracy being born in regions of centuries-long authoritarian and dictatorial rule, Georgia is also a place of delightful worship renewal. Besides leading trainings and listening to riveting stories, I was blessed to share in the rhythms of worship among the Baptists. The high point for me was Holy Week in 2005, following the Orthodox liturgical calendar, when it seemed as if the streets, sanctuaries, and hillsides of Georgia reached to the gates of heaven itself. Carrying a huge palm frond, I marched with a Baptist procession for two hours through Tbilisi on Palm Sunday. I shared Passover with the chief rabbi of Tbilisi. I preached and led communion at one Baptist church on Maundy Thursday, followed by another service at Central Baptist in which Bishop Malkhaz washed my feet along with the feet of a cross-section of the congregation. On Good Friday I helped carry a huge wooden cross through Tbilisi on a three-hour procession marked by vigils at the Catholic church, the Armenian Apostolic church and the Lutheran church before ending at the Baptist church for a worship service. The service included the Eucharist and nailing papers with our sins on the cross we had carried through Tbilisi's streets. A stunning liturgical dance followed, first of denial, then of surrender in which the sins were stripped from the cross, put into a brass bowl, and lit on fire as the dancer was draped in a red cloth from the foot of the cross.

The Easter service began at 11 p.m. Saturday evening and went throughout the night. Malkhaz and I both preached. All four of the Gospel resurrection accounts were read in full. Twenty-two people were baptized. At the end of the service Malkhaz banged on the closed doors of the church with his shepherd's staff. The doors were swung open even as the stone was rolled away from the empty tomb of Jesus, and we prayed for the world. Following a music and drama program, at 5 a.m. we all piled into buses and cars for a caravan through the city to a hillside overlooking Tbilisi. Around bonfires in the pre-dawn chill and biting winds we danced to joyous music, drank wine, and ate breakfast. As the sun rose over the eastern mountains, we celebrated a final liturgy. Somehow the poverty and struggle of these people mixed with their faith in the risen Christ produced an eruption of joy that has been a treasure for me to experience. I feel more at home spiritually in Georgia than in any other place in the world, including my own land.

A World of Books

Shortly after I published *Christian Peacemaking: From Heritage to Hope* (Judson Press, 1994) I carried about a dozen copies into a highly restricted country. I gave the books as gifts to various Christian leaders. One pastor, as he flipped through the pages and looked at the photos, said, "This could get me in trouble with the police." I offered to take the book back as I did not want to cause him trouble, but he refused to return it. Later I saw him proudly showing it off to other people, showing especially the photo of the Chinese man blocking the line of tanks, which spoke beyond languages of the power of nonviolent action.

A year later I returned to that country and met some students from a Bible college. When one of them heard my name he became very animated. He had written a paper about the Kingdom of God in the current context of his country and had used my book as the lens through which to look at the issues. I was moved by how important and useful he had found my book, and I asked how he had gotten a copy. He told me he had never seen the book; the book and its contents had been passed on orally in the class. I immediately gave him a copy as I had brought more with me on this trip.

After the conversation with this student I pondered the challenge of getting good books to poor countries in conflict to help shape the minds and skills of the emerging generation of leaders. I had seen the libraries of seminaries and universities in a number of countries. One Central American university's library consisted of one small wall of bookshelves filled with old books to serve a student body of over a thousand. Many of the libraries had old books donated from the private libraries of retired pastors. Some of the books were abysmally out of date, and other were so bound to U.S. cultural contexts that they were totally irrelevant and useless. How could we get quality new books that were cross-culturally valid and addressed the pressing concerns of countries in conflict and deliver them to the seminaries, colleges, and universities that needed them the most?

After I began working with the Gavel Fund for the BPFNA, I decided to try to purchase books on Christian social ethics to send to ten libraries in strategic settings around the world. I wrote proposals to foundations for grants and tried to find donors, but nobody was interested. The BPFNA didn't have the money to fund the project, so it appeared to be going nowhere. Then in desperation and having nothing to lose I wrote a number of Christian publishers asking for ten free copies each of a number of titles I selected from their book lists so I could send them to the libraries of educational institutions in poor and conflicted countries. Five publishers responded positively—Judson Press, Smyth & Helwys, Eerdmans, Orbis, and Herald Press—and soon my basement was filled with over five hundred new books. I sent off the first batch of books to various schools, sending some by mailbags and carrying others into various countries in suitcases.

Over the next three years I was able to enlist three more publishers to participate: Mercer University Press, Westminster/ John Knox, and Abingdon. The high point was in the third year when two publishers had major clearance sales including some excellent writings on various ethical topics. I got those publishers to send me thirty copies each of the requested clearance titles as well as ten copies for the new group of libraries to receive the collections. The new libraries received seventy books, and the libraries from the previous two years received supplemental collections of twenty books each. That year we shipped out $15,000 worth of books weighing half a ton at a cost of less than $500.

After four years of the library project I sensed some publishers slipping in their willingness to part with so many books, so I brought the project to a halt with great thanks to the publishers for their generosity over the years. We had sent collections of fifty to seventy new top-quality books to more than forty libraries at colleges, universities, and seminaries in twenty-six countries. In my travels, whenever I am close to one of the receiving institutions, I visit the library and check for our books. Joy and satisfaction wash over me every time I pull books off the shelf and see that they had been getting extensive use. Shaping and sharpening the minds of the rising generation of leaders is peace-building over the long haul.

(Left) Author commissioned as a missionary with International Ministries at the World Mission Conference; (right) Author with Rev. Abejehu Damene leads a conflict transformation workshop in Addis Ababa

Author with children at the displaced persons camp in Monrovia

(Left) Author preaching in a rural community in Ethiopia; (right) Archbishop Malkhaz Songulashvili of the Evangelical Baptist Church of Georgia

Author and Malkhaz Songulashvili (far right with hat) carry a cross through the streets of Tbilisi on Good Friday

6

HUMOR, MIRACLES, AND
THE HOME FRONT

Through the Looking Glass

Gather a group of seasoned international travelers together and sooner or later you will find them swapping tales of sickness with laughter that certainly wasn't present in the original experiences. My offering to such a yarn-fest comes from the Burma negotiations. Saboi Jum and I had flown to Bangkok with the intention of entering China for a round of meetings with Brang Seng of the Kachin Independence Organization. While I hung out at the Bangkok Christian Guest House, Saboi tried to arrange our travel into China. We quickly discovered that this was not going to be as smooth a process as we had hoped. For some reason that I could never understand, we were denied entrance into China, even though the Chinese government was hosting the talks at which we were to be present. Whether this was a matter of one department of the government not communicating well with another or an attempt to manipulate and influence the negotiations was hard to tell. The result was that for a week I grew frustrated at being halfway around the world, spending my limited program funds on doing nothing. Meanwhile the discussions about negotiations between the ethnic insurgents and the military government of Burma were held without Saboi and me. The other two members of the Burma Peace Committee had traveled with Brang Seng from within Burma to China, so at least the committee was well represented.

In Bangkok I couldn't plan any other activities because each day was spent trying to obtain permission to travel into China. I could poke around the city for a few hours, visit a temple or park in the afternoon, but I had to be ready to leave quickly as soon as we got the word. Meanwhile the talks had begun in China, and after a couple days Saboi received a call from Brang Seng. The discussions had fizzled out because the Chinese military intelligence colonel present at the talks tried to dominate the whole program. Brang Seng refused to go along, so he called us in Bangkok to inquire whether Saboi and I could get to Hong Kong the next day. There was a flight out late that evening we could catch.

Before heading to the airport we ate dinner at a Thai version of a greasy spoon. I was pinching my pennies—or baht—feeling the moral and budgetary weight of my international junket that had to that point produced absolutely nothing. Eating at that cheap restaurant was a costly mistake. We flew to Hong Kong that night, then took a cab to the hotel Brang Seng had arranged for us.

The next morning I woke up as violently ill as I had ever been. My guts were in horrendous cramping turmoil and revolt. Because I was feeling so miserable we had the peace talks in my hotel room. I lay in bed listening, giving input and taking a break periodically to crawl from the bed to the toilet. Quite a crowd gathered in the room. There were four of us from the peace committee along with Brang Seng and three of his aides and associates. We talked through the key issues that needed to be worked out in response to the latest government offer regarding direct negotiations. What had been impossible to resolve in two days with the Chinese officials we were able to work out in two hours. Though I felt utterly wretched, I was relieved (pardon the bad pun) that we had achieved the purpose of this trip to Asia.

Then Brang Seng said that he had a friend who had invited us out to lunch. I reluctantly agreed, knowing that diplomatic relationships required me to tough this one out. First we went to Brang Seng's friend's office. His friend turned out to be a multi-millionaire Chinese industrialist who had factories spread across Asia. His office was a rather stark grim-looking workplace, but we only stayed there long enough for him to gather his staff to accompany us all to lunch.

Lunch was to be at the Kowloon Club, an elegant restaurant high up in a skyscraper with a fantastic view of Hong Kong harbor. We were ushered into our own private dining room for our "lunch," which involved seventeen or eighteen courses including Peking duck. It was the most fabulous meal of my life, and I was feeling more miserable than I could remember. This glorious food would touch my lips, then I could feel it set Olympic records as it rumbled down my tempestuous gullet. Every so often I would excuse myself to go find the restroom with which I became intimately acquainted.

To top matters off, this industrialist was one of the most intelligent and articulate people I've ever met. He could talk with precision and pointed opinions about any subject. Because I was the representative of the American Baptist Churches and as the only U.S. citizen in the group, he zeroed in on me as a major partner in the verbal exchanges. I felt the weight of representing my country and my denomination as I tried to keep up with this brilliant man, all the while imposing my iron will on my roiling innards. It was exquisite torture. When our marathon lunch was finally over and we were deposited back at the hotel, I collapsed in my bed utterly spent.

During a June 1991 trip to Thailand for the Burma peace process, I had an adventure of a entirely different kind. I was in Chiang Mai for the talks with the leaders from many of the ethnic insurgent groups as well as the students and democracy leaders in exile. I'd just checked into my hotel when I heard gunfire in the street outside. I cautiously crept to my window and peered out to see what was happening.

A jeep with four men in it was racing down the road, three of the men firing steady bursts from M-16s at a motorcyclist a few yards ahead. Suddenly they all skidded to a halt, including the woman on the motorcycle. She hopped off as a man approached her wearing clothes identical to hers and adjusting a longhaired wig on his head. The man jumped on the bike and began spinning it around in wild maneuvers. Across the canal a film crew was capturing all the thrilling action. For the two days that we would be holding peace talks with guerilla leaders inside the hotel, outside we would be serenaded by gunfire as a Thai action movie was being shot. I felt as if I'd fallen through the looking glass into a land of the surreal.

At the end of those Chiang Mai meetings, as I was packing to check out of the hotel, I realized some of my belongings had been stolen. The key missing item was my camera. It was a cheap camera, not something one would think would be a target of thieves. Also taken was a small, framed butterfly I'd picked up on our visit to a butterfly farm during a break in the discussions, again an inexpensive item hardly worth stealing because of its availability in local shops. Meanwhile money was left untouched that was worth far more than all the stolen items. The theft took place a half hour before departure. The strange mix of stolen items puzzled me until a few months later I learned from Saboi that Burmese military intelligence knew everything that went on at the Chiang Mai meetings. That meant there was a government spy in the high levels of the ethnic insurgent groups, the armed student movement, or the democratic government-in-exile. The best I could figure is that my camera was stolen to get the pictures to go with the verbal report that was to be given. The other items were just a clumsy effort to make it look like an ordinary theft.

Miracles of Time and Connections

All along the peacemaking journey I've sensed that my colleagues and I were not the only actors in the dramas that were unfolding. I sincerely believe that the Prince of Peace has been working through our efforts, weaving together relationships that shaped who I was, opening doors of opportunity, and making a way where no way seemed to exist. In some cases this hidden hand was felt in seemingly innocuous connections such as my first Christian mission memory being tied to Liberia through the visit of the radio missionary Dick Reed to my childhood home and then Liberia's becoming a key focus for some of my peace work. But the connection to the Delanos was more stunning in my complete lack of intentionality and the opportune door it opened.

I first met Bob and Helen Delano through my wife. Sharon was the coordinator for the Baptist Peace Fellowship of Eastern Pennsylvania and Delaware, a regional affiliate of the BPFNA. Helen had just returned from a trip to Central America where she had accompanied refugees from El Salvador as they returned to their villages from camps in Honduras. Martin Massaglia, pastor of the Royersford Baptist Church where Helen attended, had also been part of that accompaniment journey, and Sharon invited him and Helen to share their story with the BPF group. Martin and Helen both became core members of the regional fellowship. Over time Sharon and Helen became very close friends, meeting regularly and praying together. Helen became Sharon's informal spiritual director and mentor.

Helen and Bob were retired American Baptist missionaries. They had served in northeast India among the Naga people, but at that time the mention of the Nagas just passed right over me. I had never heard of the Nagas, but I certainly knew India. Even though we had them over for dinner and spent a lot of time with them, we didn't talk about old missionary stories and adventures. There was too much going on about the wars in Central America, current church life, and children—their grown children and our young ones. Bob was going through some health struggles and wasn't as active in the current peace struggles as Helen, so I didn't spend a lot of time with him. Eventually Helen passed away, followed soon after by Bob.

A few years later I met Wati Aier and became involved with the Naga peace process. The most intransigent people we had to deal with early in the process were Isak and Muivah, leaders of the NSCN-IM insurgent group. In November 1997 Wati and I met with them for three days, stormy and tense meetings that resulted in the initial intra-Naga cease-fire. Though we had made a tentative first step toward peace Isak and Muivah were still very hard and suspicious in their relational stance towards me.

During one of our early meetings in Bangkok we went out for lunch following a round of talks. As we waited for our food to be served we chatted informally, and in the flow of the conversation Isak reiterated the common Naga refrain about how grateful the Nagas were to the American Baptist missionaries for bringing the gospel to them. I mentioned that I had known some of the American Baptist missionaries to India. Isak asked whom I had known, and I mentioned Bob and Helen Delano. The flow of conversation around us abruptly halted. Isak leaned closer and peered at me. With awe he gasped, "You knew Bob Delano!" Then he told me an amazing story.

When the Indian government expelled all the missionaries among the Nagas in the early years of the war, Bob Delano refused to go. Helen returned to the U.S. for safety, but Bob went underground to continue the ministry to which he believed God had called him. He could not abandon the Nagas during their suffering. Eventually he was captured by the Indian Army and immediately deported, but his action of sacrificial solidarity raised him to beloved saintly status in the pantheon of missionary heroes for the Nagas. Isak had worked besides Bob as a young evangelist. The fact that I was a friend of Bob Delano meant that I was now a friend of Isak. Our relationship instantly changed, and the tenor of our talks was transformed from one of suspicion to one of openness and exploration for new possibilities.

I had done nothing to create this connection through Bob Delano, and the Naga chapter of Bob's life had been basically unknown to me. I believe God wove together that relationship for the partnerships in peacemaking in Central America and Sharon's growth through Helen's friendship, but also because there was still a difficult door of trust to be opened by this deceased missionary hero. Because of our friendship, Bob was able to reach beyond the grave to make one last act for peace in solidarity with his beloved Naga people.

I experienced a miracle of timing in a country that cannot be named as of this writing due to the delicate nature of the current situation. I had been scheduled to come to the country to do conflict transformation training among the small Christian community there. The country was in the midst of a civil war that was becoming known for its ferocity and human rights violations.

Neither the government nor the insurgents were Christian; in fact, the Christian community had only recently been legalized and persecution against them lifted.

Two days before my arrival the top leader among the Christians was contacted by a high-ranking government official about opening a back-channel for possible negotiations with the insurgents. The leader, C. L. I'll call him, was taken aback. On the one hand he was honored to be given such a request, but on the other he wondered how on earth he could take on such a task and ever succeed at it. When I arrived C. L. and a couple others huddled with me in a restaurant to tell the story. The next morning I began the training in which C. L. participated fully. When the two-day program concluded C. L. and I met for a longer session to explore the current situation in his country and this incredible request for assistance. We discussed mediation processes, the risks, and the challenges. We discussed issues of maintaining the credibility of being the mediator and sustaining the trust from both sides. We talked of how to establish boundaries with two sides who were not used to respecting such boundaries even if the limits safeguarded a process both were interested in entering. The energy that flowed between us was almost electric in its intensity as we felt the historicity of a moment pregnant with possibility.

Later C. L. was called to meet privately with the country's head of state in a long interview that was more an exploration of who C. L. was than making any specific plans or requests. A similar interview was held with the top insurgent leader who summoned him. Eventually a peace accord was achieved. C. L. did not play a major role in mediating that accord, but I believe his involvement was part of building up the trust necessary for peace talks to be successfully held. In addition, C. L. and the minority Christian community earned respect as people of integrity and peace from both sides of that deeply conflicted nation. That I came at a time when the need was intense to provide training and support was certainly not in our plans as we set up the program. God knew the need and answered it while I thought we were merely working on a first step of getting to know new people and a new situation.

I have repeatedly seen these miracles of God's timing. In November and December 2002, Daniel Hunter and I were back in Kohima, Nagaland to lead the public sector organizations in a three-day training and strategizing meeting. Following the meeting, Daniel returned to the U.S. while I went on to Dimapur to teach for two days at Oriental Theological Seminary. During our time in Kohima the Indian government let the ban expire against the NSCN, both the faction led by Isak and Muivah (NSCN-IM) and the faction led by Khaplang (NSCN-K). This intentionally passive act made the organizations legal entities, allowing them to emerge from underground. The Indian government action was similar to the lifting of the ban against the African National Congress by the apartheid regime in South Africa, the step that opened up official negotiations that would lead to Nelson Mandela's release. Now in India the talks between the government and NSCN-IM could enter into the political phase. The insurgent leaders were free to move about, hold public meetings, and enter into open discourse about the future of the region. To be present in Nagaland at the moment the ban was lifted was a delightful surprise that would soon provide an unexpected opportunity.

Once I arrived in Dimapur, Wati Aier received a call from Atem, the leader of the NSCN-IM insurgency in the region since Isak and Muivah maintained residences outside the country. Atem was aware of the work I had done over the years along with my BPFNA colleagues. He had met with Daniel Hunter and me during our first trip to Nagaland back in 2000, a visit that was made in the middle of the night. Daniel and I had waited in a dark shelter while Atem's soldiers surrounded the site. After a quiet knock at the door the general slipped in quietly. When the windows were shuttered and the door closed silently, a lamp was lit for our discussions about the cease-fire and various negotiation issues. Now two years later there was no need for secrecy. Atem wanted me to meet with the NSCN-IM executive committee, which had come out of hiding and was meeting in a local Dimapur church. They were meeting that Saturday, and my schedule was open. I concluded my teaching at the seminary on Friday and was preaching on Sunday. Saturday was free, so the meeting was set up.

During the meeting with the NSCN-IM executive committee I spoke on Jesus' teachings from the Sermon on the Mount (remember, all these Naga insurgents were Baptists, some with a very pious faith). I used Glen Stassen's term "transforming initiatives," urging them to take bold and creative initiatives that would open doors of reconciliation among their fellow Nagas, particularly during this opportune moment when the ban against their organization had been lifted. Nagas in the other factions were fearful of NSCN-IM and suspicious of their exclusionary approach related to the talks with the government of India. Because of the leading role the NSCN-IM was playing both in the talks with India and in their resistance, they had the political capital to take bold steps to bring healing to the fractures in Naga society.

The executive committee members responded positively to my challenge and wanted to hear more. Could I come back on Monday and meet with them again as well as with many of their cadres? My trip was coming to an end, but in the schedule worked out months earlier my Monday was free. I had wanted to stay through Sunday so I could preach in a church. However, Air India had no flights on Mondays from Dimapur to Calcutta, so I was stuck in Nagaland until Tuesday. A seemingly wasted day in my travel schedule because of airline flight times was actually the divinely prepared opening to respond to this invitation. Two weeks earlier the NSCN-IM leaders and cadres could not have gathered for such a meeting as they were all hiding in the jungle as they had been for decades. Now they could come out to a public meeting, and I was available through what had appeared as a frustrating glitch in my schedule.

The Monday meeting was a profound training opportunity in conflict transformation. These hardened guerilla fighters, about seventy men and women, began working on new thinking related to the ways of building peace. The story of that training is told in chapter 7, but suffice it to say I have never had such an opportunity before or since to teach seasoned fighters how to resolve conflicts peacefully and move to reconciliation with their enemies. What had initially been planned as a day off just waiting for the flight home became one of the highlights of my entire ministry.

Bigger schedule snafus turned out to be divine appointments. I had two such divine "foul-ups" in 2008. The first occurred during a trip to Burma scheduled for January. The trip was scheduled for two weeks, but the plans for the second week of the trip fell apart. Every effort to arrange something to fill that time came to naught. I was frustrated because I preferred to spend time at home than hanging around in Yangon doing nothing. Then on Christmas Eve, Hindu militants in Orissa, India, launched extensive coordinated attacks on the Christian community in the Khandamal district. Almost a hundred churches were destroyed, a number of people killed, hundreds of homes burned, and thousands forced to flee into the forest. The head of the Baptists in Orissa contacted me, and there I was, scheduled to be in Asia already with an open week in my schedule. I was able to take the short flight from Yangon to Calcutta and spend a week doing nonviolence and trauma healing training with the Christians in Orissa.

A few months later I thought I'd fallen into a scheduling replay when plans for my trip to Lebanon in June fell apart. I was locked into two events at the beginning and end of the trip, but the itinerary for the week in the middle fell apart when key people had to change their plans. Every effort to come up with alternative programs fell through, and it looked like I'd be spending a week vacationing alone in Beirut. Then just before departing for Lebanon, I got a call from Wati Aier about breakthrough reconciliation talks with the Nagas to be held in Chiang Mai, Thailand (see chapter 10 for more of this story). Usually my calendar is too jammed to respond to such a sudden request, but the dates for the talks were exactly the dates I had open in Lebanon. Furthermore, the air ticket from Beirut to Bangkok was far less than from the U.S. God kept my schedule available and even helped out my over-stretched budget!

God's miraculous weaving of events and people has not always been so profound, but has been startlingly evident and even humorous. Such was the case during the gathering of participants for the second International Baptist Peace Conference held in Nicaragua in 1992. The Baptist Peace Fellowship of North America was the main organizer for the conference, and I was responsible for arranging the travel for most of our international guests. I coordinated the purchase of air tickets to Nicaragua via Miami, arranged for overnight accommodations in Miami, and collected all the information for procuring visas upon arrival in Managua.

Initially everything seemed to be going smoothly as participants arrived from their various nations on time in Miami. A Mennonite guesthouse had provided lodging and helped with pick-ups at the airport. The first wave of travelers had a wonderful evening together at the guesthouse, then departed the next morning for the flight to Managua. That's when I had the first inkling that trouble was brewing. We sent a delegation of South Africans on the American Airlines flight, but they were barred from boarding the plane because their names were not on the approved list for visas. I tried to negotiate with the airline staff, made calls to Managua, and at the last minute the South Africans were cleared to fly on to Nicaragua. This little glitch was my first warning that our travel plans might not go as smoothly as planned.

Through the rest of the day, we picked up the next wave of arriving conference participants, gathering again at the Mennonite guesthouse. The next morning the full scope of the administrative mess emerged. Seven of our travelers from India, Indonesia, Zaire, and Zimbabwe were denied entrance to the airplane because they had not been cleared to receive visas. I was also supposed to go out on that flight as this was the last major group heading for the conference. I stood at the door of the American Airlines plane with the gate agent and Ken Sehested, waiting for the call from

Managua that would clear these last seven internationals to board, but the call never came. The gate agent had to close the aircraft door, so I dumped all the registration materials, housing assignments, and other convention documents into Ken's arms. "I can't leave these folks stranded in a country they don't know," I said. "Try to straighten things out at the Managua end while I work on the situation here in Miami." Bil Mooney-McCoy, an old friend from my Boston days who was a conference musician, stayed with me to help. In those days of more relaxed security, our bags were already on board the American flight headed to Managua. I left Bil at the airport to check out the possibilities for alternative flights while I drove to the Nicaraguan consulate with our guests to try to obtain visas so they could travel later in the day.

It was July 1992, and earlier in the year Nicaragua held the election that ousted the Sandinista government and installed the opposition coalition. New officials had been appointed to various positions, including at the Miami consulate. The consul was a woman who came across as a bureaucrat with a little bit of power who wanted everyone to know that power was hers. I presented our case. A Nicaraguan Baptist legislator had assured us that he would secure all the visas for conference participants upon their arrival in Managua, but obviously that was not happening. I had sent the complete passport and registration information for all seven of those denied entrance. I knew from a list of countries the Nicaraguan government had sent me that visitors from India would be problematic, but none of the other countries represented in our group was on the short list of nations requiring a longer visa approval process. Furthermore, one Indian attending the conference was allowed to fly to Nicaragua even though I had not been given his passport information in advance, while the one who had provided information was denied. The consul had us fill out visa forms, which were then deposited on a stack of documents on her desk. When two o'clock came she got up and left as it was quitting time. I pleaded with her just to sign the forms so we could catch the late afternoon flight, but she haughtily refused, saying it was past two o'clock and they were now closed. I was angry and frustrated by the disdain she showed guests coming to a conference in her country, but there was nothing more I could do. We had no visas.

I was particularly concerned about the Indian peacemaker. He was S. K. Mohanty, a Baptist activist in a nonviolent movement for labor rights in India. Mohanty had applied for the 1988 Baptist peace conference in Sweden, but we didn't have the scholarship funds to get him a ticket. He was just the kind of person for whom these gatherings were designed, and he was slated to speak on a panel addressing nonviolence at the Nicaragua conference. Having let Mohanty down once, I was determined not to leave him stranded a second time.

That night back at the guesthouse we decided to make the most of our enforced delay, and we began our own mini-conference with lively discussions between the Baptist peacemakers and our Mennonite hosts. The next morning we checked back at the airport. The daily American Airlines flight departed in the morning without any of us receiving clearance from Managua. I kept calling the Baptist offices and every other phone number I had in Managua, but I got no answer. I sent messages with the last straggling conference participants who went out on the American flight, pleading for help to get these last seven cleared. Then we headed back to the Nicaraguan consulate.

Our visas still weren't ready, so I sat in a chair outside the consulate's door with my legs extended fully. Every time the consulate came in or out of her office she had to step over me. I kept repeating, "Just sign the forms, and we will go." She finally signed six visas, but told me that Mohanty would have to wait for six weeks to get his visa. I said that in six weeks the conference would be long over. Mohanty had come from halfway around the world at the invitation of Nicaraguan citizens, and it was ludicrous that he would be denied a visa so arbitrarily. My appeal fell on deaf ears. But with the six visas we headed back to the airport.

With the change of government, Nicaragua recently had privatized the national air carrier, Nica Airlines. The daily flight from Miami was around 5 p.m., so we had time to get tickets for everyone. I decided that I could no longer help with Mohanty at the Miami end; I had to find out what was happening in Managua and clear up the visa situation there. Our host from the Mennonite guesthouse had driven us to the airport, and he agreed to keep helping Mohanty as long as necessary. No fresh word came from Managua about his visa, so the rest of us boarded the Nica flight that afternoon.

Since it was the first week of the new privatized Nica Airlines they were engaged in a promotional campaign that included giving away free Miami to Managua round-trip tickets. As we boarded the plane a flight attendant put all our boarding passes in a fish bowl. After we were airborne she drew out a number of winning names. One of the winners was Ingrid Sabagyo, one of the Baptist peacemakers from Indonesia. We all laughed at her good fortune and the unlikely prospect that Ingrid would ever have of using a Miami-Managua ticket.

As we chatted across the rows and aisles with one another, the man sitting directly in front of me turned around and inquired about the nature of our group, clearly a group of mixed race and nationality. I told him we were Baptist peacemakers coming for a conference in Nicaragua. He told me that he worked for the immigration department and that Nicaragua could use all the people supporting peace it could get. Hearing that he was with the immigration department I immediately responded, "There's one more peace person who needs to get to Nicaragua!" I told him about Mohanty and our tribulations trying to procure visas to his country. He took down all the passport and personal information about Mohanty and promised he would act upon it. If I had been on another flight, if he and I had not sat next to each other, if our group hadn't been so stirred up to celebrate by Ingrid winning a free ticket, the contact would not have been made.

Our group finally arrived in Managua and had further adventures getting our bags and traveling the two hours to the

Pacific coast where the conference was held. Mohanty arrived the next day. Our newfound friend and traveling companion from the Nicaraguan immigration department had trumped the stubborn arrogance of the consul in Miami and cleared Mohanty's visa. We cut loose with a big celebration as Mohanty joined us for the remainder of the conference.

Another travel disaster in Asia turned out to be a divine appointment. I was flying to Nagaland. Because that particular call to go to Nagaland had not left me much time to purchase my air ticket, I could not get the normal flight from Bangkok to Calcutta. Instead I had to take Thai Airways to Dhaka, Bangladesh, to connect to the Bangladesh Airlines flight to Calcutta. From there I would fly Air India to Dimapur, Nagaland. When I landed in Dhaka, I proceeded to the transit desk to check in for the connecting flight to Calcutta.

Having traveled to many impoverished and conflict-stricken countries, I was surprised to discover a system that reminded me more of British colonial-era clerks than a modern airline. Men sat behind the counter with huge old-looking ledger books with hand-written names of the passengers. They told me that I had been dropped from the flight because I had not been confirmed. I was stunned and argued that there was no need for me to confirm as this was my initial flight to my destination, not the return. But the men behind the counter were unmoved by my plight and told me that the flight was now full. I would have to find another way to get to Calcutta.

There was one other customer in the same predicament. An Anglo woman was at the counter next to me, and she too had been bumped from the flight for "no confirmation." Receiving no help at all from the Bangladesh Airlines personnel, we sat down on a bench in the dingy terminal to try to figure out what to do. When we introduced ourselves, I discovered that she was a Baptist missionary from New Zealand returning to her work in northeast India. At least we would have something to chat about while we tried to find a way out of our predicament.

We eventually found someone from Air India to help us. Since we were both connecting to Air India flights in Calcutta, they had a vested interest in getting us out of Dhaka and on our way. As our helper left to see what he could do, the New Zealand missionary and I began to explore our common links and interests. When I told her I was going to Nagaland to work on the peace process, she became very interested. She was working in the state of Tripura. As in every other state in northeast India, Tripura was plagued by an insurgency that engaged in anti-government violence that often swept up civilians in its vicious wake. She was working closely with the general secretary of the Baptists in Tripura, and he had been trying to connect to insurgent leaders to open cease-fire talks. I had been working not just with the Nagas but also with the Council of Baptist Churches in North East India (CBCNEI) to do peace-building training. Tripura was one of two states in the region in which the Baptists did not belong to CBCNEI, so this general secretary was not in the communications loop about the training opportunities CBCNEI had developed with me and other peacemakers. Since the normal channels of Baptist life and organization could not support the peace work of this Baptist leader in Tripura, it seemed God had to bounce the two of us off an airplane to make the connection!

We shared the stories of our work in Tripura and Nagaland. I gave her a copy of my book *Christian Peacemaking* to read and then give to the general secretary as a resource of ideas and stories of others involved in mediation efforts. We continued our conversation as the man from Air India found a way to get us onto the "full" flight to Calcutta later that evening. He took us to a remote hanger to find our bags amid the luggage that had been dumped for one reason or another, but even as we walked across the runways she and I continued discussing the challenges and potentiality of the conflict situation in Tripura. We then flew together to Calcutta where we parted ways to stay in our pre-arranged accommodations for the night.

The next morning we met again at the domestic air terminal in Calcutta for our flights to the northeast. She had begun reading

Christian Peacemaking the previous night, so while we waited for our flights I began giving her one-on-one conflict transformation training that she could also pass on to the general secretary. After some delays her flight was called. We said good-bye, and she passed through security. My flight was eventually cancelled due to bad weather, so I headed back to the Baptist Mission Society compound where I was staying in downtown Calcutta.

The next morning I arrived at the airport for my rescheduled flight to find my missionary friend waiting there, too! Her flight for Agartala, Tripura, had taken off but had been unable to land because of fog, so the plane returned to Calcutta. She had finished reading my book in the meantime. We quickly got to work continuing the conflict transformation training. When we finally parted she had soaked up a lot of concepts, stories, practical ideas, and supporting Bible passages to share with the general secretary in the effort to open a peace initiative in Tripura. The travel fiasco had turned into the highlight of the entire trip, certainly due to God's redemptive meddling in human affairs.

Dress Code

Working around the world has allowed me to enjoy the wonderful diversity of human clothing. My closet looks like a tiny fitting room for the United Nations as I have either purchased or received as gifts garb from various countries, from many kinds of headgear to T-shirts, from African robes to Gandhian homespun *kadhi*. When my suitcase failed to arrive on a trip to Liberia, a gift of a beautifully embroidered shirt enabled me to preach in the pulpit that Sunday in something other than my sweat-soaked sports shirt. Naga shawls, the most common gift from a very generous people, have more than once been survival blessings as friends and I wrapped ourselves desperately in our new gifts because we were unprepared for the cold nights in the Naga hills.

On our 2000 trip to Burma, Daniel Hunter and I received longgyis as gifts on the opening day of a four-day training program. The longgyi is the traditional Burmese skirt-like clothing worn by both men and women, though each gender has different patterns of cloth and ways of wearing the longgyi. The longgyi is a large tube of cloth that is placed around the wearer then quickly folded and tied around the waist. Burmese men will re-knot their longgyis periodically throughout the day. Daniel and I slipped the longgyis over our pants and enjoyed trying out our skills at the quick maneuver to make the folds and knot, evoking much laughter from the training participants.

In a fit of cultural solidarity, the next morning Daniel wore his longgyi to class. I knew that my knot-tying skills were not sufficient to the challenge of my movements in experiential education activities, so I stuck to my Western slacks. Daniel was facilitating a particular session when his longgyi suddenly came loose from his spare frame and dropped to the floor. As we all roared with laughter, I immediately leapt in front of him, throwing my hands wide and saying, "It's time for a break!"

The training participants had organized a humorous reading of the previous day's news, writing their stories in Burmese on large sheets of flipchart paper. One story, for example, was about learning to think "outside the box." According to the story, two participants took our lesson seriously, thought "outside the workshop," and left. The workshop news reports the day after Daniel's longgyi wardrobe malfunction were all translated for us except for one story which left everyone howling with laughter. Giggling, they refused to translate it for us. After the session we asked our translator to tell us what this particular article said that was so funny and that nobody wanted to tell us—though we certainly had our suspicions. The translator refused to tell us what the article was about until the end of the entire workshop when Daniel found a written translation on his bed. The article was about Daniel suddenly revealing his "teaching tools" but not showing how they worked. The details became much worse from there. As we read each line, we laughed so hard we could hardly stand it. I vowed to myself I would never wear a longgyi in public without a safety pin.

Clothing can be a special mark of pride in one's culture. As Naga leaders were flying into Atlanta for the initial peace talks in 1997, I was responsible for picking everyone up from the airport. I had the list of various flights, and in those days you could go right to the gate to meet your arriving guests. One flight arrived with five of the Naga participants, but as they deplaned I only gathered four. As I checked off their names from my list I asked, "Where is Nagi?" They said he was still on the plane. We waited while all the passengers got off the plane as well as some of the crew. There was a long pause; then Nagi stepped off the plane. He was dressed in traditional Naga ceremonial garb. He was bare-chested with a red kilt-type outfit on. He had a red headdress with a huge hornbill feather in it. Around his biceps were huge wooden armbands. I greeted him, and we walked down the corridors of the Atlanta airport to jaw-dropping stares. He walked with pride and confidence, looking like he had stepped out of the pages of *National Geographic.*

I never saw Nagi in that outfit again as he wore Western dress for the rest of the conference. Later Nagi sent me some photos of a trip he had taken into some of the remote Naga villages to talk with some of the insurgents about the Atlanta talks and the cease-fires we were working on. The photos show Naga village chiefs and elders in tribal dress, but Nagi is sitting in the middle with an open white shirt, dark suit jacket and baseball cap!

Another Naga in a baseball cap caught my attention. During my first trip to Nagaland, as Wati and I drove to Oriental Theological Seminary we had to pass through two roadblocks, one by the Indian Army and one set up by NSCN-IM cadres. The last time we made that trip I asked if Wati could take a photo of me with the AK-47 toting insurgents. Wati negotiated with them for about five minutes before the two soldiers at the roadblock agreed to have their photo taken. I scrambled out of the car and stood next to these two teenage soldiers who didn't even come up to my shoulder. As I looked at their young faces I was surprised to find a Michigan State Spartans baseball cap on one of them. Here I was out on a rural road in one of the most remote parts of India looking at a cap from my home state.

The MSU baseball cap illustrates part of the world economy. Leftover clothing from the U.S., items that won't sell at the discount stores or even the used-clothing stores, find their way to distant parts of the globe. Clothes nobody in the U.S. wants, new and used, are bundled into massive bales that are then shipped to poor countries. In India and Congo I saw the same types of shops with disorganized mountains of T-shirts and other clothing cast off as nearly worthless. For the poor, this can become the way to look especially sharp. In Congolese churches the usher crews would all wear the same color T-shirts, shipped from the U.S. and sold in shops that were the end of the line for this global trade. Many of the T-shirts had raunchy statements and expletives in English, but dignified people who spoke Kikongo and perhaps French wore them with pride. At least all the shirts for the ushers were red, whatever they said, and all the shirts for the choir were yellow. I was not about to tell them what some of their shirts said.

I also experienced clothing in a different way as an expression of God's care. As I was packing for my trip to Liberia in 2010 I felt a prompting expressed in my mind in clear words: "Pack some extra socks to give to somebody." I've never in all my years of peacemaking travel had such an idea cross my mind, certainly not with such a strange message. Where did it come from? I believe one should take such promptings seriously. I was traveling relatively light, so a few extra socks would be no problem. I tossed them into my bag.

In Liberia one of the workshops I facilitated was at the historic Providence Baptist Church in the Monrovia city center. During one of the breaks on the first day of the workshop a young man came up to talk with me. We got into deep conversations that continued through lunch. At some point he told me he lived in a community on the edge of Monrovia. I knew that particular community and commented about how far it was from Providence. He told me he had walked for two hours one way to come to the workshop, something he regularly did twice a week because he taught Sunday school and was part of an intercessors prayer group at Providence. He had no money for the buses or taxis that shuttled people around the city, so he walked. Then he took off his hard leather dress shoes. He had no socks, and the walking in the hard shoes had rubbed awful sores across his toes and ankles. In all my travels nobody had ever taken off their shoes to show me their feet. The open sores were not a pretty sight. Infection was beginning to set in. Now I knew why I'd been prompted to pack those extra socks.

Jesus taught about how God cares for the sparrows that fall, and I believe God showed care for this man needing socks so he could walk to church. This young man wasn't going to let raw sores deter him from attending his church to pray, to worship, and to learn things to help in building peace in his country, so God took care of him by making sure I brought some extra socks from across the ocean. The next day of the workshop was his birthday, and I brought him the socks as a present. I also gave him antibiotic cream from my personal health kit, some Band-Aids, and a few other small gifts.

But if God cares for a man walking for hours with sores on his feet, what about the hundreds of thousands who were displaced and traumatized by the war? What about the maimed bodies and the shattered minds? Does God care for something so small as a person's feet and ignore the huge sorrows that overwhelm us? I pondered this disquieting question even as I marveled at how God helped me bring socks to Liberia for one particular person I'd never met. For months I constructed an answer with my theological thinking, trying to make sense of suffering that seems so senseless.

Then one Sunday months later while sitting in a worship service, something was said that pricked open my memory of the socks. I had been prompted to bring socks to meet one man's need for relief. But I was also the socks. I had responded to an invitation by Jimmy Diggs to help relieve heartache in his country by training about trauma healing and reconciliation. What I taught was part of God's healing ointment on the festering wounds of some Liberians. I wasn't the complete answer—merely a pair of socks. But God was aware of the greater suffering and responding with compassion, even in a small part, through me and the peace work I do. The socks for my Liberian friend became a parable of hope to encourage me in the face of sorrows that can be so overwhelming. I can't solve all the problems of Liberia or any other place, but I can be a pair of socks covering the wounds in front of me. God is in that simple gesture as well as in far more than I can imagine.

The Home Front

Being raised in a household of active peacemakers brought some interesting experiences into the lives of our children. From infancy they were packed up for various street vigils and demonstrations. I remember taking our oldest child, Chris, in his stroller to the Boston Common for a Good Friday peace vigil. He maintained our discipline of silence by taking his nap as I gently rolled the stroller back and forth. Later he and his little brother Jonathan would chase each other around the house yelling "No Contra aid!"—not your typical childhood play scenario!

Of course, sibling conflict was a regular part of life. I was well acquainted with such conflict in my own childhood, having tussled verbally and physically with my two younger brothers as we grew up. My mother used to say, "If the Apostle Paul had known the Buttry boys he never would have said 'Let brotherly love continue'!" Sharon's and my brood certainly were no better. We tried to put our peacemaking skills into practice in our home, using nonviolent forms of discipline such as "time-outs." As the children got older we tried various schemes that would work for a while. One of the best was the "Fight Fair Form" in which the kids had to fill out a questionnaire about their conflict, what they contributed to it, what might be done to solve the problem, and the disciplinary actions they recommended. The children were always far harsher in meting out punishments even on themselves, which allowed Mom and Dad to be bringers of grace and mercy instead of the heavy hand of justice.

One of the most notorious conflicts involving our kids was the Clubhouse War. When we lived in Pennsylvania our house was next door to a church with a large yard and cemetery around it. One summer the church had a grand old tree cut down and sawn into logs of three and four foot lengths. The wood was left piled up on the lawn over the weekend, a delightful invitation to the inventive children of the neighborhood. Chris and Jon joined with the other neighborhood kids in taking the lengths of trunk and limbs and began an impressive building project. They added a few pieces of scrap plywood scrounged from family garages and built an impressive clubhouse. The kids proudly showed it off to me, and I crawled in through the low doorway to sit with them inside drinking pop and Gatorade.

Later in the day the bigger boys banded together to exclude the littler ones even though they had all helped build the clubhouse. The big boys spray-painted insults on the plywood outside and kept the clubhouse just for themselves. Chris and Jon were among the younger group and were very upset at having been cast out of their architectural masterpiece. That night after the big kids had gone home Chris and Jon struck back. They swiped an ax from our garage and began to tear down the clubhouse, hacking up the plywood, pulling down the logs that held up the roof, and even painting their own insulting graffiti on the ruins.

After sleeping on the matter the boys realized that their destructive rampage was bound to have some unpleasant consequences, so they sheepishly approached me with the story. They took me to the churchyard to see the wreckage of the clubhouse. It was an irreparable mess. Besides the wood being torn down and scattered, the boys had broken the glass bottles of Gatorade, leaving dangerous shards throughout the grass. This carnage would require a serious cleanup effort if we were to remain good neighbors to the church.

I also knew the big boys would not be amused, so I kept my eye out for them. Fairly early in the morning the big kids discovered what had happened to their clubhouse. Chris and Jon were playing in our backyard next to the church when the big kids came storming through the gate between the two yards, bent on a mission of vengeance. I had been watching expectantly from the back window, knowing that trouble was bound to erupt. Since the

U.N. peacekeeping forces weren't available, I had to rush into the middle to prevent a massacre.

I eventually got all the yelling, protesting kids to quite down, and we began a somewhat orderly recounting of everyone's story about what had happened. As we worked through all the wrongs committed and suffered, I showed them how everyone was at fault, and that their little neighborhood war had left them all with nothing. The clubhouse was a total loss, but they could learn from this experience about life. They had all done something wrong. The big kids had unjustly excluded the little kids from enjoying the clubhouse, which everyone had helped make. The little kids had responded with destructive anger that made the problem worse rather than better. They had all paid the price for their wrongs in destruction of the wonderful clubhouse.

We talked about how grown-ups sometimes do the same thing and that such actions in the grown-up world can lead to wars and lots of destruction. We all have to learn that when we treat people unfairly and lock them out of enjoying what they produce or build, people will feel angry. Yet when we respond to wrongs done to us with further wrongdoing, the result is greater devastation. We get farther from the good we want to have.

The children were quick to apologize on each side, forgive each other, shake hands, and be friends once more. They were soon playing together again in the streets of our little neighborhood. Their story, however, became one of my favorites to tell, especially to begin a sermon from Romans 12:21 where the Apostle Paul said, "Do not be overcome by evil, but overcome evil with good." Evil had been done to the little kids as evil has been done to so many who for whatever reason are locked out and marginalized. The little kids let their anger drive them to an evil response, adding destruction to the injustice. The challenge is how to mobilize ourselves and the forces of good to counter evil and overcome it.

A few years later Chris faced a perceived injustice in middle school and wanted to use Martin Luther King, Jr.'s protest tactics to overcome it. He and his lunch-table buddies were bowling with apples. The tables were hinged in the middle, with the center going up and the ends down for storage. One of the boys sitting in the middle popped the center of the table up as the apple came rolling by. The table sprang up from the center with all the trays of food sliding down the ends and crashing to the floor. The principal acted with quick sternness, separating all the boys, sending them to various tables around the lunchroom and banning them from sitting together again.

Chris came home furious that he and his friends could no longer sit together. He felt that only the boy who popped the table up should have been punished, not the whole group. He wanted to have the boys engage in a sit-in, sitting at their old table and refusing to budge, or even sitting on the floor if necessary. As he related his plans to me he appealed to the example of Dr. King and the civil rights protest. He even dragged in the example of his old man: "You got arrested for protesting once, didn't you?" It was hard to counter such an argument and suggest that he meekly accept the punishment doled out by the recognized authority. I asked Chris if he had talked with the principal and told him that he felt the punishment was unfair. Chris had not done this, and I mentioned that Dr. King always communicated first about the unjust situation before engaging in civil disobedience. Alas, the protest fizzled out with neither talk nor action, but if Chris had been willing to make his protest in a conscientious way his Dad would have backed him up.

I had a more positive involvement with school in conjunction with Janelle's fourth grade class. While directing the Peace Program for National Ministries, I also represented the American Baptist Churches at the United Nations as their non-governmental organizations representative. In that capacity I had been involved in advocacy efforts to secure U.S. ratification of the U.N. Convention on the Rights of the Child. Janelle and I worked together to do a presentation on the U.N. and the Rights of the Child for her class. We began by showing toys from around the world, and we asked children find each toy's country of origin on a globe. I gave a brief overview of the United Nations, and Janelle read aloud a U.N. picture book on the Rights of the Child. I mentioned that 135 or so countries had ratified the Convention on the Rights of the Child, then asked if they could name one country that had not ratified the Convention. The children suggested a list of "bad" countries: Iran, Cuba, Russia. I said I didn't know about those countries, but when I identified the United States as not having ratified the Convention, one boy immediately piped up, "But I thought we were civilized!"

The final activity of our presentation was for the class to write letters to the U.S. Senate about the Rights of the Child. The teacher guided them about their form for writing: "Is this a personal letter or business letter?" The students produced a great group of letters to send off to our senators. I wrote my own letters urging ratification. I mentioned the quote from the student—"I thought we were civilized." The main reason our government had given for not ratifying such a basic statement of human rights for the most vulnerable among us was that we wanted to maintain the option to execute people under seventeen years of age who had committed murder. We have a strange way of showing global leadership for human values when we need the voice of a child to speak truth clearly!

Because of my job and Sharon's and my interest in international peace issues and Christian missions, our children interacted with people from around the world. As we would host international guests in our home, our kids got to know people such as Saboi Jum and Wati Aier. We had guests from El Salvador, South Africa, Liberia, and Japan. Our children also got to know dedicated peacemakers from the Baptist Peace Fellowship both as guests in our home and through our participation in the BPFNA's summer conference each year. These special friends would take time to connect to our children, to play or read with them. As our children grew up, they got to know some amazing folks.

In 1994 when the Rwandan genocide exploded into the news, I told my family at dinner that I had a friend who was in the middle of the violence. I had met Eleazar Ziherembere at the 1992 Baptist peace conference in Nicaragua. Eleazar became a special friend, so I asked my family to pray for him. My eleven-year-old son, Jonathan, took that request to heart. For weeks he demanded to say the table grace for every meal, and each time he would pray for Eleazar and his safety. After two months we got word that Eleazar had escaped, first to Zambia and then to Kenya. We were relieved and excited, though it was sobering to remember the million people who had not survived. When I was able to send a message to Eleazar, I told him about Jonathan's daily prayers.

A bit later Eleazar was able to come to the U.S. to visit our denominational headquarters at Valley Forge. I invited him to our home for dinner. As he came in the door, Eleazar immediately asked for Jonathan. When the two shook hands, Eleazar told Jonathan how much he appreciated those daily prayers. Eleazar said that because of Jonathan's prayers and the prayers of many other concerned people, he was alive today. Jonathan looked up at Eleazar with awe. I took Jonathan to one of Eleazar's speaking engagements, and between Eleazar's public program and our conversations at home, Jon heard many stories of sorrow, sacrifice, and loving witness in incredibly difficult circumstances. Eleazar's faith, love, and openness to Jonathan had a major influence on his developing faith. Over the years Eleazar and I have worked on a number of projects, and whenever we are together he asks about Jonathan. The prayers have gone both ways now.

Sharon and I were inspired by Paul Dekar's presentations about Baptist saints for peace and justice to develop a family observance of All Saints Day. Baptists have almost completely ignored All Saints Day, but Sharon and I thought it would be a wonderful opportunity to teach history, both our family history and church history. My father died before any of our children were born, so we were looking for ways to pass on stories about Grandpa Buttry.

At dinner on 1 November, before we said our table grace, we had each family member share the name and story of a "saint," someone who had showed the ways of God to us. As we shared the name, we would each light a candle. Sharon and I would prepare to balance the saints the children named so that we would have a range of relatives and people from history. Some peace saints the children knew from school, such as Martin Luther King, Jr. Others Sharon and I introduced to them, such as Mary Dyer, the Quaker woman martyred in colonial Massachusetts for her nonviolent witness for religious liberty. As we ate our meal we composed a poem together with a stanza for each saint we had named. Poems written by a group with young children can result in some rather odd lines, but we had fun together and reinforced the stories. Sharon wrote the finished composition on an old calendar picture and hung it up in the kitchen to remind us of our saints throughout the coming year.

One saint our children always remembered was Sharon's brother, David Crader. David was much younger than Sharon, born when she and I were just beginning to date. David joined the U.S. Army. He was in training at artillery school when Iraq invaded Kuwait in 1990. As the U.S. military mobilized for Operation Desert Shield, David's unit began preparing long-stored howitzers for shipment to Saudi Arabia. One howitzer had a stuck bolt. One of the men couldn't budge the bolt, so David crawled under the barrel and gave it a try. When David loosened the bolt the barrel of the howitzer collapsed on his head, killing him instantly. The hydraulic fluid that held the barrel in place had leaked away over the years, and there was nothing to support the weight of the cannon when the bolt was released.

At that time I was directing the Peace Program for National Ministries. I participated in many of the anti-war activities, including working with Ken Sehested to hold a large prayer service in Washington DC on the eve of launching the air war. Through the build-up period and war that followed, our family knew intimately the human toll of war. The young man Sharon had helped to raise was gone. The uncle who was visiting us when Janelle was born and who loved to hold her and look at her would never visit again. David's death has given me a poignant burden as I continue my peacemaking work. I pray and labor for the day when no family will know that loss that we have experienced.

A group of American Baptists who had family members in the Gulf was organized by a mother from Pittsburgh. We met for prayer at the American Baptist national biennial meeting. We had a variety of political views, people supporting the war and opposing it, but we all shared a concern for the well being of our family members. I was welcomed into this group, and we supported each other in our shared heartaches and anxieties.

In 1988 as I prepared to go to the International Baptist Peace Conference in Sweden and then continue on to the Soviet Union with a small Baptist Peace Fellowship delegation, my son Jon was coloring some left-over flyers from a peace demonstration. There was a human figure breaking a missile on the flyer. Jon, who was four years old at the time, was coloring this simple drawing on sheet after sheet of the flyers. He gave them to me to give as a gift to other children I might meet. At the Sweden conference I was in a small group that included a Baptist pastor from southern Russia. We were invited to tell about why we were at this conference. This Russian pastor shared that during World War II he had lost eight siblings. He was at the peace conference because he did not want his children to know the sorrow he had known as a child. His youngest child was four years old. I shared with him about Jon and gave him one of the drawings in the hope that both our children would grow up with a more peaceful future.

Another piece of Jon's artwork graced my office wall for many years. He was drawing a picture of a stealth bomber. I could recognize the attractiveness of the sleek shape and design. When Jon proudly showed me his drawing I affirmed the quality of his work and how cool the plane looked but said it was hard for me to feel good about it because the stealth existed to hurt people by dropping bombs on them. Jon went back to the table and took up his crayons once more. In a bit he returned with another picture. In the top corner of the drawing was a stealth. Falling through the air beneath it were dollar bills, hamburgers, fruit, vegetables, shirts, and pants. Jon said this was "the helping stealth," dropping gifts to people in need. I've never seen a better child-like interpretation of the vision of the prophet: "They shall beat their

swords into plowshares and their spears into pruning hooks"
(Isaiah 2.4).

Nagi in traditional Naga dress at the Atlanta airport

(Left) The Buttry family with Saboi Jum; (right) Janelle Buttry asleep in a stroller at a peace demonstration

Eleazar Ziherembere and his wife Speciose with Jonathan Buttry

7

TOOLBOX

Necessity as the Mother of Invention

Daniel Hunter and I were planning to travel to northeast India in 2000, our first of what would be many training trips together. We had never co-facilitated before, and our first training was going to be a huge test of our flexibility and skills. We had been invited to come as resource people for a training conference on conflict transformation sponsored by the Council of Baptist Churches of North East India (CBCNEI) held at their headquarters compound in Guwahati, Assam. All we knew was that the conference was for four days and that Ron Kraybill of Eastern Mennonite University would also be a conference leader. We had no idea of the schedule, the conference design, if other leaders were involved, how much time we were responsible for, or whether we had plenary sessions to lead or only breakout workshop sessions. As we neared our time to go we realized we would be designing our four-day program at the last minute whether we wanted to or not.

Daniel and I got together at my house for two days to build ourselves as a team and develop what we called our "toolbox." The toolbox was an inventory of all the learning tools we had between us, from five-minute energizer games and fifteen-minute challenge activities to one-hour group Bible studies and three-hour simulation games. We used an index card to title and describe each learning activity, then characterized its possible uses, such as whether it was a generic learning tool that could be put in a variety of content contexts or a topical tool in areas such as conflict resolution, communication, or nonviolent action. As our pile of index cards grew, we sorted them into natural topic clusters from which we could see plans emerge for one and a half to three-hour session blocks. For each session block we had a number of options available, including tools that would work better for larger or smaller groups, tools that would focus on Bible study, topic content exploration, or application.

When we were finished assembling our toolbox, we felt prepared to meet any challenge to design a workshop quickly or training in any setting, with any size group and any amount of time allotted. We arrived at Guwahati the evening before the conference began, and we met with Dr. J. M. Pau, the general secretary of the CBCNEI. He informed us that Ron, Daniel, and I were the only conference leaders and were responsible for the entire four-day program. We quickly huddled with Ron, sketched out some plenary themes we could each handle, and set up parallel workshop tracks in mediation led by Ron and nonviolence led by Daniel and me. We got a good night sleep, as much as jet lag would allow, then began the conference the next morning. Without the development of the toolbox, I would have been frustrated and angry with our hosts. With the toolbox we were able to be flexible, responding quickly to emerging needs in the groups or even opportunities to organize a spontaneous training session.

Over the years the toolbox has continued to grow as I discover new tools from other facilitators or resources, adapt old tools to new purposes, and design new tools. Like a good folk song, a tool designed by one person for one purpose can be tweaked and twisted to serve another purpose in a different setting. Everything I use is liable to evolve as I have more experiences with different groups, see their responses to the tools, adapt tools to meet various challenges and opportunities, or find ways to revitalize configurations of tools to strengthen an overall program design. It reminds me of what my Uncle Frank used to say about his sermon preparation: "I milk a lot of cows, but the cheese is mine." Other people initially designed many of the tools in my toolbox, and I am greatly and gratefully indebted to them. The way I use them, put them together with other tools, adapt them, and make the finished "cheese" of a specific program is mine, and almost every case is a unique event for a particular group of people in a particular context.

As a peace warrior I often introduce the use of experiential education tools by referring to military war games. Military forces prepare their troops by engaging in "war games," simulated activities through which the soldiers are educated. In the war games soldiers learn ways of analyzing battlefield situations, new ways of working together as a unit, and new skills to engage effectively in combat. When the soldiers are then in the actual combat situation they will be able to act more quickly and efficiently. However, my task is not to teach war but to teach the ways of making peace. As peace activists we can learn from the military's use of war games by developing our own "peace games." Our peace games can teach activists ways of analyzing conflict situations, new ways of working together cohesively with other activists, and skills to engage effectively in conflict transformation. The ends may be vastly different in war games and peace games, but there is no replacement for direct experience in developing and sharpening people's perceptions and skills.

Red/Blue Game

One of the earliest peace games I used in experiential peace education was the Red/Blue Game, but when I first came across it in an out-of-print youth curriculum the colors were yellow and blue. This game is a derivative of the famed "Prisoner's Dilemma" attributed to Merrill Flood and Melvin Dresher who worked with Rand Corporation to develop games with application to nuclear weapons strategies, oddly enough. In the Red/Blue Game two teams are paired with the goal for each team of ending up with a positive point score. Through ten rounds each team selects either "red" or "blue." The scores are calculated on the basis of the selections made by both teams. If both teams select red they both get three points. If both select blue they both lose three points. If one selects red and the other blue, the team choosing blue gains six points while the team choosing red loses six points. If the teams choose to compete in a win/lose approach, they quickly slide into negative scores, the initial approach taken by most groups playing this game. Only by taking the risk of cooperation and both choosing red can long-term positive scores be achieved for both teams. Twice during the game there are opportunities for representatives from each side to discuss and negotiate about how the teams should proceed. The Red/Blue Game is a wonderful tool for experiencing the dynamics of conflict and the benefits and challenges of win/win approaches to conflict.

I've used the Red/Blue Game in training programs across the world, and often the dynamics of a society's conflicts are reflected in how people play the game. Usually I set up two to four parallel games, both to keep the teams small enough so everyone can be involved and to maximize educational value. Parallel games usually end up with very different dynamics unfolding, so in addition to debriefing the experience of each game, we can also draw insights from the comparison of the games. The game is one of the earliest tools I use in a program to teach some of the simpler dynamics of conflict and conflict resolution. Grasping the concept of win/win solutions to conflicts is a basic component of the trainings before getting into the complexities of power differences, marginality, and nonviolent action.

In 1997, I ran the game in Liberia during a time of fragile peace following a major civil war and leading up to an election that people could already see was not likely to bring a lasting peace. During one of the games, negotiators from the two sides agreed to both play red, but then one side deliberately reversed themselves and surprised the other by playing blue, gaining a sudden advantage at the cost of the other team. Trust was shattered between the two groups with the betrayed group getting angry and determined to take down the other side even if it meant their own score plunged lower (the blue/blue option). As we debriefed what happened, we saw how the game participants had re-enacted the same strategy used by Liberian warlords to dupe others into vulnerable positions during negotiations, only to betray them to gain a short-term advantage. Of course, the cost was shattered trust and long-standing bitterness. The Liberian church leaders who had a set of proclaimed values for peace found themselves mirroring the duplicity that had become endemic in their political culture. They were able to identify the deeper issues of building trust, establishing accountability for leaders, and developing supports necessary for agreements to be sustainable.

Most of the time I facilitate the game we have a lot of fun, learn about conflict and win/win solutions, and lay the foundation for the deeper work of the rest of the workshop. Occasionally, however, this tool has opened breakthrough moments for a group. Such a time was when I led a training for Naga insurgent officers a week after the Indian government lifted the ban on their organization. At that point in the Naga story, Isak and Muivah's group (NSCN-IM) was engaged in political talks with the government of India. Other Naga political and military organizations were critical of them, calling for Isak and Muivah to first work on resolving the differences among the Nagas themselves before attempting to negotiate a final settlement with India. The terms used were "solution" and "unity," Isak and Muivah arguing for a "solution" first, taking advantage of India's willingness to talk, but leaving NSCN-IM in the driver's seat on the Naga side. The other Nagas were calling for "unity," resolving the internal rifts among the Nagas before negotiating any settlement with the government of India. Some were even saying that if the NSCN-IM came with a "solution" worked out apart from the other Naga groups that civil war would erupt. I had been hearing these two positions advocated repeatedly by one side or the other during the two weeks I had been in Nagaland.

It was while I was in Nagaland in November and December 2002 that the Indian government allowed the ban on NSCN-IM to expire. Lifting the ban allowed a measure of legitimacy to the organization that had to some degree turned aside from their pursuit of a military solution to enter into a cease-fire with the Indian Army that had lasted for five years. Political talks were underway, admittedly going very slow, but by letting the ban expire, India was allowing Isak and Muivah and other leaders to emerge from the jungle or exile and participate in more open political processes. The executive committee of the NSCN-IM invited me to meet with them on a Saturday to discuss peace building. I was scheduled to leave the following Tuesday, but we had no plans for Monday. They asked if I could do a peace-building training for their cadres, and since Monday was clear I agreed. That Monday seventy officers of the insurgency, including perhaps twenty women (all of whom a week earlier had been hiding in the jungle), gathered in a church on short notice for peace-building training.

I began with the Red/Blue Game. In one of the parallel games I had drawn together a team of women to play with a team of men. Initially they all pursued the competitive approach, choosing blue with hopes for an advantage, but both sides lost because they made the same choice. Then at the negotiation session, the representatives from the two sides both agreed to play red, to pursue the win/win option. That worked for the men's team, but the women rejected their representative's solution. They overruled her and chose blue for the next round. The men were furious and felt betrayed, so the game went back to the "I'll take you down even if I go down with you" hostility.

As we debriefed what had happened, we noted that there are two very different negotiation processes that go on in peace negotiations. Most attention is given to the negotiation between the representatives of the two sides, what we could call the "enemies" who come to the table. In the Naga context this is the negotiation where the "solution" is sought, but there is another negotiation that is equally important, the negotiation between the negotiators and their own constituency. Often this negotiation within a group is overlooked as people assume it will take care of itself. History is full of stories of people and organizations who negotiated a settlement only to have it torpedoed not by the "enemy" but by one's own people who did not participate in the negotiation process and who rejected the agreement. In the simulation game the process broke down within the women's team as the team rejected what their representative achieved at the negotiation. In the Naga context this was the reflection of the "unity" issue. The failure to maintain or achieve unity brought about the collapse of the solution. As the participants of the game unpacked what had happened they quickly grasped that the issue wasn't "unity" *or* "solution"—it had to be *both*. Both processes needed attention simultaneously. Without "unity" the "solution" could be undermined and lost. Working solely on "unity" would squander the historical moment for a "solution," a moment that might not come for a decade or more if it fell apart at this point. I'd been making little headway by talking repeatedly to leaders on both sides about these matters, but the Red/Blue Game enabled some of the lower-level leaders to grasp that working on intra-Naga peace must happen simultaneously with the pursuit of a political solution with the government of India.

Eggsercise

I developed a tool for use in a Naga training that brought me the most pride over creative design. I called it the "eggsercise." In February 1999 I was going to facilitate the training of leaders from the Naga civil society organizations, including the churches, women's organizations, student groups, business organizations, and human rights activists. Prior to that gathering, our work in the Naga peace initiative had been trying to get the Naga insurgent leaders into peace talks with each other. That process had stalled, so we decided to shift our focus toward supporting and strengthening the public sector so they could become an effective force for a just peace among the Nagas and with the Nagas and the government of India.

The problem, however, was that there was little trust among people, even people who seemed to have the same goal of peace. For decades the Nagas had been victimized by Indian authorities, who could seize and detain anyone without any regard to their legal or human rights. The army and police watched everyone. Furthermore, the vicious struggle among the Naga factions had led to many assassinations because of real or perceived leanings toward one side or the other. Naga leaders had difficulty trusting each other, wondering if anything they might say would be passed back to someone else with deadly intent. Organizations operated separately, though a few small coalitions were starting to develop.

Many of the organizations were critical of others, and the social sector organizations were critical of the church leaders even though the vast majority of all the Nagas were Baptists.

About two dozen top leaders from various Naga organizations, including the Naga Baptist churches, were gathering in Calcutta to be trained in conflict transformation and to begin planning how they might jointly work for peace. How could they grow in trusting one another? How could they break through the fear and suspicion that had kept them isolated?

Just prior to going to India I attended a Training of Social Action Trainers (TSAT) led by George Lakey of Training for Change. This was my second time in the TSAT in which we are encouraged to design tools for experiential education and practice facilitating with those tools with our fellow participants in the training. I seized the training as an opportunity to solve the problems posed to me by the gathering of the Naga organization leaders. The TSAT had stimulated my creativity, and I came up with the idea of using raw eggs. I ran the idea by George and by my small practice group in the training, then further refined it as we worked on workshop design. A few days later I used it with the Nagas in Calcutta.

I formed people into groups of three for sharing, reflection, and support throughout the four-day workshop. One day as they were gathered in their groups of three I passed out raw eggs I'd purchased from a street vendor. As the participants held the eggs in their hands I led them through a meditation on the egg, calling attention to the feel and weight of the life inside the egg, the fragile shell protecting and holding that life, and how easily the egg could be crushed as well as held gently. I invited them to think about their life, how precious it is, how fragile it is, how it can be snuffed out in a moment or held in gentleness. I invited them to identify themselves and their lives with the eggs in their hand.

Then I asked each person to pass their egg to the person next to them. They would entrust their egg to another person to take care of for the next twenty-four hours, and in turn they would receive another person's egg that would be in their care for the next day. Whatever the activity, whether studying in the workshop, doing a dramatic physical game, walking to restaurants for meals, sleeping, getting up in the morning, each person had the care of that raw egg. Symbolically we were holding one another's lives in our care.

The training participants took on the challenge with seriousness and creativity. Some made protective shelters with folded paper to keep their eggs from rolling around while we engaged in high movement activities. There was some joking, but everyone took great care to protect the egg someone else had entrusted to them. It was interesting to notice that the men were very nervous about the activity whereas the women enjoyed it, perhaps reflecting their greater familiarity with the nurturing roles of caring for others.

At the end of twenty-four hours, not one egg had been broken. We gathered again in our groups of three. The eggs were returned to the original holders. I invited the participants to express their appreciation to the ones who had carried and cared for their egg, and the response showed that people had experienced something deeper than simply carrying around an egg. They had been aware that they were holding each other, that they were entrusting their lives into the hands of their comrades in the struggle for peace. For lunch we broke all the eggs and made an omelet that we shared together in a new feeling of unity and solidarity.

That "eggsercise" seemed to break through the dam of suspicion and enable these Naga leaders to take the risks of trusting one another so that together they could take courageous action to transform their context of conflict. We did not come up with any clear strategies in that February meeting, but a new depth in relationship and commitment was reached. We gathered again in November for more training, but even more importantly for two days of planning to shape a new Naga peace movement called "The Journey of Conscience." The Journey of Conscience changed the political and social landscape of the Naga conflict, moving the civil society organizations into the forefront of defining the issues and demanding that the Naga and Indian political leaders deal constructively with the conflict. Certainly much more than mere eggs went into the creation of the relationships that bound the Naga activist leaders together, but the care of those eggs had helped them see the care they needed to give to one another if they were to be empowered to act in the face of oppression which for so long had induced fear and isolation.

Bible Studies

As a Christian and a former pastor, I have always had a major portion of my peace training and teaching tools given over to Bible studies. That pivotal conversation with my friend Christie in college when she asked me, "What does Jesus say?" inspired me to make examination of biblical teaching, especially the teaching of Jesus, a central part of what I do, at least in Christian contexts.

As a pastor I developed a "Bible Study on War and Peace," which was a fairly exhaustive set of worksheets from Genesis to Revelation. Most of my early teaching was a mix of lecture and discussion questions. Two factors revolutionized my biblical teaching on peace. One was reading Walter Wink's *Violence and Nonviolence in South Africa: Jesus' Third Way* (New Society Publishers, 1987). Wink's exposition on Jesus' teachings in the Sermon on the Mount, specifically Matthew 5:39-41 about turning the other check, giving your cloak, and going the second mile, suggested that I could dramatize Jesus' teachings, getting a higher degree of audience participation and powerful visualization of what Jesus was actually talking about. Second, attending George Lakey's TSAT challenged me to rework my Bible study methodologies to be more experiential. In some cases that meant inviting people into the biblical stories as the learning experience through group Bible studies. In other cases that meant finding creative ways of acting out stories such as the conflicts of Jacob and Esau or Paul and Barnabas.

The study on the Sermon on the Mount became one of my main components for peace education. I drew upon the work of Wink to unpack the meaning of the three actions in Matthew 5:39-

41, the work of Glen Stassen to identify "transforming initiatives" as the type of action Jesus called for his disciples to take (*Just Peacemaking*, Westminster/John Knox Press, 1992) and the New Testament Greek work of Clarence Jordan to understand that "do not resist the evil one" was more accurately translated "do not resist by evil means" ("The Lesson on the Mount-II" in *The Universe Bends Toward Justice*, ed by Angie O'Gorman, New Society Publishers, 1990). Combining these perspectives and adding my own analysis of responses to violence in Jesus' day and our own gave me a powerful Bible study session to teach nonviolent action. (See chapter 2 of *Christian Peacemaking: From Heritage to Hope* [Judson Press, 1999] for a full explication of this topic.)

In the dramatization of Jesus' teaching I would get a volunteer to act out being slapped and turning the other cheek. We would see that the person was not being cowed into submission as the backhanded slap to a subordinate person was intended to do in Jesus' day. The slapped person was still standing in front of the one who claimed superior status, yet no attack was made in return. We explored the issues of claiming our human dignity without tearing down the dignity of others.

I then became the poor powerless person brought into court by the rich landowner to legalize a loan for which I would give my cloak as collateral. I would peel off my shirt, and then following the teaching of Jesus literally, take off my undershirt to stand bare-chested in front of the laughing participants while the "rich landowner" sheepishly held my clothes. We then explored how the shame of nakedness in Jewish culture rested not on the naked one but on the one who causes the nakedness (the wealthy landlord) and those who witness the nakedness and do nothing (the court, or in this case, the rest of the participants in the class). Jesus used the powerful shame of nakedness to hold a mirror to an immoral system, exposing its evil. This dramatization has left permanent imprints on the minds of participants in my trainings.

I would then seize a workshop participant to carry my bag like the Roman soldiers impressed civilians to carry their equipment for one mile in Jesus' day. We saw the way that an act of oppression was turned into a gift to the oppressor in such a way that the oppressor was thrown off balance. We would explore the significance of all these acts in Jesus' day, asking how they all might be problematic if literally acted out in contemporary settings or cultures. Then I would give examples of how those dynamics are acted out creatively in a range of contemporary situations from one-on-one conflict situations to national moments of crisis.

Sometimes in Christian settings I will introduce the teaching of the Sermon on the Mount by turning to a fascinating book by Michael Hart, *The 100: A Ranking of the Most Influential Persons in History* (Citadel Press, 1978, 1992). Hart gives the biographies of one hundred figures in history, their impact on the world and the course of events, and the reasons he ranks them relative to other figures. I'll ask participants to guess who is ranked number one in this book, which was written by a historian, not a believer (at least not that I know or not from that vantage point). Inevitably people will say "Jesus" (and I'll say "no"). Hitler usually is mentioned, but Hart ranks him only thirty-ninth. Then I reveal Hart's ranking: Muhammad is ranked first, Isaac Newton second, and Jesus third. After Hart goes through the impact of Jesus in history, such as founding a major world religion and Christianity's influence on much of culture and history, he explores the teaching of Jesus. The most unique ethical teaching of Jesus, according to Hart, is "love your enemies." No other religion included such teaching, so Hart calls the teaching of loving one's enemies "among the most remarkable and original ethical ideas ever presented" (p. 20). Hart writes he wouldn't hesitate to rank Jesus first in the book if such teaching was widely followed. Then with a drumbeat of indictment, Hart describes how Christians do not practice or teach Jesus' "most distinctive teaching," leaving it "an intriguing but basically untried suggestion" (p. 21). Hart's critique is pretty damning. I use it to prepare people to engage with more seriousness in the study on the Sermon on the Mount, especially in its applications to contemporary conflict situations.

Over the years I've discovered and developed a large number of Bible stories to use in group studies to teach conflict resolution skills, nonviolent action, or positive action in mainstream and margin contexts. We've used the conflict between Paul and Barnabas over whether to take John Mark with them on their next missionary journey (Acts 15:36-41) to practice the steps to finding win/win solutions. There are familiar stories and obscure stories with great conflict transformation lessons.

One of my favorite stories to use in Bible study is the story of Rizpah. "Who?" most church members would ask. Rizpah is the answer for a great Bible trivia question: Who was King Saul's concubine? Cindy Weber, the pastor of the Jeff Street Baptist Church in Louisville introduced me to Rizpah when she was the Bible study leader at a Baptist Peace Fellowship summer conference. 2 Samuel 21 tells the story of a famine coming to Israel. King David inquires of God and is told that there is bloodguilt on the land. Saul had earlier committed a massacre of Gibeonites, an indigenous ethnic group that had entered into a covenant of peace with the Israelites. David confers with the surviving Gibeonites, and they decide to execute the male descendants of Saul, using a new massacre to address the wrongs of an old massacre. God is silent; the famine continues. Rizpah, the mother of two of the slain young men, begins a vigil watching over their bodies from the barley harvest till the rains come, a period that some commentators say is from October to May. David finally hears of her vigil. He comes to her, gathers the bones of her sons as well as the improperly buried bones of Saul and his other sons who died in battle, and gives them all a proper burial. Then God heals the land. I interpret Rizpah's action as a nonviolent vigil to make people face the injustice of these executions. She is one of a long line of women, especially mothers, who have protested the violence that has claimed the lives of their children. Rizpah's action brings about the public repentance and policy change by the highest leader in the land.

In the Bible study question sheet I give groups I ask, "Can you think of any modern examples of Rizpah?" I will never forget the response to the first time I used the Rizpah study in Burma where Aung San Suu Kyi, Nobel Peace Prize recipient and leader of the democracy movement, was under house arrest. Fear of repression was so pervasive that nobody would speak her name aloud. Small groups in the workshop were working with various passages in which nonviolent transforming initiatives were taken, including the 2 Samuel 21 passage. As the groups reported back, a spokesperson would stand and tell about the story and what they had learned. A young woman reported for the 2 Samuel 21 group, relating the story of Rizpah. When she finished the story she paused. She stood a little taller, threw back her shoulders, and with pride and strength in her voice proclaimed, "Aung San Suu Kyi is today's Rizpah!" It was an electric moment. This Bible story that most Christians in North America could never identify was so powerful to this young woman in Burma that it gave her strength to voice what most others in her country wouldn't dare to whisper.

After attending the STAR (Seminar on Trauma Awareness and Recovery) program at Eastern Mennonite University, I noticed that the Rizpah story contained all three of the responses to trauma. There was the victim/survivor in the person of Merab. She was a mother who lost five sons in one day. She disappears from the story, frozen in her victimhood. There were the aggressor/offenders, people who had been victims but used the trauma as a driving force to justify their own acts of violence. This response to trauma was seen in the Gibeonites, victims of genocide who became killers out of their desires for revenge. Then there was Rizpah, the victim who through transformative action moved not only herself but also the larger society toward healing and reconciliation. I refined the Bible study to incorporate these new elements of trauma responses.

In this new form, the story of Rizpah stimulated some astonishing healing in Bosnia. I was invited to Bosnia in 2006 by a Ukrainian Baptist missionary, Fyodor Raychaynets. Fyodor was the pastor of a small church in Tuzla, a Bosnian city where Serbs, Croats, and Muslims all lived together. The war in Bosnia in the

1990s brought incredible suffering, and twelve years after the peace agreement people still had deep wounds and bitterness. Communities were still divided, usually living in separate ethnically-defined enclaves. However, Tuzla was one place where people of the various ethnic groups mixed together. Fyodor assembled a small group for a Bible study workshop on trauma healing. We had six Baptist and Pentecostal Christians, including some Serbian mothers, and five Muslim men from a support group for Bosnian Army veterans with post-traumatic stress. This was not a typical Bible study group, particularly not in Bosnia!

On the first night as we started into this story, we examined the dynamics of the victim-survivor as seen in Merab. Then we looked at the dynamics of how a victim can become a victimizer as seen in the Gibeonites. We explored how the shame and humiliation of being victimized can lead to fantasies of revenge. Stories are created with a good-versus-evil narrative. The good, of course, resides in one's own people, leaving the evil solely in the enemies who have treated our group so horribly. This stark narrative dehumanizes the enemy, quickly turning into a justification for new acts of violence.

As we worked through this ancient story and the dynamics of various trauma responses, participants in the workshop recognized their own stories in the Bible story. Thinking about the movement of Gibeonites from victims of genocide to perpetrators of violence, one Muslim army veteran suddenly burst out, "Now I understand the Serbs! They used to call me 'Turk.' I'm not a Turk." He went on to relate how the Serbs were viewing him through their own traumatic experience of being conquered by the Turks. He was Bosnian, not Turkish, but both were Muslims. That was what the Serbs responded to out of their trauma memories. Through the story of Rizpah, a traumatized Muslim veteran came to compassionate understanding of his enemies. The Bible gave him a lens to see his enemy in a new way, a way that restored their humanity in his eyes.

Then a Serb mother in our group spoke up, "I'd like to pray for his healing." She looked at me and said, "I'm not asking *your* permission." She turned to the Muslim veteran who had spoken, "I'm asking *your* permission. May I pray for your healing from the traumas you've suffered?" This woman had earlier spoken about how the war had torn apart her own family. With incredible empathy from her own woundedness she offered a beautiful prayer for the healing of the inner wounds from the war for the Bosnian Muslim army veterans. After the session Fyodor said he'd never seen anything like it during his time in Bosnia.

The Muslim vets all took Bibles, and the next night they returned as we focused on Rizpah and the journey of healing. They told us that in the morning they led the Bible study we'd done the previous night with their larger post-traumatic support group, and they brought some more veterans along with them. One of the Muslim vets had testified at the War Crimes Tribunal at The Hague about the crimes he had witnessed. Reliving that wartime trauma triggered his post-traumatic stress breakdown. He brought his wife along to the second session so she could gain new understanding about him and learn how to support his healing.

We explored Rizpah's journey through victimization to grief, public witness, transformation, and healing, all recorded in the simple outlines of the biblical story. We talked about how to grieve and the importance of sharing stories. We talked about making communities of wounded healers: Muslims, Croats, and Serbs together caring for each other, risking to share their own stories, and blessing each other. One woman in the presence of these soldiers shared about being raped so violently she needed surgery to recover physically, but her pain was still so raw before us all. People who had worked with her for hours on end had never known this part of her story, yet she felt safe enough to share it in a setting with former soldiers from the other side. We blessed her as a daughter of Rizpah to break the silence of shame that keeps the victims of trauma isolated for so many years. We listened to her and prayed for her, Christians and Muslims together.

I returned to Bosnia the following year and learned that these vets continued their healing journey with Fyodor and others. The strange, awful story out of the Hebrew Scriptures had stimulated an ongoing process of healing and helped create a small community of reconciliation that is one of the signs of hope in a war-torn land.

The Village Game

In 1994 Pom, a Thai student and grassroots environmental activist, used a game to help train Thai villagers develop ways of resisting the depredations of logging companies on their land. Canadian activist Karen Ridd adapted "The Village Game" and printed instructions. Daniel Hunter introduced it to me when we were first developing our toolbox, and I have used it frequently ever since.

The game begins by dividing the participants into small groups of six to ten. Each group is given a large sheet of paper and markers. Together each group is to draw the "ideal village" or the kind of community they would love to live in. As the groups are drawing, the facilitators walk around giving affirmation and encouragement, getting everyone directly involved in the process of creating their ideal village. When the drawings are nearing completion the facilitators have everyone pause and share with the larger group what they have done in a "tour of the villages." Then the groups are given a couple of minutes to make final additions to their drawings.

The facilitators have each group stand around their drawing, which is placed on the floor, and meditate about how wonderful it would be to live in such a village or community. While the groups are doing that the facilitators quickly change into new roles as representatives of outside interests. I often put on a tie, and when Daniel and I were training we would introduce ourselves as "Mr. Banks and Mr. Moneybags of the Megacorp Corporation." We would begin circling around the groups making paternalistic comments about the "nice" and "cute" villages. Then we would note that there were no McDonalds, and we would draw a pair of arches on a key location of a village. As we went from village to village we would comment about how we were there to improve things for them, drawing power plants and factories, and polluting their rivers and skies.

The point was to see what the participants would do, how their awareness developed about threats to their community, how they organized to work together, and what strategies for resistance they might develop. Sometimes people would move quickly to resist us, perhaps acting immediately to push our hands away as we tried to draw a McDonalds or factory on their paper. Sometimes people would stand and watch with baffled expressions as we began to mar their depiction of an ideal community. As facilitators we would slowly ratchet up our actions against the village. After defacing their drawing we would begin to tear away small pieces, perhaps trees or blocks of land. Later we would take "people"—figures drawn in their village—to serve in the army to protect our national interests. As resistance would develop we would get more physical, trying to force our way into circles to tear at the villages. Then we might get more subtle, trying to pit villages against one another such as by offering to leave one village alone if they would help us seize land from another; we would even offer to pay them money or a portion of the land seized. If a leader emerged in the group we might seize the leader and try to drag them out of the room to "prison." We would keep up the activity as long as there was progress and development in the action.

Then we would debrief what had happened. We would explore issues of the development of awareness, such as "How did you become aware that we were a threat rather than friends?" How did they perceive their own power in the situation? How did they communicate with each other? What changes took place throughout the exercise in terms of their understanding of what was happening and their perceptions about what they could do? What specifically did they do to counter the threats? How did leadership emerge? What was the relationship between the villages? Usually the feelings were intense anger, pride, excitement, confusion, and solidarity.

Following the exercise I would often do a Bible study on the Sermon on the Mount, particularly on the actions Glen Stassen called "transforming initiatives" which were nonviolent ways in which people claimed their humanity, confronted evil, and opened the situations up to new possibilities (*Just Peacemaking*, Westminster/John Knox, 1992). Sometimes we would also explore different kinds of power, such as the dominating "power over" versus "power within" and "power with." These concepts gave us ways of talking about what had happened in the game and ways of thinking about applying what we had learned to the contexts of struggle for the participants. It is one of the most powerful sets of tools we use in training people facing severe injustice, threats to their communities, and systemic violence.

In January 2001, Daniel Hunter and I traveled to Indonesia to lead conflict transformation training for Baptist pastors. The previous Christmas Eve, six Christian churches were bombed simultaneously during their worship services. About twenty people were killed and more than one hundred were injured in the bombings. Victor Rembeth, the general secretary of the Baptist union with which we were training, picked us up from the airport. I told him that I had received his message about the Christmas Eve bombings just before our 10:30 p.m. worship service Christmas Eve night. I'd shared the news with the congregation, and we had prayed for our suffering Indonesian sisters and brothers. Victor expressed his thanks for our prayers but shared that in his own church in Jakarta no mention was made of the bombings. It was as if a pall of denial hung over the congregation. Violence had also shaken the Christian community in 1998 in the rioting that brought down General Suharto's government. Much of the violence focused on Chinese business people, many of whom were Christians. Furthermore in recent months there was widespread violence between Christians and Muslims, especially in Ambon in the Moluccas Islands. Churches had been burned, and extremist Muslim militias had driven thousands of Christians out of the city as Indonesian troops stood idly by. Daniel and I found denial, rooted in an overly pious other-worldly spirituality, to be one of our biggest challenges among the Baptist leadership during our visit to Indonesia.

Throughout the training with the Baptist pastors, we were challenged about how what we were doing related to the Bible. We had Bible study exercises woven throughout the training, but if there was no explicit Bible reference in any section of our plan, someone would immediately question us, usually with a critical edge to his voice. This was especially true about the experiential activities in which we tried to get the pastors engaged in the dynamics of conflict or constructive ways of dealing with conflict. They were happy doing Bible study but seemed unconcerned about activities that were rooted in regular human experience. Their response to the Village Game was particularly revealing.

When Daniel and I, with Victor as our "corporate local representative and translator," began our assault on the ideal villages the participants had drawn, the Indonesian pastors did nothing. They stood inert in circles around their villages while Daniel and I reached through, defaced them with markers, and then shredded the papers. We kept trying to stimulate them to some sort of action, any kind of response, but they remained passive. Finally, we stopped, with ripped and crumpled paper scattered on the floor. No village was even partially intact. We asked them how they felt. The posters said, "angry, hopeless, and ashamed." What had they done? Some of the participants gave answers that stunned us with their disconnection to what had just happened: They had "protested and written letters to the government." Nobody had done any such thing! We pushed them to look at the reality of what their lack of response had been and that wishful thinking was not action. They said that they couldn't do anything because we were too powerful. Daniel asked them to count: There were three of us and more than thirty of them. Finally, as we sat in the trashed room with their raw feelings hanging heavily in the air, one pastor said, "This is Indonesia."

Daniel and I could not leave the group with their despair and shame for their complete passivity during the game. We did the Bible study on the Sermon on the Mount and concluded with some exercises under heavy direction and encouragement from us so they could practice some simple transforming initiatives. We wanted them to finish with the taste of success, modest as it might be. Our lasting impression from that training was of the pastors' intense focus on the Bible while they were incapable of acting creatively with the very real threats their churches and communities were facing.

After the training with the pastors, we did a short training with the youth leaders, and the experience was wholly different. The youth leaders, who were from the same churches as the pastors, were in their twenties. Daniel and I led the Village Game with them, and these youth leaders began their resistance almost immediately. They were creative and vigorous in finding ways to protect their community. When Daniel and I tried to break up their groups by seizing leaders, they would hold on to their leaders. They folded up their "villages" and passed them around to keep them away from us and out of sight. One folded village was stuffed down a woman's pants because the group knew we wouldn't search there! As we debriefed, we found out that many of these young people had been part of the student movements that had demonstrated for democracy. We heard how Victor had stood alongside them, even visiting non-Christian students in the hospital who were injured in the demonstrations, but their culture of resistance was completely separate from their spiritual life.

In the debriefing we asked, "What minimizes your power?" The immediate response was "the Bible." We found this intriguing coming from the mouths of Christian youth leaders! As we unpacked what they were saying, they refined their answer to "the way the Bible is taught." As I led them through Jesus' teachings in the Sermon on the Mount, about turning the other cheek, giving your coat, and going the second mile, their energy was very high. In the evaluation one student said, "I never take notes in church because I don't think I'll need any of it on the street or campus. I took a lot of notes today." These Baptist youth leaders had the same division that the pastors had between their daily lives and the spirituality in the church, but it was obvious that their creative energies were with what was happening outside the church. As they found that the Bible had some powerful things to say about how they might act in situations of oppression and violence, they became very excited and connected to the Bible study.

The Village Game is no mere game. It's a simulation to help people grow in understanding the dynamics of conflict and to stimulate their discoveries about their own power and constructive ways they can use that power. The threats to communities are very real as I discovered dramatically in the Philippines in 2003. I was co-facilitating with Lee McKenna of the Baptist Peace Fellowship of North America in a series of trainings sponsored by the Convention of Philippine Baptist Churches. We traveled throughout the islands of Panay and Negros leading two major trainings and four short trainings. In all of them we did the Village Game and the Sermon on the Mount. But back in Iloilo City, a short distance from the main training site, the Village Game became a real life drama.

One hundred and twenty families in the Kalubihan barangay (*barangay* means *neighborhood* in Ilongo) had been given eviction orders from the Department of Public Works and Highways, which planned to widen the road to the airport and to provide direct access to that road for nearby wealthy homes through what had been a stable community. The government was going to bulldoze forty-five meters on one side of the road and twenty meters on the other, far more than was necessary to widen the road, but enough to devastate the poor barangay. The families would receive no compensation for the destruction of their homes, no assistance in moving, and no help finding a place to relocate.

When we heard about this threat to the community, we had to join in the actions to resist the plans. Residents took us back into the barangay to see their homes and to see how far the demolition order extended. The homes had obviously been there a long time, but just over a high wall at the end of the side street we could see the sprawling new homes of the wealthy. As darkness fell, Lee and I joined in a candlelight vigil along the road. Residents and supporters lined up for over two kilometers on both sides of the road. Sound trucks drove back and forth telling about the government's plans and calling for justice toward the community. We held signs, chanted, and distributed leaflets about the demolition to passing motorists.

The most poignant moment came for us when a young man said, "I only have one question for you: Do I have the right to protest the demolition of my home?" He felt powerless and had internalized the messages of those in power who said his voice was not worth being raised. We responded, "Yes, you do have that right!" Lee cited national and international covenants about human rights that the Philippines had signed and Filipino legislation that committed the government to provide housing for its people. Through the rest of the trip, Lee and I raised the issue of the demolition of homes in Kalubihan in sermons, talks, and a radio interview. We were no longer facilitators of a simulation but participants with local residents in a struggle to save their community.

In April 2006 I was invited to do conflict transformation training at the Mae La Refugee Camp along the Thai-Burma border north of Mae Sot. The camp was home to some 50,000 Karens who had fled the violence of the Burmese army against their people and the Karen insurgency. Saw Wado was a teacher in the Bible school established in the camp. He had been in a training led by Daniel Hunter and me while he was a student at Oriental Theological Seminary in Nagaland, so I was eager to respond to his invitation to live and teach in the camp for a week. Toward the end of the training, Wado and I led the Village Game. That evening as the vesper worship service was beginning, Wado slipped in beside me and whispered, "The Village Game is real!"

Following the close of the training session that afternoon, one of the Thai officials governing the camp met with Wado and some other leaders in that section of the camp to show them plans for new construction in the camp. The Thai officials planned to build five new dormitories and toilets that would abut the Bible school and cut through the path used by students coming down the valley to the school. Wado was concerned because of safety issues for the female students. Harassment and rape of women are severe problems in Mae La as camp residents have little control over their own security and no recourse to protest abuses. The Thai government was going to put men from another ethnic group in the dorms, exacerbating an already difficult security problem for the Karen women. Wado also was insulted by the high-handed way the official brought a "final" plan without any consultation with the people immediately affected by the plan.

That evening Wado went to the Thai camp commander to protest and present his concerns while I prayed in support of his advocacy. He came back with a positive report; the commander agreed with the concerns Wado raised and assured him that the dorms would not be built there. Wado backed up his visit with letters to the camp office, to the United Nations High Commissioner for Refugees, and to area non-governmental organizations working with the refugees. All the students at the Bible school signed petitions accompanying the letters. The project initially presented as a "done deal" was halted. Only the toilets were constructed, something which helped the community rather than dividing it and threatening its security. Wado has continued practicing and teaching in the camp about "transforming initiatives" as part of Christian discipleship.

The threats against communities like Kalubihan and the Mae La Refugee Camp are all too common, and the internalization by the poor of the messages of unworthiness handed down from on high is also tragically common. On the other hand, there are people like Wado and the Filipino community activists who organize to stand up for their communities, who claim the power that is within them and among them, and act with boldness and creativity. Through the Village Game and related Bible studies, those of us involved in training hope to support, equip, and empower local activists in their struggles for justice and basic human dignity. This kind of facilitation has been one of the most meaningful parts of my peacemaking ministry.

Walking in a Line

For any given training it is impossible to predict which tool will be the most significant or where the breakthrough for the group's learning will come. Each group has its own learning challenges and dynamics. Each group is formed within a certain historic period in their society with certain threats to peace or certain systemic injustices that must be addressed. So as a training facilitator I must be open to whatever unfolds in any moment during training. I must be tuned into the spirituality and psychology of a group so as to bring the challenges to a head. I must let the group—or sometimes even force the group—to do their own work of discovery.

A dramatic example of the interaction between a tool and the learning process of a group took place when Daniel Hunter and I were leading a conflict transformation training for Baptist church leaders in Sierra Leone in October 2004. The civil war had recently ended, and United Nations peacekeeping forces were maintaining a fragile peace in the weary and traumatized land. We were leading a three-day program in the Baptist headquarters compound in the town of Lunsar in the interior of Sierra Leone. The insurgents had captured Lunsar, and quickly the atrocities began. After telling the people that they were there to protect them the rebel soldiers were told by their officers to "pay themselves," which meant they were free to pillage and loot the community. The Baptist headquarters buildings, including a hospital specializing in eye afflictions, were gutted. Whatever couldn't be carried away was demolished. People fled from the surrounding homes into the jungle, where children and elders died from deprivation and disease. The horrors of the savage conduct of the war still lingered in the time of the peace accord as we saw beggars whose hands had been hacked off and large UN-sponsored villages for those intentionally maimed by the terror tactics of the rebels.

To match the physical devastation of the people we discovered an inward passivity, a spirit of resignation and helplessness. Over half of the gross national product of the country was being generated by international organizations working for relief and development. Daniel attended a human rights and corruption meeting when we first arrived and related to me the overwhelming attitude of despair and passivity even among those who were the leading national activists. When we began our training in Lunsar we confronted the same passivity in our participants. They were sitting back waiting for us to do whatever we would do. The challenge was for us to teach them something of value, whereas we were throwing that challenge back to them: the responsibility for learning was theirs. This struggle between facilitators and participants continued until Daniel led an activity called "Walking in a Line" or "Ankle Walk."

The group had been given a challenge to walk forward about ten meters in a line, keeping their ankles in touch with the ankles of the persons next to them in the line. If the line broke, if the feet of any of the group members broke contact with those next to them, the entire group would have to return to the starting point. It quickly became evident that it was a serious challenge for seventy people to do this exercise together. After about a half hour with a number of efforts that disintegrated into small groups trying to walk together in vain, about twenty people drifted off to the edges of the field and refused to participate, including many of the senior members of the Baptist leadership. "That's impossible!" they complained as they dropped out of the training exercise.

The impossibility of their training task reflected the impossibility of their national task. Forging peace in a country shattered by war seems impossible. How does reconciliation take place when rebels have cut off the hands of civilians, leaving a huge population of disabled people unable to earn their living in conditions that are daunting to even the most able-bodied persons? How does reconciliation take place when the bitterness is deep, corruption rife, and fear still prevalent even though UN peacekeeping soldiers patrol the cities and countryside? Peace is impossible; that was the unspoken but almost universally held assumption.

The "ankle walk" was a classic example of a peace game that seemed totally unrelated to the horrors experienced in Sierra Leone. On the surface it seemed like a foolish and perhaps fun children's game that posed the challenge of dealing creatively with a task that seemed impossible. But at a deeper level the game was bringing participants in touch with the profound social challenge before them, namely their temptation to give in to despair and helplessness. In contrast the exercise also offered them the possibility of discovering their inner capacities for meeting a daunting challenge together.

After Daniel and I huddled together to decide what to do about the rapidly disintegrating exercise, Daniel intervened to call attention to the people who had dropped out. He elicited the feelings and frustrations of the dropout group and invited those still working on the task to notice what was going on. Furthermore, he assured them that an even larger group of 150 people had successfully completed the exercise. Those still working on the task encouraged the others to rejoin them, and those who had dropped out moved back into line with the rest. They talked together, got organized, and strategized. They identified leaders to coordinate their efforts. They experimented with small groups trying various ways of coordinating their movements under guidance of a leader. Eventually all seventy participants successfully walked ankle-to-ankle in a line the full ten meters. When the line reached the finish they exuberantly cheered, celebrating their accomplishment of mastering a difficult challenge they had earlier thought was impossible.

In the debriefing Daniel led the group to identify those skills and actions they needed to succeed in the exercise. We looked at how those skills and actions would work in facing the difficult challenges of peace-building and reconciliation in Sierra Leone. At the beginning of the training we noticed that most people were passive; nationally, it seemed most people depended on the U.N. or political figures to assume responsibility for making peace. By the end of the training participants were accepting their own responsibility to be God's agents for reconciliation. Rather than saying reconciliation is impossible or if it doesn't happen someone else is to blame, the participants were excitedly and eagerly exploring what would go into reconciliation processes and discussing the specific ways they could make a difference, whether in schools and churches or in communities and the nation as a whole. These church leaders were ready to shape their own destiny, and Daniel and I could never have predicted that as simple a tool as having people walk with their ankles touching would prove the experiential key to unlock their personal commitment to responsibility.

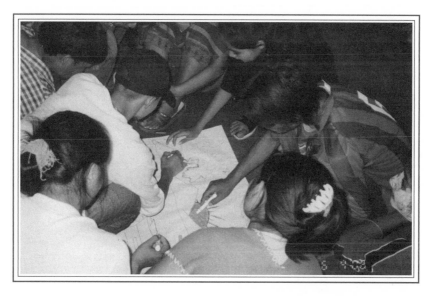

Karen refugees in Thailand draw their "ideal village"

Workshop participants in Kenya proudly show their village

Wado (left) and friends walking in the Mae La Refugee Camp at the Thai-Burma border

Walking in a line in Sierra Leone

8

PEACE ON THE STREETS

The Gang Peace Movement

After living for nine years in Dorchester, Boston's largest urban neighborhood, I had some experience and concern about issues of violence in our cities. Though most of my focus was on international peacemaking after I went on staff with National Ministries, I certainly believed that peacemaking in our urban streets and neighborhoods was just as important as in any of the other conflicts that demanded an activist's attention.

I met Carl Upchurch at the first summer conference I attended for the Baptist Peace Fellowship of North America. Carl was from central Ohio and attended the First Baptist Church of Granville. He had grown up in Philadelphia, Pennsylvania in a very violent neighborhood and had witnessed the murder of an uncle. At a young age he entered into a life of crime, and soon he was serving ten years in a federal prison for armed robbery. In prison he turned his life around. He made a commitment to follow Christ and earned two college degrees. After his release he founded the Progressive Prisoners Movement to advocate for prisoners' rights but also to encourage prisoners to take responsibility for themselves. As Carl often said, "Just because they treat you like an animal doesn't mean you have to become one."

Carl and I began a relationship that slowly developed over the next few BPFNA conferences. At times he wasn't sure he belonged in this context of mostly middle-class white folks who were concerned with the nuclear arms race and the wars in Central America, but I talked with him about working in the same struggles against those forces that grind people down and rob them of life. We were in the same struggle, just working on different fronts. There were ways we could support each other, particularly at key points when we needed extra help or extra bodies on the line. The alliance we made as international peacemaking and U.S. prison system activists would be put to the test following the 1992 uprising in Los Angeles. When the police officers who beat Rodney King were acquitted in the beating that was captured on video and televised across the nation, the city erupted.

As Los Angeles smoldered, a wonderful invitation to search for peace came out of the very heart of the L.A. culture of gang violence. The two most notorious gangs in Los Angeles, the Bloods and the Crips, had begun a hesitant cease-fire effort. As gang leaders had grown up and had children who were beginning to enter gangs themselves, leaders began to look for help from the community to find a way out of the cycles of violence. The OGs (Original Gangsters) were getting weary of the terrible death toll their violence was claiming, but out of fear and suspicion nobody would help them.

A few of the gang leaders involved in the cease-fire effort stumbled across a brochure for the Progressive Prisoners Movement (PPM). They were impressed by all the positive comments in the brochure from prisoners, ministers, wardens and politicians—people whose help they would need but from whom they were alienated. Perhaps PPM's executive director could help them. They called Carl Upchurch; Carl called me. He had no money to go to Los Angeles and spend a month with the gangs to explore what was going on and to build relationships with the gang leaders who were seeking peace on the streets. I talked with my supervisors at National Ministries, and they were very enthusiastic about supporting this venture. Creative and bold action was needed to halt the spirals of violence that were killing so many young people. We came up with funds to help send Carl to Los Angeles to take the first step in working with the gangs for peace.

Upon his return a month later, Carl submitted a stunning report. He quoted a gang member who said, "We wanted to get [the gangs] unified first and to realize we're all the same people striving for the same goals. We wanted them to come together and stop killing each other. The truce just caught on everywhere." But the overwhelming concern was providing real jobs for young people caught in despair and the destructive cycles of racism, poverty, and violence. Carl also challenged the organizations that sponsored his trip to get more deeply involved. Peace groups had been active with the situations of gross injustice in Central America and South Africa, but South Central L.A. was devoid of any presence of those peace groups. Distilling the messages from the streets and his own vision, Carl called for a gathering of key players in urban peacemaking for a dialogue to design strategies, followed by an ongoing structure to implement action ideas coming out of that discussion. Thus the idea of a "gang summit" was conceived.

Carl returned to Los Angeles with Jim Wallis of *Sojourners* and Ben Chavis of the NAACP for further discussion. Connections were made with gang peace movements in other cities such as Minneapolis and Boston. Plans were made for the gang summit to bring all these grassroots gang peace movements together along with supportive peace and religious groups, but many cities were reluctant to host such a gathering of individuals viewed with suspicion and fear by the larger society. Finally Kansas City offered to host the summit, thanks to a mayor who was also a Christian minister with a vision and heart for peace. Rev. Mac Charles Jones, a leader in the National Baptist Convention and a board member of the BPFNA, offered his church, St. Stephen Baptist Church, as the meeting place for the summit.

From 29 April to 2 May 1993, about 140 urban gang leaders and community and church activists from more than twenty cities met. Those of us in support roles were asked not to attend the working meetings of the summit due to the delicate and volatile nature of the relationships and the issues needing to be hammered out. Instead, we prayed fervently, with the BPFNA board meeting nearby and receiving daily briefings on the events from Mac.

The summit got off to a rough start with the media almost immediately. No Kansas City gangs were involved in the summit because there were no truce efforts underway there. The major Kansas City paper ran a front page article questioning whether such an event could produce anything good, accompanied by a photo of Kansas City gang members posing with armaments that would delight a liberation army. The summit leaders were furious and took action. First, because they saw the media as unsupportive of their efforts, leaders banned the media from the rest of the summit. Second, they sent a delegation to the local gangs pictured in the paper to tell them they didn't know anything about what was going on and inviting them to join the summit meetings. Out of that invitation came one of the strongest on-going metropolitan gang peace initiatives in the whole country.

The summit was an immediate success in that all the participants were able to talk through difficult issues and forge a common commitment to work for peace on the streets. The top issue they raised repeatedly was the same one raised in Carl's first trip to Los Angeles: jobs, jobs, jobs! The gang, community, and religious leaders came out with specific recommendations about jobs development, rebuilding the urban community infrastructure, establishing community-based citizen patrols to monitor and protect against police abuse—issues that over the years before and since have seen very little attention from national and state governments. In spite of this marginalization and the deaf ears on which the advocacy for justice fell, the summit participants also took responsibility to do what they could to maintain momentum for peace. Specifically, they set up a coordinating group to take the summits to various metropolitan areas so that efforts at building gang peace and coordinating with community leaders and city officials could happen at a level where substantive decisions could be made.

To parallel the gang peace coordinating group, we established a support group, of which I was a part, called Things That Make for Peace. That network included denominational staff, national Christian development organizations, and representatives from local gang peace projects in Kansas City, Boston, Minneapolis/St. Paul, Santa Cruz, and Los Angeles. We worked with Carl to seek out resources to continue the peacemaking efforts and to undergird the local summits and resulting projects with logistical support. For about three years we met in various cities to encourage the urban peacemakers and link up various efforts so they could learn from each other. I went with Carl and a number of the leading activists to the United Nations to meet with various non-governmental organizations. We asked from them the same level of awareness and commitment for our urban war zones that we give to more traditional areas of civil and international conflict.

I worked closely with two efforts: In Minneapolis/St. Paul and Pittsburgh. We organized gang summits for both cities. I attended the summit in Minneapolis/St. Paul in the fall of 1993 and witnessed the power of bringing young adults and teens from the gangs together in a secure atmosphere to discuss ways they could participate in turning around the cycles of violence in their own communities. The Nation of Islam provided security, passing everyone through metal detectors and providing escorted bus service through warring neighborhoods. Leaders like the comedian/activist Dick Gregory and Jim Brown, the Hall of Fame football running back, connected the earlier freedom struggles to the struggles for justice and peace in the ghettos. Local pastors committed themselves to get out of their sanctuaries and work with the youth on the streets. One pastor, Rev. Jerry McAfee, who worked closely with the entire gang peace movement in Minneapolis, told us that after the summit he did one funeral for a victim of gang violence in over a year, compared to many funerals a month before the summit. Rev. McAfee developed a housing rehabilitation program that trained and employed gang youth. Whether long-term structural change came or not, there was at least the blessing of an easing of the horrific levels of violence for a while.

Pittsburgh had only recently seen the development of major urban gangs, but the growth of those gangs and the rising violence made the city a key location for a summit in 1994. Pastor John Cook of Victory Baptist Church was a host pastor and organizer for the summit. At one point the gang members at the summit got into a scuffle, but the fighting was quelled quickly to enable the summit participants to press on. A truce was forged at that summit for many parts of the city, a truce that held through the hot summer that followed.

I was supposed to attend the Pittsburgh summit as I had worked closely with Rev. Cook in the planning, but I was ill that weekend. However, we followed up with a "pastors' summit" to look at gang ministry and the issues raised at the summit that presented a serious challenge to the churches. We brought in four of the gang leaders from the Pittsburgh Bloods and Crips (no relation to the L.A. gangs of those names, other than emulation) who had committed themselves to the truce. I moderated the discussion between the gang members and the pastors. After hearing how difficult the life of the gang members was, including the high level of violence they lived with, one pastor asked why they stayed in the gangs. The answer came back immediately: "Because they love me."

Gang members are ready to die—and kill—for their "homies." Are church members committed to each other enough to sacrifice their comfort, let alone their lives? Rev. Bruce Wall, who followed me as pastor at Dorchester Temple Baptist Church and has a powerful ministry among gang members on the streets of Boston, said that lack of love among church members is the biggest problem for bringing gang members into the churches. Gang members are used to a radical—though often twisted and abusive—form of love. These summits have revealed what it would take to truly bring peace to our streets. It's not a new solution, but one we don't try very often: radical love and doing justice (jobs, jobs, jobs!).

Sleeping In

As I worked with the "Things That Make for Peace" network, I also was tapped to work as National Ministries staff with the Violence Task Force for the board of the American Baptist

Churches to shape a new policy statement for the ABC on violence and an appropriate Christian response. From my connections with various urban peace efforts and my awareness of a number of creative initiatives going on across the country, I put together a series of exposures for the task force. We met in Oakland, California, to learn about church-based antiviolence educational efforts from preschool to youth. In 1995 we met in Oklahoma City to learn about Native American experiences with violence and to reflect at the ruins of the bombed-out federal building. One of the most interesting meetings we held was back with my old friends in ministry in Boston. There we learned about efforts to confront violence as a public health issue and to study the TenPoint Coalition.

The TenPoint Coalition was launched in 1992 when a young gang member ran into a Baptist church during a funeral and stabbed another young person. In the wake of that incident that made national news, Rev. Eugene Rivers said, "If the churches don't go to the streets, the streets will come to the churches." A large ecumenical group of urban pastors gathered to hammer out a plan that would dramatically and thoroughly engage the issues of youth violence. That plan took shape as a ten-point call to action. The foundation for the TenPoint Coalition was that local churches adopt local gangs as a focal point for their ministry. The church folks had to get out of the sanctuaries and into the street, engage in prayer walks, talk to young people on the corners, offer mediation services in the criminal justice system, mentor young people, establish viable employment opportunities to counter the drug economy, establish shelters for battered women and children, initiate or participate in neighborhood crime watches, and establish a Black and Latino curriculum to build self-esteem.

The TenPoint Coalition grew as it made an impact on the streets and in the halls of political power. As violence dramatically decreased, police departments from other cities sent delegations to Boston to see what happened. National news magazines and CBS's *60 Minutes* covered the story.

Rev. Bruce Wall was part of the TenPoint Coalition, but he had been involved in gang and anti-violence ministry for many years. While I was still pastor at Dorchester Temple, Bruce led a movement called "Drop-a-Dime" in which he and other activists would occupy a vacant house on a street where drug dealing was going on. They would organize the neighborhood and confront the drug dealers to drive them out. Bruce organized one effort just a block from our church, drawing upon some of our members for local support. Once Bruce became pastor of Dorchester Temple, he began looking at the neighborhood with a plan to take back the community from the drug dealers.

They discovered that the library across from the church was a drop-off point for drugs. Kids would walk into the library as if they were going to study and make the drug exchange in the study carrels. Bruce worked with the probation department to make the library off limits as a term of probation. That restriction, backed up with knowledge of the kids' identities and quick calls to the probation department, soon cleaned up the library.

Bruce's next action target was Roberts Park, two blocks from the church. He began with a prayer walk in the park involving members of the Gangs Anonymous group meeting at the church as well as other church folks. Then they put out the word through flyers in the neighborhood that they were going to sleep in the park as part of "Operation Spiritual Liberation." I didn't know anything about these plans when I called Bruce to let him know that I would be in town that weekend for meetings with the ABC's violence task force. He invited me to join them for the sleep-in occupation of the park. I couldn't make the first night because of meetings but agreed to join them on Saturday night before preaching at Dorchester Temple on Sunday.

Bruce and the activists from Gangs Anonymous and the church gathered at the street entrance to the small park. Many people were skeptical, expressing doubts that their action could make any difference in the face of the drug dealers. Sure, they were shutting down business for a night or two, especially with all the police presence, but the dealers would be back. For Bruce, however, the key matter was not just sleeping in the park for a few nights, but mobilizing the community for action as they overcame their fear.

That was exactly what happened. About 9 p.m. as the group was singing and praying in the park, they heard noise from down the street. They could see flickers of flame and hear voices raised in song. As the people drew near they could see it was a candle-light procession of neighbors, including babies in strollers, singing "He's Got the Whole World in His Hands." The neighbors joined the vigil for the evening, and later provided food, mattresses, and anything else needed to aid the occupiers of the park.

When I joined them the next night I got no sleep. All through the night, people passed by along Washington Street. We had some fascinating conversations about what was going on. I heard feelings ranging from despair to renewed hope and appreciation. One neighbor said about the drug dealers, "They'll be back." Bruce responded, "We'll be back, too." The church was just down the street, and these active members weren't going to back off from the challenge to keep their neighborhood clean of drug dealers and violence.

Nine months later I was back in the neighborhood to film a video report for National Ministries on anti-violence ministries. I related the story about the occupation of the park standing in the places where our sleeping bags had covered the concrete. What encouraged me most was talking to some of the people out in the park that afternoon. They told me that the park had been clean of drug dealers ever since the occupation. That nonviolent action mobilized a community that had given in to fear. People kept coming to the park, bringing their families, and calling the police if a problem developed. The community, stimulated and inspired by the church activists, reclaimed that space as theirs and has maintained it as a public resource.

From Mugging to Hugging

My family sometimes got involved in efforts to bring peace to the streets. In 1993 we all went down to Washington DC for the thirtieth anniversary of the March on Washington where Dr.

Martin Luther King, Jr. delivered his "I Have a Dream" speech. A march was planned down the Washington Mall from the Capitol to the Lincoln Memorial. The day before, however, the Baptist Peace Fellowship of North America planned to join another demonstration in solidarity with Rev. Al Gallmon, pastor of the Mt. Carmel Baptist Church in DC. Every week Rev. Gallmon protested in front of the headquarters of the National Rifle Association. Out of his concern for the impact of violence on his community he decided to raise his voice on the unrestricted manufacture and sale of guns. Sometimes he was a lonely though determined voice, so we thought it would be helpful for some of us coming for the thirtieth anniversary march to come a day earlier to support him in confronting a burning contemporary concern. The BPFNA was joined by members of the Southern Christian Leadership Conference, the Fellowship of Reconciliation, the American Jewish Committee, and Dick Gregory.

We formed a line with our signs and banners around the center of the traffic circle across from the entrance to the NRA headquarters. Our whole family was there, with the kids plastering anti-handgun stickers on their faces and T-shirts. Ten-year-old Jonathan had such a charmingly boyish face that photos of him holding his sign—"Guns are killing our children, our families, our dreams"—appeared both in *Fellowship* magazine and on the cover of *The Baptist Peacemaker*. A cute activist kid! Later when I published *Christian Peacemaking* with sixteen pages of photos in the center, I had to include the cover photo of Jon. I figured I couldn't be just acting as a proud parent to include the photo if two magazines thought his image was worthy of publication!

While we stood in the traffic circle with our signs, I did my own informal survey of people who were supportive and people who were against our witness. The overwhelming majority of people who made disparaging remarks or gestures towards us were younger white males. I expected that. I was surprised, however, to discover that the strongest support for our message came from younger black males. I had expected to find more women in support, but black men are the ones dying in horrifying numbers from this plague in our cities. The profits from gun sales, legal or illegal, make their way to the well-manicured wealthy communities of Connecticut, home to major gun manufacturers. Meanwhile in the hospitals of our cities young people bleed out from gunshot wounds. In front of the National Rifle Association young black men were honking their horns and encouraging us in our cry to halt this slaughter.

Joseph Lowery of the Southern Christian Leadership Conference came a bit later in the demonstration. He spoke to us from the center of the traffic circle for a few minutes about the issues of urban violence and gun control. Then he asked where the NRA building was. We pointed across the lanes of traffic to the black glass structure. "Well, what are we doing standing here? We should be over there," he pointed. "We don't have a permit to be there," Rev. Gallmon advised. "We need to do our praying right there at their door," Rev. Lowery countered. He began to cross the street, and we all followed. Rev. Gallmon muttered to some of us, "I can't get arrested today; I've got to pick up my car from the repair shop!" But nobody was stopping Rev. Lowery from taking his prayers to the door of this symbol of our national love affair with guns. We formed a circle across the entrance of the NRA building and held a prayer meeting on the sidewalk. My son Chris stood there and held Joe Lowery's hand with no idea who this veteran civil rights warrior was. Nobody was coming or going into the building. It seemed all closed up, so no protest was raised to our presence. No police bothered us. No arrests were made. Rev. Gallmon could pick up his car that afternoon. But we all had a chuckle at our own timidity that was challenged by Rev. Lowery's extra measure of boldness.

Our family had a direct experience with handguns when Sharon was held up at gunpoint going into work one morning. At that time Sharon was the executive director of Friendship House, a Christian neighborhood action center in Hamtramck, a diverse urban municipality completely surrounded by Detroit. She had pulled our van into her parking spot behind Friendship House, and as she was tidying up the inside of the van, a man with a gun came up and pointed it toward her belly. He demanded money. Sharon told him, "You picked the wrong woman to rob today. I only have a dollar. I just gave my kids their lunch money for school." She kept up a stream of conversation that she had credit cards but would cancel them. She suggested that she and the robber go through her purse together to see what they could find. As she talked, she took control of the situation and presented herself as a human being—not an anonymous victim.

When Sharon presented her purse the man put the gun on the seat of the van. She thought for a moment about trying to grab the gun, but that would have changed the whole dynamic of the situation into one in which she was now threatening the robber. The potential for violence would have dramatically escalated. Instead she continued her conversational connection with the man robbing her.

As the man went through Sharon's wallet he discovered that, sure enough, there was only one dollar. He began to cry. "I guess I'm not very good at this," he said. Sharon asked him what was the matter, and he began to unfold the story of his troubles. He had no job. His wife had recently left him and his eleven-year-old daughter. He had to care for his daughter, but with no work, he had no money to feed her. Furthermore, his mother had just died, and his confusion and grief had been bubbling close to the surface. "What would your mother think of you doing this?" Sharon inquired. She asked the man if his mother was a praying woman, which he affirmed. So they prayed, the robber with his eyes closed, Sharon with hers open!

Sharon said, "Maybe you did pick the right woman to rob today." They sat together on the floor of the van by the open side door, and Sharon counseled him for a while. She found out he had taken the gun from his father's house. She told him to return the gun to his father, confess what he had done, and ask forgiveness. He had been drinking to gather the courage to commit his robberies, and since Sharon's policy was never to provide direct assistance when someone was under the influence of alcohol or drugs she asked him to come back sober later in the week so she could help him look for work. They set an appointment and exchanged phone numbers. The man repeatedly sought assurances that Sharon wouldn't call the police.

The robber started to walk away, then turned and came back. "You won't call the police?" he asked. Sharon replied that just as Christ had forgiven her, she had forgiven him. That seemed to reassure him. He started to leave again, then returned and said, "Could I ask for one thing more?" Sharon expected him to ask for a cigarette, the common request she got on the streets of Hamtramck, even as a nonsmoker. Instead he asked for a hug! Sharon hugged the would-be mugger, the man who had held a gun to her half an hour earlier.

When the man failed to show up for his appointment, Sharon called him up saying they had made a deal and reassuring him that she was serious about her offer to help. He came back to Friendship House two days later. Sharon helped him develop a plan and made some contacts. Within a couple of weeks he had landed a job. He would come visit her occasionally, once saying, "Rev. Sharon, I'm so happy now!" He even volunteered for a bit at the food bank that Friendship House operated and joined a men's Bible study at the food bank. Once when Sharon drove him back to his ravaged-looking street, he assured her that she would be safe in his neighborhood. Everyone knew what she had done—the man had been telling the story of the mugging that turned into a hugging in his neighborhood even as Sharon and I were telling the story in our circles. I continue to tell this story as an example of the nonviolent transforming initiatives Jesus calls us to take.

Peacemaking in the Schools

When I was directing the Peace Program for National Ministries and working on the Violence Task Force for the board of the American Baptist Churches, I connected with a variety of peacemaking initiatives in local schools. I discovered many educational programs to teach conflict resolution skills to children from preschool all the way to high school. Many schools had developed peer mediation programs in which older children would mediate conflict resolution processes with younger children. Churches were sponsoring after-school programs to teach conflict resolution skills. Some churches were establishing adult accompaniment patrols to walk school kids safely through dangerous areas. These acts to protect children going to and from school saw an increase in grades as the children could concentrate more fully on their studies. I helped promote these programs and ideas through the various means of communication at my disposal.

My most direct involvement in local schools, however, came through Sharon's involvement in the Hamtramck school system. Though Detroit is severely racially segregated, Hamtramck is the immigrant gateway into the Detroit area. In Hamtramck High students from more than fifty nationalities speak more than twenty-five languages. An English teacher began an extracurricular group named the Nonviolent Student Peace Force. Some of the kids wore combat fatigues as a mark of their group discipline and engagement in tough community concerns, apparel that I couldn't criticize in my self-image as a "peace warrior"! The group lead in various community projects, bringing people together to clean up a local park and paint outdoor murals about community harmony.

Later Sharon and I were invited to lead the Nonviolent Student Peace Force in a Saturday training on conflict transformation. We met at a local community center and began with the Red/Blue simulation. We had first-generation immigrant kids from Poland, Iraq, Cuba, and Yemen as well as African-American and "blended white" kids who could no longer identify a specific national background. We had a great time going through the simulation and discussing ways to turn conflicts into positive experiences.

Then Sharon and I were invited to lead a session at the "alternative" high school for the youth who just could not fit into the public or parochial school systems. Many of these kids were in trouble with the law, on probation, or in some other form of close monitoring. As the kids filed into the small room we had for the session, they filled all the desks and sat with bored, suspicious looks. I thought, "This is going to be rough," not trusting Sharon, myself, or our teaching techniques.

Our plan, however, turned out to be an excellent one. We immediately showed the kids this would be a highly participatory class dealing with their real issues. We broke the kids into groups to talk about conflicts they had directly experienced or witnessed at their work places. Then we asked them to pick one and develop a skit to show the conflict to the larger group. We had the groups act a couple skits out, doing a "freeze-frame" where we halted the skit at critical decision points. We asked the kids where the situation was headed, then had them brainstorm options that might move the conflict into a more positive direction. We snuck in little bits of information and terminology, such as "win/win," as we were facilitating their high-energy involvement in the skits and brainstorming. When we ended the session the enthusiasm of the students was exciting to see. They were so eager that the session was hard to end. Smiles had replaced the stern, aloof looks.

Because key leaders graduated, Hamtramck High's Nonviolent Student Peace Force fizzled out after a couple of very productive years. The teacher-adviser next organized a local chapter of the national student movement called Peace Jam. Each week the group met after school to study peacemaking practices and engage in community projects. Once a year there are multi-state conferences that a Nobel Peace Prize laureate attends to interact with the students. Sharon also became an adviser to the group, working with the teacher to plan activities. I was invited to come and share some of my global peacemaking work and to lead the group through basic conflict resolution practices such as the steps to come to "win/win" solutions. We practiced the steps by setting up a sample conflict of two people wanting the same orange. The creativity and "outside the box" thinking of the kids from so many different cultures was a delight for me as a facilitator.

At the 2005 Peace Jam weekend conference for the Great Lakes states, Bishop Desmond Tutu met with the students. Sharon joined the kids for the 2006 conference at which José Ramos-Horta from East Timor was scheduled to be the participating Nobel laureate. Unfortunately, severe violence erupted in East Timor, requiring Ramos-Horta to return to his homeland since he was foreign minister. Peace Jam was able to hook up a live video feed from East Timor so the students could see him and he could see the students. Sharon enjoyed his gentle spirit with the youth. She was especially taken with his vision of a "Truth and Friendship" process with the former invading Indonesians. The goal was not just ending the strife but creating friendship with the neighboring country that had brutally oppressed East Timor for decades. For Hamtramck youth to encounter such a person was a window on the wider world, a world that was shaping their own community whether they were aware of it or not, and a world within which they need to grow up capable of shaping in a positive way.

9

JIHAD FOR SALAAM

First Encounters

In recent years the encounter between Christians and
Muslims has been a significant component of my peacemaking
both close to home and around the world. Christian/Muslim
conflict goes back to the early days when Islam swept out from
Saudi Arabia, overwhelming ancient Christian communities in the
Middle East. The Crusades of the Middle Ages were captured in
romantic lore through stories I read such as Sir Walter Scott's
Ivanhoe and the mascot of my college, Wheaton's Crusaders. I
thought nothing much negative about that chapter of history.
Muslims were distant and alien to me.

In 1975 I had to drop out of seminary because I'd lost my
part-time job in a lumberyard during a major downturn in the
construction industry. I scrambled around to find any kind of
work and landed a job as a waiter at a special school for Algerian
students learning English prior to studying for engineering
degrees. The school was set up just for the thirty students who had
been cloistered in a former Catholic monastery. I worked in the
dining room, waiting on the tables two meals a day. The students
were preparing to enter the Algerian oil industry following their
training. They were all from wealthy families except for one
economically lower-class student whose brilliance had somehow
caught the attention of Algerian educators and enabled him to
enter the engineering program. Most of the rich students treated
the two of us as unworthy of their interest. The two of us
connected, began to talk with each other, and started a friendship.

As we shared our faith we decided to begin a joint Bible and
Qur'an study after my evening work shift was over. We had a
couple sessions with a few of the other students joining in. We

read portions of the Bible together and then the Qur'an, each choosing whichever passages we wanted to share with the other. After a week my boss informed me that I was no longer allowed to meet with the students socially, especially for the Bible/Qur'an study. A friend informed me later that one of the students was an agent for the Algerian secret police whose job was to monitor the students and keep them away from any corrupting influences. Inter-religious contact was viewed as too threatening for these students, at least by those responsible for security. It was a sobering start for my interfaith relationships.

In 1988 when I was directing the Peace Program for the ABC and working at the United Nations I joined a coalition planning major peace demonstrations during the U.N.'s Third Special Session on Disarmament. I volunteered to organize a daily religious vigil during the session across the street from the U.N. at the "Isaiah Wall." The Isaiah Wall is a beautiful curved wall alongside a staircase coming down the bluff from Second Avenue to First Avenue. Engraved in the wall are the words from the prophet Isaiah: "They shall beat their swords into plows and their spears into pruning hooks, neither shall they learn war anymore." It was a great location for religious vigils for peace during the special session considering how to end the nuclear arms race.

I planned to have a vigil day for every identifiable religious community that was interested. There was a day for the Catholic Pax Christi group, a day for the Jewish Peace Fellowship, a day for the Buddhist Peace Fellowship, and a day each for various Protestant groups, including a day for the Baptist Peace Fellowship. (Ironically the only day it rained during the vigils was the day for the Baptists. I joked as we opened the vigil that God knew the Baptists could handle water just fine!). We found Bahá'ís willing to keep the vigil and Orthodox Christians, but nobody in the peace activist networks in New York could recommend any Muslims.

Because I lived in the Philadelphia area, my own contacts in New York City were limited, but somehow I heard about a Muslim study center. I called and shared about the daily vigils with the man whose name I'd been given. I asked if he would be interested in joining us and leading a peace prayer vigil out of the Muslim faith tradition. His response was overwhelming gratitude. I have never been on the receiving end of so many "God bless yous!" as from that Muslim leader. He was so excited to have been considered and invited. That brief encounter showed me that there was much about the Muslim community that I did not know, including a passion for peace that was very different from the terrorists whose hijackings and kidnappings were periodically making world news.

Christian/Muslim Joint Conflict Transformation Training

When our family moved to Detroit, I was called to be co-pastor of the First Baptist Church of Dearborn. I knew nothing about Dearborn but quickly discovered that it was the epicenter of the Arab Muslim community, both in Detroit, and even in the U.S. Through our Dearborn Ministerial Alliance I got to know Imam Mohammad Elahi of the Islamic House of Wisdom and Imam Hassan Al-Qazwini of the Islamic Center of America, two large Shi'ia mosques in Dearborn. I visited their mosques during our rotation of clergy meetings. Later Imam Elahi and I had lunch together, sharing our experiences of providing pastoral care to our congregations.

Meanwhile Ken Sehested of the BPFNA had gotten to know Rabia Harris, director of the Muslim Peace Fellowship (MPF), through the common link of being religious peace fellowships affiliated with the Fellowship of Reconciliation. Rabia was on the editorial staff of *Fellowship*, FOR's monthly magazine. Ken introduced Rabia and me to each other, and we began an e-mail conversation about the possibility to doing training in conflict transformation with Christians and Muslims together.

When the terrorist attacks of 11 September 2001 took place, this established web of relationships supported some quick responses. We had a prayer meeting at First Baptist Dearborn that evening, praying through psalms of lament that had never spoken so powerfully to me before. We poured out our hearts in anger, grief, and confusion. One of our members prayed for our Arab neighbors who feared violent reprisals. As she prayed, I knew we couldn't just offer such a prayer to God and do nothing. We had to love our neighbors and not just pray for them, so in the middle of the service I asked the congregation if they would like me to go to Imam Elahi and invite him and his congregation to join us for Sunday worship and offer to join them at the Islamic House of Wisdom for Friday night prayers. The response was quick and unanimous in favor of the idea.

The next morning I went to meet with Imam Elahi, and he greeted the suggestion for joint visits with an enthusiastic endorsement. Friday evening a delegation of Baptists arrived at the House of Wisdom where we were warmly greeted. We were not segregated by gender, but were ushered to seats behind the congregation as they sat on floor mats for Elahi's lecture and the prayers. One member of the mosque instructed us on the meaning of the prayers and the postures used during praying, providing a handout with stick figures in the various prayer positions and translation of the prayers into English. Following the prayers we were treated to a delicious meal of Middle Eastern food. We sat around tables, our congregants mixed with members of the mosque, getting to know each other as neighbors and people of faith. I was the only person from our church who had been in a mosque before, and the church folks spoke with delighted wonder about the warmth of the hospitality they had received.

On Sunday morning, 11 a.m. arrived, the time to begin our service. Though nobody from the mosque had arrived, we began. As we were singing the opening hymn, Imam Elahi walked in with eighteen members of his mosque. In typical Baptist fashion, our congregation had filled in from the back of the sanctuary, so the only open pews were in the first two rows. The ushers escorted our Muslim neighbors right to the front. We gave the Imam an opportunity to bring greetings, then I preached from Romans 12:21: "Do not be overcome by evil, but overcome evil with good."

During the sermon I related a story that appeared in a letter to the editor of the *New York Times*. The writer had been in the market in Damascus when he saw a collision between a man carrying a crate of oranges on a bicycle and a man walking with a heavy load on his shoulder that obscured his view. When they collided the crate of oranges spilled, something I demonstrated as I was telling the story by carrying a basket of oranges that I dumped at the front of the sanctuary. Immediately one of the Muslim visitors jumped up to help pick up the oranges. I had to work graciously around him to say how the two men began circling for a fight with the on-lookers yelling and choosing sides. Suddenly a small elderly man stepped out of the crowd and kissed the fist of one of the protagonists. The angry man relaxed. His opponent relaxed. Everyone started to pick up the oranges, which my eager helper and I then did together in front of the congregation. "Who will kiss the fist?" I asked.

Our congregation provided refreshments for our guests and a warm time of sharing with each other. Further exchanges and interaction took place over the months to come. But the most significant interaction was to take place later and was sparked by a telephone conversation with Rabia.

Rabia and I had been making plans for our joint conflict transformation training, but I said that the 9/11 attacks challenged us to put our plans on the fast track. We eventually pulled together a team from the BPFNA and MPF to plan our joint activities. Rabia and Mas'ood Cajee came from the MPF, while Ken Sehested and Lee McKenna joined me from the BPFNA. Rabia and Ken began to work on a booklet called "Peace Primer" that had quotes from Christian and Islamic scriptures and traditions. In that booklet Rabia wrote about *jihad* meaning not "war" or "holy war" but "struggle." *Jihad* as "struggle" can refer to war, but Muhammad spoke of war as the "lesser *jihad*" and imposed strict limits on war including the protection of noncombatants and the refusal to hate. The "greater *jihad*" was dealing with one's own self, removing evil and selfish motives and attitudes. For Rabia and many Muslim peace activists nonviolent action can be viewed as the perfect instrument of engaging in struggles for justice, peace, and the protection of one's community. Rabia's understanding of *jihad* resonated with this peace warrior.

Rabia, Mas'ood, Lee and I laid the plans for facilitating together a training program on conflict transformation involving participants equally drawn from Christian and Muslim backgrounds. In April 2002 we held the training in Dearborn. We began on Friday evening by participating in the prayers at the Islamic House of Wisdom followed by workshop sessions. After we went around the circle introducing ourselves, I said, "Before we get started I have to say...Rabia, I cannot wait until I can baptize you in the name of the Father, and of the Son, and of the Holy Spirit." Rabia responded, "Dan, I cannot wait until I can witness you say, 'There is no God but Allah, and Mohammad is his prophet.'" Then we turned to the group and said, "In the meantime, how are we going to live together and even build community together?" We wanted to acknowledge the missionary drives within both faiths, yet also raise the vision and challenge of how with integrity, and even delight, we can work at building rich and just relationships with each other.

For Saturday and Sunday we moved the workshop to First Baptist Church in Dearborn. The team worked well together as we led the groups through the teachings of the Bible and Qur'an related to peacemaking and explored the challenges of religious extremism coming out of both our faith communities. We participated in Sunday morning worship at First Baptist, then spent the afternoon working on the themes of truth, mercy, justice, and peace. From the Christian perspective, we used the text of Psalm 85:10, which says "Truth and mercy will embrace; peace and justice will kiss." From the Muslim perspective, four names of God were used related to these four attributes. We asked people to form groups around the attribute that most reflected the strongest interest in their lives. Christian and Muslim participants self-selected to be in each of the four groups. The dialogs within the truth, mercy, justice, and peace groups were very rich, and when shared with the larger group helped us to see many areas of common concern and possibility for collaborative work in the world.

Interfaith Partners

The evening after the 9/11 terrorist attacks, a meeting of interfaith clergy from across the Detroit area was held at a Dearborn mosque. Muslim, Christian, and Jewish leaders shared their perspectives of what was going on and its impact in our community. We shared our hopes and ideas for ways to bridge the gaps between us.

After the session Victor Begg, a Muslim businessman, contacted those of us who had been more assertive and radical in our comments. As Victor often put it, he wanted to connect with people who were interested in "doing more than just praying and holding hands." Six of us—three Muslims and three Christians—met on his boat at the Detroit Yacht Club. Victor felt that September 11 was the beginning of a new calendar and that we had to find new ways to relate to each other as religious people. We shared our analysis of the inter-religious conflicts and what we thought we could do in a metropolitan area to bring the various religious communities together.

For a few months we had discussions with an expanding circle of Christian and Muslim leaders. We realized that in Detroit and across the U.S. we were linked to the conflicts in the Middle East. We couldn't make progress either in the Middle East or in Detroit without also involving the Jewish community. So we invited some key leaders of the Jewish community, immediately making the discussions far more complex. Instead of just two communities facing each other with their histories, we now had three communities, each with complex histories with the other two. The work we had done, the assumptions agreed upon and vision shared, had to be undone so we could go right back to the beginning. The Jewish community couldn't simply be added to what we Christian and Muslim leaders had done. Rather we had to start fresh so that the Jewish leaders could struggle with us through the building of trust, the articulating of hopes, and the hammering out of assumptions and a group vision in terms we could all accept. The process was long and slow, but that very process was perhaps more important than the outcome. Without taking the time to travel together, no outcome would have been worth much.

We finally took shape in a network from the Abrahamic faiths that we called Interfaith Partners, which we linked to the local chapter of the National Conference on Community and Justice (NCCJ). Our mission was to create deeper understanding among the three Abrahamic faiths and to improve social welfare through dialog and cooperative projects. We convened gatherings of people to share "holiday/holy day" experiences. We participated in service projects such as a blood drive, raising contributions for food banks, and joining in a Habitat for Humanity project. I met a young Muslim man to whom I became a mentor when we were hanging up a window together on a Habitat site. That was one of many relationships being established by people coming together in different settings so that we could meet each other, learn from each other, and experience the joys of working side by side for the good of our community.

We also began to be present with one another in the face of the challenges and tragedies that touched us from the broader world. When a synagogue was bombed in Turkey, Christian and Muslim partners joined in the mourning observances with the Jewish community. When copies of the Qur'an were desecrated by U.S. military guards at the Guantánamo detention camp, Jewish and Christian partners joined with Muslim leaders in a public witness calling for respect for people's religious practices and scriptures. When Christian churches were attacked in Iraq, Jewish and Muslim partners joined with the Christian leaders in calling for respect of all places of worship. That solidarity in advocacy could not always be achieved as we found that the political differences about Israel and Palestine especially made it difficult to always speak with one voice. Yet we were determined to stick together to speak as one where we could, with the hope that as we continued to dialog we might be able to expand the circle of mutual understanding as to how our values of justice, peace, and respect for human dignity could be applied in the complexities of the deeply rooted conflicts that profoundly involved our faiths.

One of the great successes of Interfaith Partners was The
Children of Abraham Project. It began with a conversation
between two of our partners, Brenda Rosenberg and Imam
Abdullah El-Amin. Imam El-Amin referred to the verses in
Genesis that spoke about Isaac and Ishmael coming together to
bury their father, Abraham. "Wouldn't it be wonderful," he said,
"if today's children of Isaac and Ishmael could come together
around their common father, Abraham" (Genesis 25:7-10). That
night Brenda dreamed of a stage on which Isaac and Ishmael were
standing together. An angel "Raphaela" helped them tell their
stories, and at the end the two brothers' faces shone with deeper
understanding. To bring the dream to life with the endorsement
and support of Interfaith Partners, Brenda enlisted the Mosaic
Youth Theater in Detroit to begin a four-step process of
exploration and healing, working with young people around the
theme of having a common father, Abraham.

The first step was to "break bread." Christian, Muslim, and
Jewish high school students were invited to meet together over
pizza. In that context the second step began, "to listen with
compassion." The youth shared their stories of being victims of
hate and prejudice, of how they grew up with the various beliefs
they had, both of their own religious faith and their beliefs about
other people. They learned to speak with and listen to those who
were initially strangers or even viewed as enemies.

The third step was to "be the other." Using theatrical tools of
improvisation, the adult advisers assisted the youth in role
playing. They acted out the ancient stories of Abraham, Sarah,
Hagar, Ishmael, and Isaac. They acted out the stories that had been
shared of their own experiences in high school, the Detroit
neighborhoods, and even countries of origin of the immigrant
youth. Students would step into other people's experiences
through the role-plays, which brought new empathy and
understanding. They learned that they did not need to agree with
someone in order to express empathy and validate feelings.

The fourth step was "to create something new together."
Working with a professional theater director and a professional

playwright through Mosaic Youth Theater, the youth wrote a play titled *The Children of Abraham* based on the story of Abraham, Sarah, Hagar, Ishmael, and Isaac. The play wove together the ancient story and the experiences of contemporary youth. It also wove in the current conflict in the Middle East. Topics that adults were too cautious to handle were tackled by the youth with courage, openness, and astonishing creativity. The role-plays used in the healing process and even the story of the project's history were incorporated into the drama. Music was also used, from the opening vigorous dance of "Father Abraham" to beautiful songs out of Muslim and Jewish traditions and the closing phrases from John Lennon's "Imagine."

As the script was being developed, Brenda gave me a call for help. They wanted to have scenes with religious leaders from the three faiths speaking about peace from within their particular faith tradition. She wanted me to write what the Christian pastor might say. This was far more challenging than writing a sermon. What could I say about peace that would be authentically and specifically Christian, that all Christians—Catholic, Orthodox, mainstream Protestant, evangelical, Pentecostal—would recognize as true for them? How could I do that in a paragraph, a minute of dramatic speech? It was a delightful challenge. I offered these words to be added into the script for a young person to present in the role of a Christian pastor:

> Jesus said, "My peace I give to you." God gives us peace deep within our hearts when we respond to the love God extends to us in Christ. We can know we are God's children, created to reflect God's goodness into the world as a mirror reflects light. That inner peace we have then works its way into the world by how we live for God. We become peacemakers. Jesus said, "Blessed are the peacemakers, for they shall be called the children of God." So if you are working for peace, if you are working to bring healing to all the broken relationships in your lives and even in the larger world, then you are following in the

footsteps of Christ. When we worship we often greet each other, "Peace be with you...and also with you." That is the spirit we are to have between us and to extend to all we meet. (*Children of Abraham*)

There were other challenges far more difficult to deal with in the script, challenges not so much for the youth as for the larger supporting adult communities. Should the term "Zionism" be used in the script? For Jews this was essential if their hearts and dreams were to be present, yet the Muslim advisers said that using the term "Zionism" would make the play a non-starter for the Muslim community. After a couple days of intense discussion, the Jewish and Muslim advisers agreed to not use the term but to include the concept of what the homeland in Israel means to Jews. Issues were also raised about how to dramatically depict those viewed as prophets by Islam: How can you do a play about Abraham and Ishmael if you can't show depictions of them? As a result, an understanding was written down and articulated in the play early on that these were not depictions of the prophets themselves but role-plays.

When the Interfaith Partners board was invited to the first dramatic reading of the script, I was overwhelmed at what had been done. I sat next to Abdullah El-Amin. When the reading was completed, we turned to each other with emotions of wonder and joy on our faces. There were rough spots to be dealt with, refining still to be done, but the result of the eight-month-long journey of youth and their advisers was a powerful expression of faith and hope. We gave our critiques. I gave specific suggestions for how to strengthen the Christian presentation, which I felt was weak at key points and had too negative an image of evangelism. Those suggestions were incorporated into the final script.

I have now seen *The Children of Abraham* live three times, plus watched recorded versions of it many times. Every time I am brought to tears for the passion, the pain, and the struggle of hope to be born through this younger generation into the harder hearts of more battle-weary adults. The live performances of the play have been discontinued after a very successful run in many local congregations and theaters. Each performance was sponsored by local interfaith coalitions with follow-up discussions or panels. CBS did a special program on The_Children of Abraham Project. As the live performances came to an end, Brenda began work on a multi-media program titled "The Children of Abraham Project" with major sections of the play interspersed with the story of the project and testimonies of the youth who were involved. She continues to use the multi-media production as a key program piece for gatherings of Jewish, Muslim, and Christian congregations to begin their own journeys of interfaith understanding and community-building.

The Call to Prayer and Action

In July 2004 a controversy in Hamtramck made national news. The Al-Islah Islamic Center, at that time one of five mosques in Hamtramck, approached the city council about broadcasting the Muslim call to prayer. The leaders of this Bangladeshi mosque wanted to initiate their action in a positive and cooperative way with the larger community. The city council negotiated with them an amendment to the city's noise ordinance to allow for the call to prayer within the hours of 6 a.m. and 10 p.m.

When some of the non-Muslim citizens of Hamtramck found out about this, they launched a petition drive to overturn the ordinance. In one of the ironies of the campaign that was overlooked by those who began it, overturning the ordinance would also ban the ringing of church bells, a Christian form of calling people to prayer. Such concerns were overshadowed in the hysteria that Hamtramck's Polish Catholic heritage was being swamped by an influx of Muslims. The petitions succeeded on putting the repeal of the ordinance to a special vote. News of the issue spread and brought outsiders into Hamtramck to protest the call to prayer. "The Lord's Mighty Men," a group from a fundamentalist church in Ohio, protested on the grounds of religious liberty—not that Muslims could exercise their religious liberty, but that the public call to prayer was an infringement on the religious liberty of others who would have to hear it.

Amid the hullabaloo, some of the Muslim and Catholic leaders in Hamtramck gathered together to explore ways for community peace. The priest of St. Ladislav's Catholic Church, who was a leading figure for community harmony and justice, said that Rev. Sharon should be at the meeting. None of the Muslims knew her even though Sharon was a key figure in much of Hamtramck because of her community work as director of Friendship House. At the first meeting she attended, she spoke about the Baptist heritage of standing for religious freedom and how allowing the call to prayer to take place was a religious liberty issue. Her statement was so eloquent that the group immediately made her their spokesperson.

As the campaign developed to vote against the repeal of the city's ordinance, allowing the call to prayer to continue, the interfaith group decided to focus its message less on the political action and more on their vision of a unified community that celebrated its diversity. Sharon and Abdul Motlib from Al-Islah became the leadership team of the movement, speaking to the local and national media and organizing people for action. My role was to help Sharon with any small tasks to be done, such as setting up chairs for press conferences and joining with other colleagues in Interfaith Partners to provide support for the movement from the larger metropolitan community. Interfaith Partners supported the Hamtramck interfaith group as they came together and strategized not just about the immediate election issue but about the ongoing work of building relationships across religious lines. On election day the citizens of Hamtramck overwhelmingly supported the city council's action and turned aside the campaign against the call to prayer. We all celebrated the victory, but even then we were looking ahead to deeper relationships and continued partnership.

When Sharon stepped down as director of Friendship House, Abdul Motlib was one of the most concerned and supportive people for her. He had a day of prayer and fasting at the mosque "for Rev. Sharon to get another job in Hamtramck." His prayers were answered as Sharon took a position with a creative urban church-planting ministry called Acts 29 Fellowship. She continued her interfaith leadership, working closely with Muslim and Catholic leaders in town. They connected with a Jewish congregation in nearby Oak Park to begin interaction between the three Abrahamic faiths. Youth group visits were planned. Sharon and I went to Al-Islah to talk with their youth about Jewish synagogues and prepare them for their first visit to a house of worship outside their Muslim tradition.

From her leadership at the local level in Hamtramck and the trust she had earned within both the Muslim and Jewish communities, Sharon was enthusiastically endorsed to become a congregational organizer for Interfaith Partners. For a couple years she has worked as part-time staff to involve Christian, Muslim, and Jewish congregations directly with each other in educational encounters and service projects.

During the war between Israel and Hezbollah in 2006, the Jewish and Muslim men in the Interfaith Partners network broke off most of their communication. The politics of the Middle East spilled over into our relationships in Detroit. However, the women refused to be divided by the distant war that was touching our lives. Jewish, Muslim, and Christian friends formed WISDOM, the Women's Interfaith Solutions for Dialog and Outreach in MetroDetroit. Sharon joined the executive committee of WISDOM and became active in their programs. She was part of the "Five Women, Five Journeys" panels that would go to various houses of worship to share their spiritual stories. She told of her interfaith journey in the book WISDOM published, *Friendship and Faith* (Read the Spirit, 2010). It has been very special for us as a couple to share the interfaith activities together.

During spring 2011 our interfaith community was jolted by the news that Terry Jones was coming to Detroit, specifically to Dearborn to protest at the Islamic Center of America, the largest mosque in the U.S. Terry Jones was the pastor of a tiny independent Pentecostal church in Florida. He made world news by threatening to publicly burn a Qur'an, which he eventually did in early 2011. His action provoked riots in Afghanistan in which a number of people were killed. Now he was coming to our community. Furthermore, he picked Good Friday as the day to hold his protest. I had sent two letters to Jones and received no reply. I felt it was imperative to act.

Our Interfaith Partners had reorganized as the InterFaith Leadership Council (IFLC) with which I served as board secretary. I said that the Christians especially needed to be in the lead in making a constructive response to Terry Jones. IFLC leaders met repeatedly with the leaders of the Islamic Center along with the mayor and police chief of Dearborn. Eventually we conceived the idea of an interfaith prayer service to be held at the mosque on the Christian holy day of Maundy Thursday. This would enable us to pre-empt Jones's Good Friday action by sending the larger community a message of respect and cooperation in contrast to Jones's message of disrespect and hostility. Furthermore, following brief statements and prayers inside we would bring the prayer meeting outside the mosque to turn it into a nonviolent peace parable in action.

By the time the decisions were made, we had just a week to publicize the action and mobilize religious communities to participate. How many people would come on such short notice? Our action was planned for 4:00 p.m. so that the Catholic archbishop could participate and still make his scheduled Holy Thursday mass. Many people would still be at work. I worked with the Young Muslim Association from the mosque to coordinate crowd control as we sought to move people quickly and quietly from the conference hall in the mosque to form a protective arc around the front of the mosque. We would then stand in a silent prayer vigil outside until my "Amen!" called an end to the witness.

On Holy Thursday we still had no idea how many people would come. I was hoping for a couple hundred. Instead we were stunned as the crowd grew to a thousand: Muslims, Christians, Jews, and Baha'is. More than one hundred Christian and Muslim clergy came, many dressed in their clerical robes. Terry Jones had stirred the religious community from their isolated lives of worship to seek a way to express a different vision of what our faiths stood for. Our planned action gave the perfect vehicle for this vision to be made tangible. As we closed the vigil in silence outside, the news helicopters circled overhead. Our message would set a high standard in the news cycle that would minimize Jones's extremist approach.

As I worked with the Muslim young people I talked with them about the power of nonviolent action to transform negative experiences, such as Jones's visit, into positive ones as we were experiencing in this large interfaith community gathering to witness for respect and peace. I shared with them about Muslim practitioners of nonviolence and about Jesus' teaching in the Sermon on the Mount. After the vigil was over, the youth were ecstatic about the event, feeling that they had made a difference in the life of our city. We had not gotten hooked into the cycles of hatred Jones was stirring up. Rather we had acted in a transformative way that gave powerful and exciting visibility to interfaith peacemaking.

A picture of me and one of the Muslim young women beaming at each other with hands over our hearts was splashed across the *Detroit Free Press* along with photos of Christian and Muslim clergy standing side by side. Jones came and did his thing, but he ended up as the side story instead of the main feature. We successfully seized the initiative and controlled the prevailing message.

There is a postscript to this story from the other side of the world. I had been engaged in peacemaking efforts in the Indian state of Orissa since the outbreak of violence by Hindu militant nationalists against the Christian community during Christmas 2007. In July 2011 I returned to Orissa to speak at an interfaith conference convened by Baptist leaders. Present were various kinds of Christians as well as Sikhs, Muslims, and Hindus, including a few of the extremists. I shared specific practices that could help shape an interfaith movement to transform a situation of violence into one of building a delightfully diverse and peaceful community. One point was about defending those who are vulnerable from attack by one's co-religionists. I told the story about Christians taking the lead to defend the mosque from Terry Jones's provocations. Christians, Muslims, and Hindus all spoke to me about how powerful that example was to them. The story of our action in Detroit broke through the more abstract political, sociological, and religious discussions to show the simplicity of acting boldly and nonviolently for what was right and just. Our interfaith example in Detroit encouraged the growth of interfaith peacemaking in India.

Global Challenges for Interfaith Peacemaking

Being rooted in the United States in interfaith peacemaking gives me a special vantage point in pursing peacemaking in some of my global contexts where religious difference was one of the aspects of severe conflicts. I developed an early awareness of some of those challenges during my college years. Sharon and I were in a group that met every week to pray for Christian ministries in Afghanistan. This was in the days before the Soviet invasion brought Afghanistan into the awareness of many U.S. citizens. We were interested because we were considering joining a mission called Dilaram House that reached out to the young people from Europe and North America traveling the "Hippie Trail" from Amsterdam to India and Nepal. Kabul, Afghanistan, was a major stopover on the Hippie Trail, a place that often turned into a nightmare for these Western travelers. Afghanistan had severe drug penalties, and many of the hippies were carrying and using drugs. They would end up in jail, dropping out of sight to become forgotten and lost. Dilaram House was a Christian community that reached out to the hippies, trying to turn their lives around and rescue them from drugs and prison.

In our prayer group were two children of Dr. Christy Wilson, the only Christian pastor in Afghanistan. He was pastor to the international church that served Christians in the business and diplomatic communities. Besides praying for Dilaram House, we prayed for Dr. Wilson's church. When a radical Islamist coup overthrew the king, the church was destroyed by the new government and Dr. Wilson deported. The Soviet invasion and the installation of a Communist puppet regime that followed brought about the closure of Dilaram House. The tragic flow of events over the next decade would show the futility of dealing with religious extremism through violence. Afghanistan became a center for inspiring and training extremists who would use terror in the name of their God. Violence begat more violence, a cycle of misery continuing in Afghanistan today which has spun out to many parts of the world including New York, Washington, and Pennsylvania then coming back to Afghanistan with the long war of the U.S. and its NATO allies against the Taliban.

I came very close to touching some of that violence when I was in the Philippines in 2003. Lee McKenna and I were scheduled to fly to Davao City on the southern Filipino island of Mindanao to do some training. The week before we were to fly, while we were leading trainings in Iloilo City further to the north, one of the Muslim insurgent groups planted a bomb in the Davao City airport. Twenty people were killed including a Baptist missionary. Our Filipino Baptist hosts were distraught and, worried for our safety, cancelled the trip to Mindanao where the violence was taking place. A few days later we read in the papers about a public bus in Mindanao that was stopped by Abu Sayyef, the most extreme Islamist group in the Philippines. The gunmen culled the Christians from the Muslim passengers and then shot them.

The Saturday evening following the airport bombing in Davao City we were involved in a peace conference at a hotel in Iloilo, talking with Filipino activists. Just as we were closing the conference, we learned that there was a bomb in the street outside the hotel. The police demanded to know the names of everyone inside. When we would not give the names since some of the activists were fearful of the police, we were sealed up in the hotel. We sat on the floor in the center hallway away from the windows. After about fifteen minutes the police agreed to let us go without getting our names. We were escorted out the front door and walked single file past the police cordon. The bomb squad was working carefully on a package a mere ten meters from us. I felt a huge wave of relief washing over me as well as agitated nervousness once we were safely back at our own hotel. The bomb turned out to be a fake, though it was deliberately made to look like a bomb. We never learned whether our peace conference group was the target or not. It was also never made clear who planted the fake bomb—Abu Sayyef, one of the Moro insurgent groups (fighting for independence or autonomy for the predominantly Muslim island of Mindanao), or the New People's Army (a long-standing Communist insurgency), or even the police trying to scare the activists who were meeting with us. Going through these experiences made inter-religious violence immediate and emotionally charged rather than a distant or merely academic matter.

I had seen the impact of religious violence in other contexts. In Jakarta, Indonesia, I'd seen a church marred by a bomb blast during Christmas Eve services. I heard a pastor tell about how his church was severely vandalized by gangs of Muslim youth as he and his family hid terrified under their beds in their upstairs apartment. I'd talked to victims of a radical Muslim militia in the Moluccan Islands and watched with them the videotape of the violence. I saw the Indonesian Army troops standing idly in the background while the militia members were beating and shooting Christian civilians and looting their homes and churches. I watched the pathetic sight of frail elderly people being hoisted by ropes out of rowboats up onto larger ships so they could flee their burning city of Ambon. I looked at photo after awful photo of the victims of the violence in Ambon as the survivors pleaded for help.

I heard the same stories and saw similar photos from Nigeria. A pastor from Kaduna, Nigeria, participated in a training I led in Cameroon in 2001. He told about the riots between Christians and Muslims in his city that led to hundred of deaths on both sides and the destruction of many churches and mosques. In so many countries interfaith relations, particularly between Christians and Muslims, were being expressed violently. Sometimes underlying issues were ethnic, economic, and the balance of power, but religious differences added to these issues became extra inspiration for intensity of passion and violence. God was claimed to be on one side while the others were infidels or unbelievers.

Even in these situations I saw signs and heard stories that showed a counter trend of religious tolerance, respect, and even willingness to take huge risks for people from other religious communities. In the Philippines I heard a Baptist talk with empathy about how the Moros in Mindanao ("Moro" is the term used for Muslims in that southern region of the Philippines) had been targets of prejudice and discrimination from the Christian majority in the country. He understood their anger. Though Baptist churches in Mindanao had been burned and people killed in the violence, this Baptist did not demonize those who committed those acts. Instead he had the compassion that allowed him to see the needs of the Moros for justice if there was to be a genuine solution to the conflict.

In Indonesia one pastor told about a Muslim neighbor who took the pastor's family into his home during a rampage of violence by Muslim extremists. I had grown up with the stories of Christians like Corrie Ten Boom's family who had hidden Jews during the Holocaust; we can tell the stories that make our own community look like it had some people who did what was right. But here was a Christian telling a story in which a Muslim was the hero providing shelter in the violent storm. Even in a conflict situation, when their own religion has become captive to extremism, hate, and violence, there are people who go deeper into the values of their faith to practice love, justice, and peace, even at great risk to themselves.

While Daniel Hunter and I were doing the training with the Baptists in Lunsar, Sierra Leone, a local Muslim imam came over to the Baptist compound during a break. The general secretary of the Baptists introduced me to the imam, and I could see the personal warmth in their relationship. They talked about the shared suffering of the people and how they worked to assure that religious difference did not become a part of the war. Now they were trying to rebuild together. Even though both Christians and

Muslims have been strongly involved in conversion efforts, they are striving to keep their relationships across religious communities strong and respectful. These efforts don't make the world news, but it will take the work of such people multiplied across many cultures and continents to counter the seeds of discord and suspicion sown by extremists of all kinds.

Healing Together

The war in Bosnia was one of the most vicious conflicts in recent years with religious difference playing a significant role laid over and reinforcing ethnic difference. When I arrived in Bosnia in 2006, about ten years after the war ended, the lines of division were still evident in symbols and maps. Bosnia itself is still divided between the Muslim/Croat Federation of Bosnia and Herzegovina, and the Serbian Republic, a Bosnian Serb entity. Each has their own president, parliament, and police, yet these two political entities are supposedly one country. Unlike states or provinces in most countries with boundaries that follow rivers, mountain ranges, or straight lines drawn by surveyors, the Serbian Republic is sprinkled throughout Bosnia, non-contiguous enclaves here and there, defined solely by the Serb majority living in that section. It is totally untenable as a long-term solution, a conflict on the verge of reigniting. I was told that militants on all sides were just waiting for the international peacekeeping forces to depart to resume their killing. The evidence of the war was seldom far away. Though Sarajevo has experienced much reconstruction and one can feel the vibrancy that had once made it such a cosmopolitan city, the scars of the war pockmark houses like a bad case of acne. Outlines of shell-bursts still stain the pavement.

Some memorials reflect a vision of unity and healing even amid the grief, such as the white marble walls marking out a square in the park in Tuzla. Here the names of all the people from Tuzla killed in the war are together, chiseled into those gleaming walls: Bosnian Muslim names, Croat names, and Serb names. However, just a few steps beyond that memorial is a special memorial cemetery for about fifty young people who died in the main square in Tuzla when Serbian militia artillery shells exploded during an evening of festivity. In that incident about seventy young people were killed from all three of the ethnic groups living in Bosnia, but only Muslims are buried in this public cemetery in the park. Croat victims were buried in the Catholic cemetery, and Serb dead were buried in the Orthodox cemetery. The tragedy was compounded by dividing those who had died together.

Amid the long-lingering bitterness and sorrow in Bosnia, I experienced some astonishing healing across the religious lines of division. Fyodor Raychynets, a Ukrainian Baptist missionary who was pastor of a small church in Tuzla, invited me to do conflict transformation and trauma healing work in Bosnia. He gathered together a small group of Baptist and Pentecostal Christians, mostly women, and Bosnian Muslim army vets suffering from post-traumatic stress disorder. In chapter 7 I described the healing unleashed in that group through the story of Rizpah in 2 Samuel 21. One Bosnian Muslim spoke about how he now understood the Serbs who had brutalized him, seeing them with compassion as fellow tormented and traumatized souls. A Serb woman then prayed passionately for the healing of these Muslim vets. The next night a Serb woman told about being raped, a story she had never shared until feeling safe enough in this strange group of wounded people helping each other heal. The Muslim men joined in prayers for her.

After I returned to the U.S., Fyodor told me that the connections between his church members and these Muslim veterans continued as they sought to build community upon what was begun during those sessions. A year later he invited me back, and we had further sessions on trauma healing and reconciliation with the same group of Muslim veterans and Baptists coming from all the sectors of Bosnia's frayed ethnic quilt. It seems that there is no end to people who are willing to speak and act to deepen the rifts between people, to accentuate the differences and create a demonic enemy to fear and attack. But there are also people sprinkled around in every situation I have seen, people like Fyodor, the Serbian mother, and the leader of the Bosnia Muslim veterans support group, who are willing to risk being vulnerable though they have been wounded so deeply. They are willing to listen to a story, hear something new, learn from the experience of another, and connect at a human-to-human level.

During that return trip to Bosnia in 2007 I visited Srebrenica. Srebrenica is the little town nestled in hills where on 11 July 1995 the Serbian militia massacred more than 8,000 Muslim men and boys. It was the worst massacre in Europe since World War II. The week before I arrived in Bosnia the International Court of Justice ruled that Serbia did not commit genocide related to the massacre, merely that they failed to stop the Bosnian Serbs who did the killing. No one was being held politically liable for the massacre.

Srebrenica is almost like a ghost town, having experienced little of the rebuilding seen in other parts of Bosnia. It is a somber testimony to the success of ethnic cleansing. Most of the Muslim survivors from the town live elsewhere. Ironically the memorial for the massacre is guarded on the outside by Serb policemen from the Serbian Republic, which includes the "cleansed" Srebrenica. The killers still live in town and perhaps are even among the police.

At the memorial the names of all those massacred are carved into massive granite blocks, 8,000 names from this one little place. As mass graves are found and unearthed, the remains that can be identified are placed in fresh individual graves. I was visiting on 11 March, and on the 11th of each month the Mothers of Srebrenica hold special vigils. I walked and meditated among the grieving, praying mothers. I was most deeply moved by their testimony carved into stone, even in the face of the killers of their loved ones just beyond the gate.

There is a prayer on a pillar erected by the mothers among the grave markers. It reads, "In the name of God the Most Merciful and Most Compassionate, we pray to Almighty God, may grievance become hope, may revenge become justice, and may mothers' tears become prayers that Srebrenica never happen again to no one nowhere." To no one nowhere—not just to *our* people, but to *all* people. Here under the eyes of the killers was a stunning expression of compassion for all people in a context where ethnocentrism was fought over most savagely. This compassion was extended by grieving—and freshly offended—Muslim mothers. I also found a Muslim memorial with this quote from the Qur'an, again stunning given the context of Bosnia: "It may be that God will bring about friendship between you and those whom you hold to be your enemies."

A few days after I returned from Bosnia, I met a professor of evangelism from a Christian college. This man, so wonderful in other ways, was talking about the conflict in the Middle East and said, "I wish they would just bulldoze all the Palestinians into the sea!" He gave no thought of the humanity of all those Palestinians—whoever they might be. He gave no thought that many of those Palestinians are his brothers and sisters in Christ. He gave no thought that as an evangelist he should recognize that Christ's sacrifice and gospel did not stop at the thresholds of Palestinian homes. Perhaps he didn't think at all, but he certainly did not exhibit the love of the Jesus Christ he claimed to honor, at least not in that moment.

What a contrast I saw between the mothers of Srebrenica and this Christian evangelism professor! Who showed God's heart? We can sometimes be surprised to find positive core values of our faith expressed more in people who claim a different faith than ours. These shattered Muslim mothers showed more of the spirit of Jesus than the Christian professor. It is an experience I have had repeatedly in my interfaith encounters.

Jihad is a term many Western Christians have linked to suicide bombers and grainy videos of masked men cutting off the heads of kneeling prisoners. *Jihad* has a much broader and more honorable meaning. Simply put, as Rabia Harris taught me, it means "struggle." Muslims teach that we are to struggle with those things within ourselves and in the world that are wrong and seek to establish what is right and just. *Jihad* as applied to warfare is more akin to Christian traditions of just war theory. However, just as some Christians have been so swept up in twisted piety that they engaged in Crusades that butchered both enemies and innocents in the name of God, Muslim extremists have claimed *jihad* to justify their own crimes committed in the name of God.

Meanwhile Muslim peacemakers struggle for peace, engaging in nonviolent actions and the hard work of reconciliation. They struggle to create community out of the injustices and conflicts of our world just as Christian peacemakers and peacemakers of other faiths do. I have found more spiritual kinship with them, and they with me, than either of us have with our co-religionists who claim heavenly blessing on earthly acts of brutality, war, and terror. Looking into the future we can see a world that is neither Muslim nor Christian. We must either find ways to live well together or damn ourselves and our children to hopeless, unending violence that shames our God.

Joint Muslim Peace Fellowship/BPFNA Conflict Transformation Training (Rabia Harris at far left)

Author talking with an imam in Dearborn

Fyodor Raychynets and his children read some of the 8,000 names of men and boys killed in Srebrenica

Names in granite at the memorial for those massacred in Srebrenica

10

NAGA BREAKTHROUGH

Chiang Mai

After a couple years of no significant development in the Naga peace processes, 2008 provided a breakthrough. It all began with a small charismatic Naga prayer group who felt they had been given a prophecy from God about reconciliation between the Naga factions. The members of the prayer group contacted Wati Aier, and Wati began trying once more to pull together a face-to-face meeting with high factional leaders. That had been the plan in Atlanta in 1997, and it had fallen short then and every time since. This time would be different.

A meeting was planned for Chiang Mai, Thailand, and all the key groups had agreed to come: the old Naga National Council (NNC), the National Socialist Council of Nagaland-Isak and Muivah faction (NSCN-IM also now known as the NSCN-GPRN), and the Khaplang faction of NSCN, now called the Government of the People's Republic of Nagaland-National Socialist Council of Nagaland (GPRN-NSCN). The meeting was set for May, but I was unable to attend. A team of British Quakers with a long history of reconciliation work in Nagaland was asked to facilitate the process. John Sundquist, former executive director of International Ministries who also participated in the Atlanta talks, was able to go to represent the American Baptists who shared so much mission history with the Nagas. Wati had also gathered a number of Naga leaders from the civil society organizations, most of whom had been involved in the Journey of Conscience campaigns in 2000.

At the last moment, the delegation from a key group was unable to attend. It seemed that a replay of the disappointments of Atlanta was developing. Though this group did not show up, the delegations that did come made a commitment to Wati and the other civil society participants that they would continue pursuing a reconciliation process. The civil society groups organized themselves as Forum for Naga Reconciliation (FNR) with the sole purpose of facilitating the process of forging some sort of reconciliation between the factions. Wati was selected as the FNR convener. People left Chiang Mai feeling hopeful in spite of the one group that did not show.

Another round of talks was quickly scheduled for June, again at the YMCA in Chiang Mai. I was teaching in Lebanon, but in a scheduling miracle, all the plans had fallen through for the very days of the Chiang Mai meeting. I was able to fly from Beirut to Thailand round-trip, and for a cheaper airfare than if I'd gone from the U.S. I joined with the Quakers as the facilitation team working at the invitation of the Forum for Naga Reconciliation.

The Chiang Mai 2 meeting, as it came to be called, was the moment we had worked toward for twelve years. We finally had all the key groups together, face-to-face, not the very top leaders, but the next level. They were leaders who could talk substantively and who carried weight in their organizations. They could take some initiative in the talks, not just spout party lines then report back to headquarters. We also had traditional tribal leaders from three of the major Naga tribes that were on different sides of the factional fault lines. The factional leaders and the tribal leaders were not completely aligned, but there were similar deep divisions. The FNR also had some of the conflict divisions within themselves, for Wati had worked intentionally to bring civil society people together who had leanings toward one faction or another or who were aligned with various regional tribes. The FNR felt the strains of these divisions, but the FNR members were bonded with a commitment to the work of reconciliation. Together they were going to forge the bonds that would allow the tribal leaders and the political faction leaders to begin their own journey toward reconciliation.

I had never met any of the Quaker team members before although they had been part of a tight-knit Quaker Naga interest group for many years. We had arrived at Chiang Mai a day in advance of the meetings so we could get to know each other and plan how to work together to assist the process as best we could. We quickly developed patterns of working smoothly together and sharing our various support and facilitation roles. We knew that ultimately we were not going to be the critical difference-makers; rather it would be the Naga peace activists who would prove to be the real heroes and leaders for the process. Our role was to support them in their work and facilitate some portions of the process within the overall design from the FNR leadership. After all, peace was something the Nagas would have to create and hold for themselves, not something we as outsiders could create and give to them as a gift.

For four days we worked on a host of issues, closing the sessions in a passionate time of prayer. A joint statement was prepared for public release, short but with a clear commitment by all sides to keep the process going. I had to return to Lebanon just before the meeting formally ended.

When I got back to Lebanon, I learned that all hell had broken out—well, not quite, but it felt that way after the emotional high of the bonding that had been achieved after over thirty years of division in some cases. Just as the conference participants were leaving Chiang Mai, fresh fighting had erupted back in Nagaland. Many people viewed the reconciliation process, which had been kept out of the media, as futile. The fragile web of trust that had been built in Chiang Mai 1 and 2 was frayed by the new violence. We knew that there were people within each faction in addition to people outside the Naga groups who did not want reconciliation, who had vested interests in keeping the conflict boiling. Would they torpedo the process that had achieved such a hopeful moment?

Football? Football!

Wati worked desperately to schedule another round of talks—Chiang Mai 3. A larger group gathered. The Forum had grown, broadening the base for the peace constituency demanding reconciliation. Tribal leaders from some of the other tribes joined.

Again all the factions came with high leaders. The mediation team worked through a tentative schedule for our delicate work. Then, just as we were preparing to open the sessions, Wati came in talking about playing football ("soccer" to an American). Football? All of us on the mediation team were taken aback, thinking Wati was surely joking. This was a very serious situation. The process was about to blow apart because of the bitterness and mistrust from the recent violence. Football? Wati kept talking about it. We had prepared a full, demanding schedule of sessions, but Wati insisted that we carve out most of an afternoon for a football match. This was serious business, not a sports camp, for heaven's sake!

One of our team members reminded us that Wati was in charge as convener of the FNR. We were there to serve the process under his leadership, so reluctantly all of us on the mediation team submitted to Wati's agenda. His football match was either a stroke of pure genius or the prompting of the Holy Spirit—or both. On the afternoon of the second day of our four-day meeting schedule, we all piled into the covered pickup trucks Wati had hired. We drove to a raggedy, overgrown soccer field somewhere on the edge of Chiang Mai. Some of the grass was a foot high in huge tufts. It was like running through a vacant lot. There was no clear sideline, only the higher grass at the edge of woods on one side and the rise up to the road on the other. But at each end were the netless metal goal frames. We had our venue.

Wati had assigned all the factional leaders to the same team, called the United Nationals, along with some of the FNR folks including himself. The other side, called the Naga Parliament, was made up of the traditional tribal leaders, and the other half of the civil society activists. That was my team. The grand old man of Naga peacemaking, eighty-year-old Rev. V. K. Nuh, was my team's goalie.

Following a lot of stretching, laughter, and stripping off dress shirts, play commenced. The Nagas know how to play football. Wati, well into his fifties, was able to run circles around many of the young activists. V. K. Nuh made a couple saves. The regulation time ended in a 2-2 tie. The friendly competition was running strong, so the teams demanded a deciding shoot-out. The tribal leaders' team won 4-2 on penalty kicks. V. K. Nuh was named man of the match for his saves in goal. But none of that mattered; before the game reached half time everyone in the game knew something profound was happening. Zhabu Terhuja, the general secretary of the Nagaland Baptist churches, gave voice to the vision that had crystallized on the football pitch. "We have to do this in Kohima," he said. Putting the enemies on the same team had given the reconciliation process the tangible symbol of togetherness that was lacking. All the factions could be on the same side striving for the same goal. All the tribal leaders could be on one team. The score didn't matter, what mattered was that long-standing enemies were playing together. As we drove back to the Y in the covered pick-up truck, Zhabu convened a planning meeting, talking about some of the specific things needing to be done to bring a similar match to the main stadium in the Naga capital.

The tenor of the Chiang Mai 3 meeting had changed from anger over the past to hope for the future. There was still a lot of difficult work to be done in the sessions, but a new energy was unleashed. Participants got to work on the substance of building reconciliation, including how to take the Chiang Mai processes back to Nagaland. The FNR in particular was growing in the relationships between its members and their clarity about the steps they could take to make reconciliation substantive.

Akum Longchari, the human rights activist and journalist, had worked alongside Wati as the key behind-the-scenes organizer for the FNR. He was brilliant at articulating the consensus emerging in the group, so he drafted a statement that would become the first major public presentation from the reconciliation process. He presented it to the plenary, and all the factions and all the tribal leaders responded positively to the commitments outlined in the draft. After minor refining of some wording, the ten-point "Covenant of Common Hope" was agreed to by all parties: political factions, tribal leaders, and civil society leaders.

Back in Nagaland the papers announced the "Covenant of Common Hope." The story of the reconciliation football match was published. Zhabu convened a Nagaland Council of Churches meeting so that the Kohima football match would be sponsored not by the Baptists alone but by all the religious communities. Most of the other components for the FNR's agenda set out in Chiang Mai 3 were acted upon. A series of meetings was held with factional representatives to hammer out details to address the points of contention between their armed forces. A choir was drawn together from cadres in each factional group that provided music at public events the FNR sponsored to promote reconciliation.

On 9 October 2008 the big football match was scheduled for the stadium in Kohima, the Naga capital nestled among the high hills of the Naga heartland. A few days before the game there was a clash between Khaplang's forces and Isak and Muivah's soldiers. A number of the cadres were killed. The football match looked like a foolish enterprise before the rising old feelings of mistrust, hatred, and bitterness threatening to reignite the violence. Zhabu, Wati, and the FNR pressed ahead with the match. The factional players had to come to the stadium without their weapons, and many feared an ambush. The FNR provided their own members as nonviolent escorts to the stadium for the factional players; any attack would be a strike not only at the other faction, but at the Naga public. With trepidation the football players came from each side.

The match was a great success. The game was surrounded by a day of prayer for Naga reconciliation. Again, all the factions were represented on one team called Team Hope, playing against a team from the civil society called Team Faith. Thousands of people cheered the factional team, as just their presence on one team meant more than the score of any game. Within five minutes of the start of the game the emotions were transformed. Tension was replaced with laughter as teammates shouted encouragement to each other. One moving moment was when the oldest player on Team Hope, a sixty-seven-year-old veteran from the NNC, was near exhaustion. Two teammates, one from NSCN-IM and one from GPRN/NSCN helped him back to the bench for a replacement. One gently teased him, "You played well. You will be a really good player when you grow up!" Team Faith won the match, but the growing spirit of fun on the factions' team was more important. One cadre speaking of the whole experience said, "Suddenly we were made to eat and sleep with the very people we had been so carefully avoiding. We didn't know what to do except look at each other and grin nervously." When the teammates parted they exchanged warm handshakes and hugs.

Another match was quickly organized in Dimapur, the largest city in Nagaland. Besides the prayer held around the event, a special presentation was arranged before the game began. Widows and orphans of men who had been killed in factional fighting met on the field with the players from the various factions. They presented each player with flowers and words of forgiveness. They encouraged them to continue the process of reconciliation. The hope-filled emotions in seeing the factions come together for the game were spilling over into some of the deep places of pain from the war. Football had become a peace game.

A Covenant of Reconciliation

The momentum for reconciliation was gathering power, especially in the Naga public. Problems still arose. Scheduled meetings between factional representatives to work on modalities related to disengagement of forces had to be postponed because one side's delegates could not come. Indian army roadblocks were blamed for blocking access to talks, but representatives from the other sides didn't trust that excuse. Some factional leaders who had not participated in the Chiang Mai talks made provocative statements in the press that violated the commitments in the Covenant of Common Hope. None of these problems was serious enough to derail the reconciliation movement. The FNR pressed ahead with determination, and key leaders among the factions maintained their commitment in spite of their own frustrations and perceived provocations. Meetings continued to be held in Chiang Mai and in Nagaland, keeping at least a structure to the commitment for reconciliation even if the substance was lacking at times.

Then in June 2010 the next major breakthrough occurred. Wati was still trying to get the very top leaders to sign on to the reconciliation process personally. He kept encouraging a face-to-face meeting, but something always developed to prevent such an encounter from happening. That June Wati prepared a written statement, a "Covenant of Reconciliation." He approached the top leaders of each of the Naga factions to get their agreement to sign it, pledging not to make it public until all had agreed. Wati had to travel back and forth to meet with them in places viewed as safe. He finally got them to sign: Isak for the NSCN-IM, Khaplang for the GPRN-NSCN, and S. Singnya, president of the NNC (Federal Government of Nagaland). When all their signatures were affixed, the "Covenant of Reconciliation" was announced to the Naga press.

Though all the groups had top leaders now committed in writing to the reconciliation process, there was still a major step missing. Some of the key leaders, such as Muivah for NSCN-IM and Kitovi for the GPRN-NSCN, had not affixed their signatures to any document. Furthermore, these key leaders had not met face-to-face, which had been such a powerful part of the Chiang Mai process. Wati and the FNR continued their persistent work of prodding people toward the next steps, a process that at times was agonizingly slow and frustrating.

Then in early September, Wati contacted many of the international friends, urging us to pray. Something big was brewing. On 18 September Wati and the FNR convened a meeting in Dimapur that included Muivah, Kitovi, and Singnya. Together they affirmed that they were reconciled on the basis of the "Historical and Political Rights of the Nagas," a statement that the FNR had worked out as a Naga consensus. They also affirmed, "Henceforth, we commit to working out our differences as outlined in the 'Covenant of Reconciliation.' Furthermore, we commit to cessation of all forms of hostilities including any territorial expansion. For this the JWG [Joint Working Group—established by earlier negotiations in Chiang Mai] will meet from time to time" (Press Communique, September 19, 2010: FNR," FNR Press Release printed in various Naga Newspapers).

The FNR announced the meeting and affirmation of the three leaders as a "historic landmark," calling it "the beginning of a new phase of Naga reconciliation." The Naga state politicians who were aligned with Indian political parties, both the party in control of the state chief minister's office and the opposition, hailed the agreement as a positive step. It had been a long, long time since the Naga situation had looked so positive.

The Road Ahead

The signing of the Covenant of Reconciliation by the Naga leaders was not the end of the overall conflict, however. The initial conflict between the Nagas and the government of India still remains. In spite of a formal cease-fire still in place, there were two confrontations in 2011 between Naga factional forces and the Indian army's Assam Rifles unit, resulting in casualties. In two major incidents the two sides came to a standoff with the Naga cadres under siege by the Indian militias. Civilian leaders engaged in direct negotiations with the military leaders on the ground. After some days, both incidents ended in a peaceful separation, but the tensions between the Nagas and the Indian army remain high.

How the Nagas engage with the government of India in the political talks is still one of the large issues to be worked out. Isak and Muivah have been the ones sitting at the table with Indian leaders, while those in the other groups have felt left out of the process. The FNR still has their work cut out for them as they try to help the Naga political leaders come to answers to this and many other challenges.

Furthermore, the Naga neighbors have grown increasingly nervous as they have witnessed the reconciliation process. Many of them fear that united Nagas could demand the reorganizing of political boundaries leading to further destabilization of already volatile situations. Many people in the state of Manipur, just to the south of Nagaland and with a large Naga population, fear that the Nagas will try to carve up their small state. Manipur has other insurgent groups that are active, and the state is under the Indian Armed Forces Special Powers Act just like Nagaland. Already violent clashes have occurred in Manipur as Naga reconciliation is perceived by many non-Nagas as flexing of Naga muscles for pulling Nagas out of Manipur.

Seeing these conflict ripples move out from Nagaland, I have given more time to working alongside religious and civil society peace activists in the neighboring states, including Manipur. I've found other Baptist leaders with courageous hearts for peacemaking like Wati, Zhabu, and others in the FNR. Through my Baptist contacts I've been invited to work with an interfaith group in Manipur that has members from the Hindu, Muslim, and Baha'i communities as well as from traditional tribal religious groups. I've held a number of workshops and training programs in the region to strengthen civil society leaders committed to peace.

Northeast India remains a very volatile place, but it also is a place where people from many tribes and religions are growing in their commitment to peace and in their skills to build that peace. Coming to peaceful and mutually agreed solutions to the Naga internal conflicts and the conflict with the government of India will likely unlock many positive dynamics in the region. The Nagas do not want to return to the old times characterized by cycles of violence, hiding in the jungles, and burying their children. Now Nagas are working together to give their children a fresh start with the hope for a peaceful life that they had never known. Surrounding people look to the Nagas with fear that growing Naga political cohesion could lead to instability in relation to the neighboring tribal groups and states. But they also are inspired and encouraged by the success of the Naga civil society to develop a peace constituency and facilitate a viable reconciliation process. Links of peacemakers across tribal, state, and religious lines could provide creative new opportunities to explore new solutions to the problems and identity issues that have long plagued this region. Hope is growing in a place where the future seemed doomed to be a repeat of the violence of the past. With a lot of hard work and faith-filled persistence, peace is being shown to be genuinely possible.

Author greeting the choir at the Kikwit airport

Author with representatives of the two NSCN factions at the Chiang Mai talks

Author (center with hat) in the Chiang Mai soccer match

Participants in the Chiang Mai soccer match pose following the game

11

DEEP WELLS AND OLD WARRIORS

Drying the Tears of Jesus

"Mbote, mbote, mbote"—the beautiful strains of the music floated toward us from beyond the Kikwit airport fence. We had just landed after flying over vast swaths of lush green Congolese forest. We had deplaned but were standing on the sweltering tarmac watching the baggage being unloaded and waiting for our papers to be processed. As this wonderful music wafted over the fence and across the field to the airstrip, I turned to Virgil Nelson, the American Baptist missionary to Congo who was traveling with me, and said, "Looks like some VIP flew in with us." I could see a large crowd on the other side of the fence with about sixty colorfully clothed women in the choir.

After a half-hour wait our documents were all cleared and we could claim our bags that had been piled on the asphalt. We passed through the gate into the parking lot to discover we were the VIPs! Virgil Nelson and Rev. Ikomba, general secretary of the Community of Baptists in Western Congo (CBCO for its French acronym) had invited me to Congo to lead a series of conflict transformation training programs in Kinshasa and Kikwit. After leading the training programs in Kinshasa, the three of us had flown into Kikwit for two and a half days of training for pastors and other church leaders in that district. What a welcome we received!

A little girl presented a bouquet of flowers to Rev. Ikomba. Twenty pastors greeted the three of us while the choir continued to sing the exquisite song of welcome: "Mbote, mbote, mbote." I asked what that word was that I was hearing repeatedly and was told *mbote* is a word of greeting in the Kikongo language that incorporates also the sense of blessing and expressing peace, much like *shalom* in Hebrew or *aloha* in Hawaiian. After greeting each pastor, we continued down the receiving line to greet the choir members as they continued to sing and sway. Eventually we formed a caravan that traveled the three kilometers from the airport to the church where the training would be held. The choir members climbed into the back of a large open-bed truck, standing and singing all the way.

At the church there were more people eagerly waiting to greet us. They picked up the song of greeting from the choir. Children from the school were out for the celebration. As we got out of the car, we had to push our way through the joyous throng, shaking hands and receiving greetings. We finally made it into the church where we were treated to a service of welcome, complete with yet more music from the choir. I was dressed in blue jeans for the travel day, yet I was ushered straight to the front of the sanctuary along with Rev. Ikomba and Virgil. A church service began that was one of the most energetic and happy services in which I've ever participated.

I was overwhelmed at this unexpected outpouring of welcoming joy. I had never been greeted so enthusiastically in all my travels. The celebration, the singing, the running and shouting children reminded me of that first Palm Sunday when Jesus entered into Jerusalem. Jesus received an effusive welcome as people waved palm branches and put their cloaks on the ground under his donkey. Shouts of "Hosanna" echoed from the stone walls of Jerusalem. Jesus was welcomed with the kind of unrestrained joy I was experiencing in Kikwit.

Amid the celebration Jesus wept. When he came over the brow of a hill and saw the glories of the city, Jesus wept and said, "Would that even today you knew the things that make for peace! But now they are hid from your eyes" (Luke 19:42). As I sat in front of this jubilant crowd I felt a clash of joy and sorrow in my heart. I knew Jesus was weeping over Congo. Congo was suffering from the bloodiest war since World War II, a conflict that has claimed more than four million lives and at times drawn the troops of seven surrounding nations into combat. While I was in

Congo the latest twist in the war was taking place with Rwandan troops pushing into Congolese territory. In Kikwit we saw a couple hundred new Army recruits quick-stepping toward their induction point, more fodder to fuel the war. As in most wars, the chief victims are civilians—the women, children, and the elderly, people who just want to live their lives in peace yet can lose everything as the dogs of war snap, snarl, and tear about them. Surely, Jesus was weeping over us in Kikwit even as we rejoiced.

"If only today you knew the things that make for peace." I was in Kikwit precisely to teach the things that make for peace. We were going to study the Scriptures and work through various challenges to practice skills in communication, nonviolence, and peace-building. So as I experienced the joy wash over me from the greeting from the Baptist brothers and sisters of Kikwit and with the mandate of the training clear in my mind and heart, I had an image of us together drying the tears of Jesus. As we learned those things that make for peace, I sensed that we would be bringing comfort to the soul of our Lord. Then I was asked to stand before the crowd and bring greetings. I had nothing planned as this entire event was totally unexpected, so I shared my gratitude for the warmth of their welcome and the vision of Jesus weeping over Congo. We could now dry the tears of Jesus by learning and doing the things that make for peace. In the days that followed as we worked through the training and saw the profound responses from the participants, I knew we were dealing with matters that were close to the heart of Jesus. These long-suffering people received the tools of conflict transformation as eagerly as food and drink.

Whether I travel to new places like Bolivia or to familiar places like Thailand, I see people hungry for the things that make for peace. As we learn those things I imagine us drying the tears of Jesus. I am keenly aware of Jesus weeping over all these places of violence and war, including my own country that throughout my life has always been at war somewhere. If our inability to see what makes for peace brings profound grief to the heart of God, then when we learn how to deal positively with our conflicts God must rejoice over us like a parent seeing a hard-to-teach child finally grasping the lesson.

My personal journey of peacemaking began when Christie confronted me with that inescapable question: "What did Jesus say?" My work as a preacher, teacher, and trainer has been to bring those words of Jesus to people in such a way that they could understand what Jesus was saying and could apply his words in real conflicts. The image of drying the tears of Jesus through this work has brought encouragement to my heart as I am coming closer to the end of my career than the beginning. Wiping away divine tears is a good legacy.

Spiritual Disciplines

"What did Jesus say?" was the question that started my peacemaking journey and gave shape to the place of Bible study in the training workshops I designed. That question was also a driving question for my personal struggles on the interior front. My Christian faith, understanding, and action have been shaped by regular reading of the Bible.

Beginning in my Wheaton College days, I read the Bible through many times, becoming familiar with the overall flow of the Scriptures as well as the themes of each book. I was a Bible major, so I delved deeply into the texts, supplemented by taking two years of New Testament Greek. Through all these studies, the teachings of Jesus became the lens through which I would interpret other passages, rather than *vice versa*.

On the question of war this interpretive starting point is critical. If Jesus is the ultimate interpretive lens, then loving one's enemies and nonviolence become central ethical components. The wars of the Hebrew Scriptures must be seen in light of the final revelation in Christ who gave his life in transforming love rather than destroying his enemies. Christian interpretations that accept violence as an appropriate action have to minimize Jesus' teaching in some way; some other theological theme—covenants, dispensations, or even political realism—trumps the clear radical statements of Jesus. For me, that was unacceptable. If Jesus is the Messiah, the one who reveals God to us, God incarnate in human flesh, then he is the point toward which all the other teachings of the Bible are either headed or from which they are coming.

My personal Bible study with a rigorous concern to examine the issues of war and peace prompted me to engage in a deep and thorough systematic study of the topic. From Genesis where conflict erupts between Adam and Eve in the third chapter, followed by Cain killing Abel in the fourth chapter, to Revelation 19 where Jesus wages war against the dragon and beast, I examined every teaching and story I could find related to war and peace. I systematized my discoveries in a Bible study guide that followed my hermeneutical principle of centering on Jesus. I began the study by examining the teachings and life of Jesus. Then I went on to the practice and writings of the early Christian community who had the freshest way of living out the teachings they had received. Then I examined the Old Testament teachings, finding a progressive development from God teaching Israel to trust in God as their Warrior to the prophetic visions of peace achieved by the sacrifice of the suffering servant. I used that Bible study at Dorchester Temple Baptist Church. When I went to National Ministries it was published in both English and Spanish as a resource that was distributed extensively.

Bible study is the easiest spiritual disciple for me as it appeals to my intellectual and activist sides. I am constantly reading, engaging ideas, and working on ways to implement what I believe must be done. Prayer, on the other hand, has been a challenge for me. My high energy levels make me skittish to get on with things rather than be still in prayer. My tendency has been to rush through whatever list of concerns needs to be covered with divine blessing, then bounce on to what really matters. I almost talk to God over my shoulder as I'm on to the next item on the activist agenda.

Back in my Dorchester days one of the church members, Scott Heald, was a mentor in prayer even as I perhaps encouraged him in action. We met regularly to eat lunch, talk, and pray. Scott introduced me to the Quaker Thomas Kelly and his *Testament of Devotion* (Harper, 1941). I was challenged by both Kelly and Scott to open myself to the presence of God in all that I did. I did not need to reject my activism, but rather to open myself up in my activity to the constant companionship of God. Or to turn things around, that God was the activist in the world inviting me to be a companion. I was joining the God who had been acting for justice and peace long before I arrived on the scene, who would be truly faithful compared to my wavering dedication, and who would be at work long after any memory of me had been blown away by the winds of history. I began letting prayer seep into my action, creating cracks of spiritual awareness.

Sharon also began to teach me about imaginative prayer and centering prayer, two forms of prayer she was discovering in her spiritual journey. I was not able to become a dedicated practitioner of either form of prayer, but I did learn enough to begin creating more space in my busy days for stillness with God in one form or another. I realized that the life of deep prayer was a weakness for me. I did not need to feel guilt over it, but I had discovered at least a taste of the blessing and power that could be tapped into through such prayer. I re-read Kelly and also discovered the writings of Brother Lawrence and Thomas Merton.

When I was working with National Ministries I wrote a booklet called *A Peacemaker's Journal*. The journal was a series of quotes on various aspects of the spiritual challenges for long-term peacemakers. Each quote was followed by extensive blank space for the reader-journaler to draw or to write prayers, reflections, or poetry. The journal came not from a source of strength but from my own struggle to connect to the deep wells that keep one energized for a life-long quest that is bound to fall short. I remembered a talk with a wonderful older peace activist who had lost hope because the world was still a very hostile place. I did not want to see my youthful zeal fade into aging despair. Just as there were old gnarled trees that could stand strong for centuries because of their deep roots, I wanted to have my roots deep enough to keep my spirit fresh, open to new discoveries, and connected to the One who holds the end as well as the beginning.

This did not come easy or naturally to me, so I searched for supports along the way.

During the Burma peace initiative I got to know the British Quaker John McConnell. John combined the kind of activism that I admired with the contemplative life that felt distant from me. We roomed together during the peace talks with the Burma opposition groups in Chiang Mai, Thailand, in June 1991. Throughout the talks I was impressed with John's wisdom in our mediation sessions. What impressed me more, however, was his daily discipline of prayer and meditation. Every morning he began with a long period of quiet. From this quietness of spirit centered on God came the depth of compassion and insight we all saw amid the complex and sometimes contentious discussions we had during the rest of the day. I longed for that type of spiritual calm and steadfastness.

My interior life was more ragged. Over the years my prayer life ebbed and flowed. Sometimes I felt closer to God and was able to maintain better disciplines of time for stillness and prayer. At other times I knew I was drawing down on my spiritual savings account. I was as active as ever, and to the eyes of the world, doing as well as ever. Inside, however, I knew that my life was drier than I desired or than was spiritually healthy. I was not drinking from the deep wells. My personal times of spiritual devotion, whenever I took the time, were often perfunctory, a brief panting stop as I rushed from one task to the next.

During one such time of inner dryness I stumbled into a divine appointment with Frank McAuley. While I was pastor in the Detroit area I was asked to lead a workshop at a prayer conference in Michigan. My workshop was on "Praying for Peace," such a perfect title for me! The workshop was scheduled to run twice, but when I got to the conference I found that one of the sessions had been cancelled due to a low number who had signed up for the workshop. I was stuck far from home with nothing else to do, so I scanned the workshop list. My old friend Frank was leading a workshop on "The Celtic Rule of Life." I had no idea what that meant, but I had known Frank from years earlier when he was the leader of the Baptist Peace Fellowship of Michigan. I thought, "Let's see what Frank's up to," and popped into his session with no deep concern or expectation. That moment was a major turning point in my inner journey.

Frank shared about the spirituality of the early Celtic Christians of northern England, Scotland, and Ireland. I was taken by their deep prayers that poetically praised the Triune God, echoed the praises of nature to God, and welcomed Christ's presence into every part of life and being. I was challenged by the marriage of prayer and activism in their ministries. I was also moved by the community base for their mission work, the relationships and accountability they had with one another. I discovered an ancient form of Christianity that in many ways pointed to how I could be a more faithful Christian in this contemporary age. Frank had introduced me to a heritage of faith with deep spirituality practiced by activist Christians. I felt I had discovered cool water in a land that had been parched too long.

Immediately after getting home I ordered a book Frank recommended, *Celtic Daily Prayer*, by the Northumbria Community in England (HarperCollins, 2002). Sharon and I began to pray the prayer book's daily liturgy, whether we were together or separated by an ocean. The daily liturgy became an important bond between us, knowing we were reading the same Scriptures and meditations and praying for the same concerns.

The heart of the morning prayer is a canticle inspired by the traditional "Deer's Cry" or "Patrick's Breastplate." As I have prayed its phrases day after day and year after year it has become a part of my way of thinking and feeling:

> Christ, as a light
> illumine and guide me.
> Christ, as a shield
> overshadow me.
> Christ under me;
> Christ over me;
> Christ beside me

on my left and my right.
This day be within and without me,
lowly and meek, yet all-powerful.
Be in the heart of each to whom I speak;
in the mouth of each who speaks unto me.
This day be within and without me,
lowly and meek, yet all-powerful.
Christ as a light;
Christ as a shield;
Christ beside me
on my left and my right.[1]

The repeated phrase "lowly and meek, yet all powerful" was a tremendous anchor for my spirit when I felt totally inadequate to some of the challenges I faced in my peacemaking travels. I knew I did not personally have what was needed to meet the challenge before me, but with Christ in me I could be creative and bring a gift of healing, grace, or transformative power to the situation. I was not alone but surrounded, kept, and empowered by the life-giving Christ. This discipline has been a great source of strength and has calmed the fears that would rise within me at times.

The closing blessing in the daily liturgy has also been especially meaningful:

May the peace of the Lord Christ go with you,
wherever He may send you.
May He guide you through the wilderness,
protect you through the storm.
May He bring you home rejoicing
at the wonders He has shown you.
May He bring you home rejoicing
once again into our doors. (p. 19)

---

[1] © 1990 Birdwing Music [ASCAP] EMI CMG Publishing Co., used with permission, pp. 18-19.

"Wherever He may send you" has covered a lot of territory for me over the past years! Some of those places have felt like wilderness areas, some have felt like storms. To keep this daily focus on the One who has sent me and accompanies me has helped me stay calm and centered even when plans fall apart and the unexpected becomes the norm. I have grown ever more confident that God is in those unexpected moments and crises. The last phrases tie me back to home and Sharon, my partner in life. However remote I may be I can think of that precious moment of return, coming through the door and receiving her embrace. I always have stories to tell of the wonders I have seen in people or experiences I've encountered. What will be that wonder, that story that is just beginning to unfold as I pray the liturgy in the morning in some distant land? That expectancy has grown in me through the discipline of daily prayer year after year. I feel as if I'm on my toes, ready to bound quickly in any direction as God calls me to deal with a new challenge each day.

Some of the challenges that unfold in the day bring a heavy weight of sorrow and disappointment. I hear stories of war's viciousness and heartbreak. I run into the hard walls of human stubbornness and fear. I make my own mistakes in spite of all the prayer and love that supports me, mistakes small or large that fill me with shame and self-critique. The evening prayers from *Celtic Daily Prayer*, which I don't pray quite as much as the morning prayers, have spoken powerfully to my heart again and again.

> Lord, You have always given
> bread for the coming day;
> and though I am poor,
> today I believe.

> Lord, You have always given
> strength for the coming day;
> and though I am weak,
> today I believe.

Lord, You have always given
peace for the coming day;
and though of anxious heart,
today I believe.

Lord, You have always kept me
safe in trials;
and now, tried as I am,
today I believe.

Lord, You have always marked
the road for the coming day;
and though it may be hidden,
today I believe.

Lord, You have always lightened
this darkness of mine;
and though the night is here,
today I believe.

Lord, You have always spoken
when time was ripe;
and though you be silent now,
today I believe.[2]

I have prayed that prayer following threats of violence. I have prayed that prayer following my own personal failures. I have prayed that prayer when I was confused and unsure of what to do next. I love the prayer's honesty and faith. Sometimes I have felt like the man who came to Jesus for the healing of his son and said, "I believe; help my unbelief" (Mark 9:24). This prayer has

---

[2] Reproduced from British Council of Churches' Week of Prayer for Christian Unity 1988 resource "The love of God casts out all fear" with permission from Churches Together in Britain and Ireland [CTBI], pp. 22-23.

helped me to hold the mix of faith and doubt before God, yet come down finally on the side of faith. "Today I believe"—I make that affirmation again and again. I also plead for God's help for my unbelief when I feel poor, weak, anxious, tried, lost, in the dark, and facing the silence of God. I believe I would have been worn down a long time ago without these disciplines of the spirit to anchor me to "a rock that is higher than I" (Ps 61:2).

Feelings and Support

When I began my first major international peacemaking venture, the Burma mediation, I felt I was in a situation completely over my head. I had been thrown into the deep end of the pool and could barely dog paddle, let alone swim. Saboi Jum had a trust in me that seemed more rooted in the historic saintly aura of Adoniram Judson than the person I knew myself to be, especially as a rookie at this major league level peacemaking initiative. Because I knew I couldn't deal with this challenge alone, I intentionally gathered two circles of support.

One circle of support was made up of American Baptist colleagues from National and International Ministries. I especially leaned on Keith Tennis, the area director of IM who covered Burma, and Pat Magdamo, IM's staff person responsible for social and political issues. Pat had been born in Burma, and her wisdom, guidance, and encouragement were especially helpful. This group was effective early on, but it fell apart during a major leadership transition at National Ministries. However, the advisory links have continued informally with key people who have knowledge of either the situation in Burma or of the institutional context in which I must work.

The second support group never met as such, but it played a critical role. I asked six people to pray for me and my involvement in the peace initiative. I knew that if they promised to pray for me they would be faithful to that commitment. Three of the people were from the BPFNA. They knew the situation in Burma and were passionate about peace. The other three people had no discernable involvement in peace issues, but I had very good relationships with them and trusted their commitment to the work of prayer. I called this group Gideon's Band after the Bible story of the small group God had Gideon recruit so that it would be clear that any victory achieved was due to God and not to human endeavor. Success in Burma would be a miracle, especially with my lack of understanding and experience. I sent the members of Gideon's Band periodic prayer updates, keeping them informed of my activities and upcoming key points in the process. The support of Gideon's Band enabled me to move forward with humble confidence. When my role in the Burma mediation project came to an end, I thanked the group and released them from their commitment.

My most profound support over the years has come from my wife and peacemaking companion, Sharon. We wrote our wedding vows and included a vow that we said as one to the assembled family and friends. We pledged, "Together we offer ourselves to God as a living sacrifice to be his ministers of reconciliation, seeking out those in need, not turning aside from any who ask." Throughout our marriage we have shared a sense of calling in God's service for our lives separately and together. Sharon has always encouraged me to step forward in faith rather than to hold back.

Many friends have commented about how courageous Sharon is to send me off to what are perceived as dangerous places. I tend to downplay the danger that people imagine because the work I do is seldom in the war zones themselves. Mediation venues are chosen specifically because all parties view them as safe spaces, as neutral zones. Training also usually takes place in settings that are apart from the severe conflict, quiet spots where people can relax a bit and enter fully into the educational experience. Sharon, on the other hand, works every day in a neighborhood with a high crime rate. She is the only one of us who has had the business end of a gun pointed at her in a threatening way. She has the same passion for her urban ministry and community transformation work as I have for my peacemaking work. We both know the fear of parting, which we intentionally overlay with our blessing and prayer. We regularly trust each other into God's hands.

I have often been able to share in Sharon's urban ministry. My nine years of being an urban pastor and community activist in Boston gave me first-hand experience and a love for that kind of work. We lived for eleven years just off the notorious Eight Mile Road that separates predominately black working-class and poor Detroit from predominately white working-class Warren. That neighborhood is a place where the races mix, for the most part peacefully but without much bonding or community cohesiveness. Now we live in Hamtramck, an incredibly diverse, largely immigrant community that is completely surrounded by Detroit. I have a good feel for the day-to-day context of Sharon's ministry because I live it with her when I'm not traveling.

It has been harder for Sharon to have that feel for my context of ministry. We have had many international peacemakers as guests in our house, including Saboi Jum and Wati Aier. Friends like Ken Sehested and Daniel Hunter often have stayed with us and sat around the table sharing stories and making plans. I've brought home photos and told stories. In the earlier years of my travels I would make maybe one phone call per trip to stay in touch. The advent of e-mail allowed for almost daily contact and a richer, fuller sharing of the details of each day's events. Still, I felt a gap between my experiences and the understanding of my life companion, and because of our closeness in every other part of our lives this gap brought a dull ache to my heart. We had no money to buy Sharon international plane tickets, so we had to be content with whatever form of communication was available to keep in touch while apart and to share the story when we were reunited.

When I began my work with International Ministries this changed. In 2003 Sharon received a sabbatical grant that enabled her to travel outside North America for the first time in her life. She traveled across Europe, spending most of her time in Poland, including many days with the Polish Baptists. During that time she worked with Ryszard Gutkowski, a Baptist involved in urban social ministry in Warsaw and Bialystok. Together they laid the plans for the first-ever Social Ministry Conference for Baptists in Poland. Sharon returned to Poland with me in 2004, and together we were the resource people for the conference. Through her travels alone she experienced much of what I have gone through in discovering new places, new cultures, and new friends. She now knew first hand the disorienting challenge of travel in a country where you don't know the language. When she returned she told me that she understood so much better what I go through in my travels.

Once I was working full-time with International Ministries, my frequent flyer miles piled up, and we could used these miles to buy tickets for Sharon to join me on one trip a year. Because of her own skills in conflict transformation, community ministries, trauma recovery, and experiential education, she could join me as a co-facilitator in the training programs. Following our trip to Poland to lead in the Social Ministry Conference, we led trainings together in Thailand, northeast India, Italy, Ethiopia, Kenya, Burma, and the Philippines. We experienced together the pathos of listening to heart-rending stories, the joy of seeing new ideas and skills electrify people facing huge challenges, and the tension of waiting at military checkpoints while our papers were checked by soldiers our friends viewed as an oppressive, occupying force. She knew what it was like to stay in a two-thirds-world context, to not use tap water to brush your teeth, and to get violently ill from bad food or water far from home. She knew the awe of seeing a glorious landscape unlike anything in the U.S., the mental haze of severe jet lag, and the laughter and grace of trying to communicate across languages. I felt a deeper connection to Sharon simply knowing that she shared these experiences from my international work first-hand. She could do more than listen with an empathetic and supportive ear as I related my various adventures; she could feel with me. Even when I came back from a solo trip, our sharing of stories and experiences was much deeper and fuller.

I have occasionally felt fear in my journeys. It took a night of prayer in Liberia to face the fear that welled up as I thought of doing nonviolence training in a context dominated by Charles

Taylor's henchmen. I was robbed once in the wee hours of the night when I arrived jet-lagged in Mumbai (formerly known as Bombay) and was steered to a dishonest cab driver. I was able to stay calm enough to master my anger and get out of the cab with my bags minus some money rather than see the situation deteriorate on lonely streets. I've known the anxiety of being detained by soldiers or armed officials for interrogation as I entered or departed certain countries or restricted areas. I am always honest, but I don't offer what isn't asked! I recall acting calm during the bomb scare at the hotel in the Philippines, then shaking when I was alone at night in a typical physical release of traumatic stress.

These fears have been assuaged by God's mercy as I have prayed and by the expressions of support in prayer by a circle of family and friends. An image has spoken to this peace warrior out of a Bible war-story to give me peace amid the threats of violence. Exodus 17:8-13 tells about the battle of the Israelites with the Amelekites. As long as Moses stood over the battlefield with his rod raised in the air, Israel prevailed, but as the day grew long Moses wearied. When his arm holding the rod sagged in fatigue, Israel began to lose. Aaron and Hur stood beside him and held up his arms when he could no longer do it himself. When I have felt overwhelmed by fear or any other powerful emotion, I imagine all those friends and loved ones praying for me, holding me up like Aaron and Hur held up Moses. That circle of prayer support means a great deal to me, so I in turn encourage those faithful supporters by telling them of specific needs or challenges and then later sharing the stories of how God answered our prayers.

I have felt a different kind of fear, though, which can easily strike those who give their lives to the work of making the world a better place. What if all our work is undone? What if everything that people of good will try to do is destroyed by the foolishness, the vanity, or the arrogance of people in power? Someone pushes the button, and nuclear weapons incinerate all the hard labors of peacemakers. We work for ten years on a delicate peace and reconciliation process only to have it all blown apart by an assassin's bullet or a terror bomb blast. We pick up litter, recycle waste, and try to live responsibly in the world only to see the planet get warmer and warmer because of our insatiable lust for oil and short-sighted political leaders. The fear is that for all our efforts the future will be worse than the past, or perhaps that we humans will have no future at all. The fear is that all is in vain.

For me this deeper fear has been countered by three witnesses. The first witness I met was Dietrich Bonhoeffer, the German theologian who was executed by Hitler for being part of the German resistance. The fear of what the future will hold can be countered with cynicism, a feeling I knew well in the early 1970s as I was discovering how badly national political leaders and even religious leaders could act. The cynic makes philosophical or even comedic observations that give the speaker a sense of moral superiority with no responsibility for acting for what is good, right, and just. Cynicism turns fear of the future into a swagger and a sneer, and it is very tempting for anyone who feels the pain of what is wrong with the world. I fell to that temptation during my senior year in college. Then I stumbled across a line from Bonhoeffer's *Letters and Papers from Prison* that changed my life: "Anyone who tells the truth cynically is lying" (Macmillan 1971, p. 163). The cynic ignores the presence and action of God in the present and the future. So whatever the cynic says is not the full truth but a deliberate ignorance of the most crucial part of the truth. Bonhoeffer, speaking from a Gestapo cell and under the looming shadow of his own martyrdom, refused to give in to cynicism. I knew I had to hold onto enough faith to let God always hold the bleak present and the clouded future.

The second witness was an indigenous Ecuadoran whose name I forgot but whose witness is burned into my soul. I met him in 1990, the week after the Sandinista government in Nicaragua was voted out of power by the U.S.-backed UNO coalition. I had worked long and hard with many people to support a popular revolution that had dared to stand up for national self-determination in the face of brutal U.S. political and military pressure that tried to crush the hope rising from Latin America. I was not under any illusion that the Sandinistas were a great government, but they were far better than anything the Nicaraguans had experienced before and were certainly far better than the vicious regimes in Guatemala, El Salvador, and Honduras supported by massive U.S. military aid. To see how the Nicaraguan people were ground down through war weariness under the U.S. "low intensity conflict" made me heartsick. It was my first experience of major defeat in something I had believed in and worked for passionately.

That's when I attended a workshop led by an indigenous man from Ecuador. He confronted directly the despair that my friends and I felt. He spoke of the five hundred years of struggle since the Europeans invaded his homeland. We were tasting our first defeat, but he and his people had known centuries of heartache and oppression. Still, here he was full of hope that was a source of energy driving him to maintain the struggle for justice. He told me that his people thought of their actions in terms of the good they were doing for the seventh generation. I had known immigrants who sacrificed so their children could have a better life, but his long-range vision of the fruit of our labors helped me to lift up my despairing eyes. We live and act not to serve ourselves or even bring God's peace and justice in our time but to make life better for the seventh generation from now. We take a small step now, which will make the journey easier for those coming behind us.

Ken Sehested, my old friend from the Baptist Peace Fellowship, is the third witness. He told about how most of our peacemaking was like growing pumpkins. Pumpkins are annuals; you sow the seed in the spring and harvest the fruit that fall. Most of our peace campaigns—the nuclear freeze, Contra aid, the B-1 bomber, the "Star Wars" outer space defense shield, the war in Iraq—are short-term. They are the hot topic in the news for a year or two or three. Campaigns are mobilized, action taken, victories achieved, or losses suffered. The most important peacemaking tasks we do—raising our children to deal in a just and peaceful way with their conflicts—are more like planting date trees. Ken told us that date trees take so long to come to fruit-bearing maturity that the farmer who plants a tree often has died before that tree's fruit can be enjoyed (my Yemeni friends in Hamtramck have confirmed this). The farmer plants date trees for succeeding generations, not for himself. None of us would be able to relish dates if people had not planted in a hope beyond themselves. We need that hope if the best peace-work is to be done now for the sake of our children, grandchildren, and the generations to follow.

The witness of Bonhoeffer, the Ecuadoran Indian, and Ken are all echoes of the hope in the Biblical message. In Revelation, the Apostle John rejoiced in hope even though he was sitting in exile on the rocky island of Patmos under the power of one of the most brutal emperors of the massive Roman Empire. John saw a vision of Jesus who is the Alpha and Omega, the beginning and the end. History, even with all its terrifying and destructive apocalyptic horsemen, does not have the last word. God's redeeming work is the last word. All we do now is held in that embrace of Christ's beginning and end. If Bonhoeffer, Ken, indigenous folk from the Andes, and the aged exile John could find hope, then I and all my peacemaking colleagues can find hope as well. The empires will not win; they will all go the way of proud Ozymandias (and who was he whose moldering visage the poet Shelley contemplated?).[3] I just need to tend to myself, that I

---

[3] I met a traveler from an antique land
Who said: Two vast and trunkless legs of stone
Stand in the desert. Near them, on the sand,
Half sunk, a shattered visage lies, whose frown,
And wrinkled lip, and sneer of cold command,
Tell that its sculptor well those passions read
Which yet survive, stamped on these lifeless things,
The hand that mocked them, and the heart that fed;
And on the pedestal these words appear:
"My name is Ozymandias, king of kings:
Look on my works, ye Mighty, and despair!"
Nothing beside remains. Round the decay

stay rooted in the messages of hope no matter what today's headlines proclaim.

Mentors and the Next Generation

Daniel Hunter, Ron Kraybil and I were sitting around a table in a restaurant in Guwahati, India. We were facilitating a four-day conflict transformation seminar, the first time we had worked together in an educational context. Daniel was eighteen, making his first international training trip. Ron and I talked wistfully about the learning opportunities Daniel had already received and that were still available for him. When I was in college there were no peace study courses, no degrees in conflict resolution, no academic departments packed with experienced and intellectually astute practitioners. As I told Ron, we were making this stuff up. How I wish I had the opportunity to study today!

Of course, I did not learn in a void. I have read avidly and extensively, and garnered as much knowledge as I could in conflict studies through short-term courses and training seminars. None of us comes to a position in life without someone who guided us along the way. Ka Tong Gaw was a professor at Wheaton College in sociology. Sharon took his class on racism that was structured with an experiential education foundation. The class began with an exposure to the realities of life in Chicago, the first steps in Sharon's radicalization and journey toward urban ministry. Our senior year we worked closely with Ka Tong, absorbing his deep questioning of what was going on in the world and a radical commitment to faith that engaged social issues.

In seminary Stephen Mott became my next intellectual mentor. He taught social ethics. I took most of the classes he offered and worked as his student assistant. His classes always included a practicum in community work, taking the ideas we were studying into the struggles of the real world. For his classes I worked in an advocacy organization, helping with some of the mundane tasks that are the basics for success in every political

---

Of that colossal wreck, boundless and bare
The lone and level sands stretch far away.

movement. I studied the community organizations of one of the small, declining industrial centers in Massachusetts, which enabled me to understand the institutional opportunities and challenges related to community transformation. Steve was also rooted in biblical teaching, reinforcing my belief that working for justice and peace was not a so-called "liberal" or "humanist" agenda but was God's agenda and received more attention in the Scriptures than almost any other topic.

When I arrived in Boston, Father Robert Branconnier became my mentor in peacemaking. He taught me about faithfulness in witness. I saw his courage in making solitary witness. He practiced Jesus' mustard seed perspective that God's reign comes through actions that may seem small and insignificant at first, so we need to be diligent and dedicated in those small actions outside the attention of the majority of the world.

As I moved into more leadership positions, my mentors were people who perhaps thought of me as a peer. In the Baptist Peace Fellowship George Williamson, Ken Sehested, Paul Dekar, Paul Hayes, and Glen Stassen stood out. We worked together on the BPFNA board, sharing rooms together in travels near and far and working side by side in many struggles. At times I was in awe of their experience and insight, and I soaked up what they said like a sponge. George, a veteran of the civil rights lunch counter sit-ins, challenged me with his outside-the-box thinking and understanding of the revolutionary humor of God. Glen taught me the concept of transforming initiatives in Jesus' Sermon on the Mount and provided a role model of someone who thoroughly practiced the reconciling message he preached, even in the most mundane contexts. Paul Dekar opened me up to the vast cloud of witnesses we have in our heritage of peace and justice "saints." Paul Hayes pushed the boundaries of being a peace activist pastor, never losing a pastor's heart for the people even as he gave his heart to suffering people around the world. Ken was our prophetic poet, driving us all on by his creative thinking and his willingness to put himself on the line again and again. There were many others with whom I shared so much. The network of religious peace activists became my emotional and spiritual home.

George Lakey, founder of Training for Change, revolutionized my teaching methods. Sharon took his Training of Social Action Trainers workshop one weekend and said it was more profound than anything she learned in her seminary training or her master of social work program. She insisted that I take the workshop, so I did just before we moved to Detroit. I repeated that workshop two more times and finished the three week workshop course George calls "The Super-T." These workshops taught the principles, practices, and tools of experiential education, a form of participatory education that empowers the learner to become a change agent in society. The educational methodology puts justice and peacemaking values into the way we engage in learning and teaching. But more than the educational philosophy and methodology, I learned from George's strength of vision, non-defensive openness, and joy as an activist. Sharon would often face challenging situations with the question "What would George do?" His creative application of nonviolence prompted us to get outside the constraining boxes of our programmed responses to conflicts. George gave us a host of flesh-and-blood examples of people who lived out the biblical injunction to "overcome evil with good." He spurred our imagination and confidence in our own capacity to act creatively.

"You have to reproduce yourself," Sharon told me. So many people helped to shape me. I needed to help prepare the next generations for their leadership roles in peacemaking. Just as my African-American pastor friends could identify their "sons and daughters in the ministry," I needed to be able to identify people who were taking on my gifts and vision, mixing them with their own creativity and calling, and taking the work of peace into the decades ahead.

I have sought to encourage and support peacemakers developing their gifts in training and leadership by providing counsel and coaching, by pointing toward educational opportunities and resources, and by working together as a training team. Some of those I've been mentoring have been younger activists while others have been people closer to me in age who are sensing a new call to work in conflict transformation. Some are from the U.S., while others are from countries where I've worked over the years. I have been able to share training facilitation as a way to mentor through experience these younger activists.

Akum Longchari is a bright, intense Naga human rights activist. He participated in the two training workshops I held for the Naga civil society groups in Calcutta in 1999. He earned a master's degree in conflict transformation at Eastern Mennonite University. He began conducting his own workshops around Nagaland with the Naga Peoples' Movement for Human Rights. We eventually had the opportunity to co-facilitate a three-day training for Isak and Muviah's insurgent group on conflict resolution and negotiations. Akum and I have consulted frequently with each other, appreciative of the insights we each bring to a struggle that means so much to us. Now he is a leading force in the Forum for Naga Reconciliation, helping shape in a positive way the history of his people.

The person from the rising generation with whom I've shared the most is Daniel Hunter. Daniel attended a conflict transformation training I led during four afternoons of the BPFNA's summer conference one year. He was fourteen years old at the time. When the training had concluded he said, "This is what I want to do with my life." We discussed some of the steps he could take to prepare for that career. He enrolled in Earlham University when he was sixteen, then took a year off when he was seventeen to attend "The Super-T" at Training for Change, travel with an Indonesian anti-sweatshop labor activist, and conduct workshops at campuses around the country, as well as a number of other experiences to stretch and shape his thinking. When I was planning a training trip to northeast India, Daniel, who was also serving on the BPFNA board as a representative from "The Next Generation," asked if he could go with me as a trainer. He was still a teenager, which would give many people pause, but Daniel was extremely gifted and had already gone through more training in experiential education than I had. He also had quite a bit of experience leading workshops. I welcomed him to join me.

Before our trip we spent two days together designing our toolbox (see ch. 7) and working out the understanding for our relationship. We decided together that he would not be an apprentice, but a co-facilitator. We would be a team, and I would support him in the face of social customs that devalue youth, especially in Asian cultures that place a high value on elders. I quickly came to trust his skill in facilitating group processes. Again and again, key turning points in our workshops happened because of Daniel's adept reading of the group and pushing them to break through at their points of greatest challenge. I know that I taught him many things about faith and peacemaking, but I was his student, too.

Daniel and I traveled together so much that we developed the ability to communicate in the middle of training sessions just by looking at one another. We knew when the other needed help, and we knew when to relax even when the other was doing some tough group facilitation. Through all the long flights, waits in airports, meals together, jolting car trips down deep-rutted roads, Daniel and I shared many, many stories. When he said to me, "You've told me that story before," I thought I was hearing my wife talk. It was delightful payback when I could throw that line back at him as he was winding up for a tale he'd already told me!

From our initial travels to Asia, Daniel went on to the staff of Training for Change. Daniel became one of the trainers in their network, helping to lead portions of "The Super-T" and other activist workshops. He and George Lakey collaborated on the 200-page curriculum for the three-week intensive training of the Nonviolent International Peace Force, a nonviolent, non-governmental counterpart to U.N. peacekeepers. Daniel also did independent work, leading training programs for the anti-globalization movement and consulting on the design of a massive and humorously creative protest campaign for the Canadian postal workers union. He provided creative leadership for a grassroots struggle against bringing casinos into Philadelphia. I was privileged in 2006 to finish my own participation in the Super-T with Daniel as one of the co-facilitators guiding me in my learning. After George Lakey retired, Daniel became a co-director of Training for Change. Wherever his activist journey will take him in the years ahead, I'm sure he will make an impact for justice and peace with creativity, joy, and passion.

For my fiftieth birthday Sharon presented me with an oil portrait. The painting was of Daniel and me taken from a photo when we had received beautiful red and black wool shawls from our Naga activist friends. I am a half step in front of Daniel, but Sharon also painted me slightly to the edge of the canvas. I'm in the lead but my time is coming soon to move off the stage. Daniel is moving toward that center. Sharon's gift moved me to joyous tears. Others are taking on the work that I've been doing, and they will go much further than I have. I received the baton from those who went before me. I've been running my leg of the race for many years. Now I'm running step for step with those who will lead for the next portion. We are together, holding the baton as we share the race. I'll be letting go soon to cheer my teammates on with their fresh legs and fresh hearts. That's the way it has always been. None of us run this race alone; it takes a community spanning the generations.

Fading Away?

When General Douglas MacArthur was appropriately relieved of his command in Korea by President Truman, he gave a farewell address to the U.S. Congress. Referring to an old military ballad, MacArthur said, "Old soldiers never die, they just fade away." Old peace warriors need not fade away. One of the advantages of being a peace warrior is that different demands are made on the peace warrior than on military personnel. Old soldiers may move into other careers or sit around in legion halls swapping stories with other vets. They may show up with their beribboned chests for holiday parades and memorial ceremonies. Combat requires young bodies to deal with the stress and strain of life-threatening massive violence. But old peace warriors can stay active to the very end.

A peace warrior who died too young and has never faded away, Dr. Martin Luther King Jr., spoke in his book *Why We Can't Wait* (NAL, 1963) about the demands and equal opportunity for the nonviolent army:

A nonviolent army has a magnificent universal quality. To join an army that trains its adherent in the methods of violence, you must be of a certain age. But in Birmingham, some of the most valued foot soldiers were youngsters ranging from elementary pupils to teen-age high school and college students. For acceptance in the armies that maim and kill, one must be physically sound, possessed of straight limbs and accurate vision. But in Birmingham, the lame and the halt and the crippled could and did join up.... In the nonviolent army, there is room for everyone who wants to join up. There is no color distinction. There is no examination, no pledge, except that, like a soldier in the armies of violence, you are expected to inspect your carbine and keep it clean. Nonviolent soldiers are called upon to examine and burnish their greatest weapons— their heart, their conscience, their courage and their sense of justice. (pp.38-39)

I have been blessed to witness many of the older peace warriors who have continued to be active long into what many think of as the years of retirement. Helen Delano, a retired missionary, was in her seventies when she went to Honduras to accompany Salvadoran refugees as they returned to their home village. Olive Tiller, a board member of the BPFNA, spent weeks as a volunteer working with women in a refugee camp who had fled the wars as Yugoslavia disintegrated. Norman Kember, a leader in the Baptist Peace Fellowship in Great Britain, joined a Christian Peacemaking Team delegation in Iraq when he was seventy-four. He was determined to step up his peace witness from the protest demonstrations in front of the prime minister's office. He was kidnapped by Iraqi insurgents along with three other team members, one of whom, Tom Fox, was executed by their captors. These are just a few of the elders I have known who have continued or even increased their peace activism in retirement.

When I head to the airport for another flight across an ocean I feel like the aging football player who gets up from the ground and slowly moves back to the huddle. You can see the aches and pains in that battered body. Then the ball is snapped, and the old star moves once again with grace that befuddles the opposition and delights the fans. I wonder how long I can keep up the fatiguing pace of international travel, pushing through the protests of my body. Ah, but then I meet my friends struggling for justice and peace. I start training with a new group hungry to learn "the things that make for peace." The adrenaline of the struggle is pumped back into my blood, and I know I'm not ready to quit yet.

As long as I have breath and brain I need not quit. I'm sure the day will come when I will have to tone down my travels. I will have to "retire," but there is no need to fade away. The nonviolent army still will need people to write letters, vigil, and march. I will joyfully continue doing that. The nonviolent army will still need people to teach and pass on the wisdom gained from many years of struggle. My role may change, but my calling will continue. I can still burnish those weapons of heart, conscience, courage, and sense of justice needed by the nonviolent army.

Even if my body gives out I can still be a peace warrior. My grandmother, Francena Arnold, was known as a "prayer warrior." She would pray for people around the world. My grandfather, Frank Arnold, had been the business manager at Northern Baptist Theological Seminary in Chicago. They had nurtured many young people who returned to their home countries to serve as church leaders or people who left to U.S. to become missionaries in distant lands. Grandma and Grandpa prayed faithfully and diligently for those who had received their hospitality. It was said that the sun never set on people being prayed for by the Arnolds. When Grandma was confined to her home because of her physical frailties, she continued in her prayers, including praying for her young grandson who came to study at Wheaton College nearby. I marveled at her faith and her wonderfully tough spirit. If my lot is to be frail and in bed my last years, Grandma will be my role model of a warrior who keeps on as long as there is breath in the body. I will pray for the peacemakers, especially that new rising generation who will be taking the torch from those I mentored. I will watch the news and pray for those who are not mentioned but are working for peace behind the scenes. I will know they are there because I was there. I live and labor in hope because of the promise of God. The Hebrew prophets proclaimed a vision that is engraved in my heart:

> They shall beat their swords into plowshares,
> and their spears into pruning hooks;
> nation shall not lift up sword against nation,
> neither shall they learn war any more....
> (from Isaiah 2)

> For I am about to create new heavens
> and a new earth:
> the former things shall not be remembered
> or come to mind.
> But be glad and rejoice forever
> in what I am creating...
> No more shall there be in it
> an infant that lives but a few days,
> or an old person who does not live out a lifetime...
> They shall build houses and inhabit them;
> they shall plant vineyards and eat their fruit.
> They shall not build and another inhabit;
> they shall not plant and another eat;
> for like the days of a tree shall the days of my people be,
> and my chosen shall long enjoy the works of their hands.
> They shall not labor in vain,
> or bear children for calamity;

for they shall be offspring blessed by the Lord—
and their descendants as well.
Before they call I will answer,
while they are yet speaking I will hear.
The wolf and the lamb shall feed together,
the lion shall eat straw like the ox;
but the serpent—its food shall be dust!
They shall not hurt or destroy
on all my holy mountain.
(from Isaiah 65)

When that day comes I will gladly lay down my calling.

Ken Sehested with Atem from the NSCN-IM at Naga reconciliation
talks in Chiang Mai

The author hoisted on the shoulders of students at the Arab
Baptist Theological Seminary in Lebanon following the completion
of the peacemaking course he taught there

Author presents the Dahlberg Peace Award from the
American Baptist Churches to Ken Sehested

Author and Daniel Hunter received traditional shawls from leaders of the Naga
Peoples Movement for Human Rights

APPENDIX 1:

JOURNEY ON HOLY GROUND

What follows is a version of a presentation that began percolating in me following visits to the Peace Park in Hiroshima and the Yad Vashem Holocaust Memorial in Jerusalem. The first version appeared as an article titled "A Shadow Over Holy Ground" in The Baptist Peacemaker in summer 1995 to commemorate the fiftieth anniversary of the bombing of Hiroshima. In October 1999 I was invited to address the American Baptist Churches' Public Mission Team (PMT) at a consultation held in Boston. The theme was "Grounded in Hope: Discerning God's Presence Amid Conflict and Violence." In addition to my visits to Hiroshima and Yad Vashem, I wove in experiences related to a couple visits to the Lorain Motel in Memphis with the board of the Baptist Peace Fellowship.

Following the September 11, 2001, terrorist attacks I reworked the presentation for the first anniversary commemoration at Prairie Baptist Church in Prairie Village, Kansas. That version was later published in a revised interfaith form in September/October 2003 issue of Fellowship magazine for the Fellowship of Reconciliation.

I've chosen to include the Public Mission Team version in this book because it deals directly with more of my experiences than the other versions, and it has never been published in this form.

"Journey on Holy Ground"

Text: Exodus 3:1-10 NRSV

Moses was keeping the flock of his father-in-law Jethro, the priest of Midian; he led his flock beyond the wilderness, and came to Horeb, the mountain of God. There the angel of the LORD appeared to him in a flame of fire out of a bush; he looked, and the bush was blazing, yet it was not consumed. Then Moses said, "I must turn aside and look at this great sight, and see why the bush is not burned up." When the LORD saw that he had turned aside to see, God called to him out of the bush, "Moses, Moses!" And he said, "Here I am." Then he said, "Come no closer! Remove the sandals from your feet, for the place on which you are standing is holy ground." He said further, "I am the God of your father, the God of Abraham, the God of Isaac, and the God of Jacob." And Moses hid his face, for he was afraid to look at God.

Then the LORD said, "I have observed the misery of my people who are in Egypt; I have heard their cry on account of their taskmasters. Indeed, I know their sufferings, and I have come down to deliver them from the Egyptians, and to bring them up out of that land to a good and broad land, a land flowing with milk and honey, to the country of the Canaanites, the Hittites, the Amorites, the Perizzites, the Hivites, and the Jebusites. The cry of the Israelites has now come to me; I have also seen how the Egyptians oppress them. So come, I will send you to Pharaoh to bring my people, the Israelites, out of Egypt.

The theme of this consultation is "Grounded in Hope: Discerning God's Presence amid Conflict and Violence." In his message in the consultation brochure, Hector Cortez writes about the holy ground we can find amid settings of conflict and violence. Some Mennonite conflict resolution practitioners have spoken of conflict itself as "holy ground." Tonight I would like to work on that theme of holy ground, particularly bridging the sub-themes of today and tomorrow, namely the roots of violence and redemption.

I am particularly grateful for the invitation to come to this PMT consultation. As a former staff person with National Ministries and a former member of the PMT, it's always good to be with you, my friends and colleagues. I'm particularly glad to be in Boston. This is my old stomping ground, the only place in my life I have known as home in the richest sense of that word. Dorchester Temple, where we will go tomorrow, is the church I once was blessed to pastor.

But my unique perspective to bring to bear on this consultation is that from my experience. I bridge the global and the local in terms of conflict and violence. I have worked on issues of local violence, particularly urban violence. I have also worked on issues of international violence and civil wars across the globe. So allow me to bring that global perspective to bear on our journey together.

Violence may be, as Jesse Jackson has said, part of the American lifestyle, but violence is not American. I have seen the horrors of violence on every continent and witnessed its scars upon people of many different cultures and countries. Violence is a human phenomenon, something that should not surprise us as Christians rooted in the biblical story.

So let us take a journey to Holy Ground. I've been on Holy Ground. I've experienced it. I've been to places that speak as archetypes of violence in our world. Every place was a place of conflict, awful, dreadful conflict. But in each place I sensed I was on Holy Ground.

Holy Ground. Ground Zero. As I stood in Hiroshima's Peace Memorial Park looking at the stark ruin of the domed building over which the bomb exploded, I sensed a bit of the horror of that day in August 1945 when nuclear weapons were first used against other human beings.

There is a statue of Sadako Sasaki, the girl who died from leukemia following the bombing. Thousands of brightly colored paper cranes lovingly laid at the base of the statue commemorate her prayer for peace and healing. A mass grave with the ashes of ten thousand people stretched my imagination beyond its capacity. The most emotionally ripping moment for me was to look at a burned, empty school uniform, knowing in an instant the terrible fate of the child who put the uniform on that morning. As an American walking through this Japanese park, grief and tears were my constant companions. I was on Holy Ground.

Holy Ground, Yad Vashem. Yad Vashem is the Holocaust memorial in Jerusalem. The eternal flame burns over a stark black surface with the names sculpted in metal: Auschwitz, Bergen-Belsen, Terezen Stadt, Babi Yar, Dachau, Treblinka, Ravensbruk, Buchenwald. Six million Jews perished in an extended and systematic act of genocide, but each was a person with a name. Each was a person loved by others. Names are important at Yad Vashem, part of the remembering. There is a special place for families and friends to list the names of their loved ones in the memorial.

The pictures in the historical museum were familiar to me, but it was the art that revealed the heart of both the horror and the determination to survive. *All That Remained* is the title of the work that tore my soul: a sculpture of a pile of shoes—women's shoes, men's shoes, children's shoes. All that remained. In the museum a single shoe of a child made the work of art even more graphic. That shoe was not a work of art, but an artifact, the shoe of a real child with a real name who vanished into the ovens. The shoes had been removed not in respect of God but in brutal violation of God's image in Jews and the millions of others viewed as unfit to live by the Nazi regime.

For all its horror, I was standing on Holy Ground.

Holy Ground. The Lorraine Motel. I entered the National Civil Rights Museum in Memphis. As you first step in, you are greeted by a massive work of art, ebony as the people it celebrates in their struggle for freedom. You look at the newsreels, the photos, hear the sounds on the tapes. You step on a bus. It's all another museum until you enter an ordinary motel room, like so many I've stayed in—bed, nightstand, low dresser, bathroom to the side. You are drawn to the open door at the balcony. You remember the photo of men pointing to a distant building while at their feet Martin Luther King, Jr.'s lifeblood poured onto the concrete. Holy Ground.

These places, and so many others like them, are Holy Ground. For from these places there is an echo heard from an ancient patch of soil. From these places we can hear the blood cry out even as the blood cried out from the ground when Abel was murdered by his brother Cain. The Holy Ground cries out with the blood of the slain. These places, places of conflict, places of violence, places of death are also places of Holy Ground because here God's image is seen. God's stamp has been placed upon our humanity. It is the essence of our very being as humans. And so when violence seeks to erase a human being by an act of murder, what God has put upon us, that divine stamp, that divine image, that divine reflection of the glory of the Creator cries out. God's image within us will not be silenced no matter what Cain and all his violent progeny may do. Holy Ground.

But there is a shadow over Holy Ground. These holy places are not pure places. The shadow comes not from the violence that shed the blood but from the human beings much like us who raised the memorials.

Holy Ground. Ground Zero. At Hiroshima twenty thousand Korean slave laborers perished in the bombing. Japanese racism toward Koreans had led to invasion of the Korean peninsula, the exploitation of Korean people, and the sexual enslavement of tens of thousands of Korean women. Thirty thousand Korean laborers worked in Hiroshima in August 1945, and twenty thousand of them died. Following the bombing of Hiroshima, the Korean dead were not buried but were piled up to be left as carrion for the birds to devour.

When the Koreans wanted to build a memorial for their dead in Hiroshima, it was not included in the Peace Park itself but is across a river from the park. Though the intersection is on the tourist maps, and many less significant points of interest are noted, there is no indication of the Korean memorial on any of the guide maps. The shadow of racism has crept into the Holy Ground where 100,000 human beings were slaughtered.

Holy Ground. Vad Vashem. The historical story of the Holocaust in the museum at Yad Vashem concludes with the achievement of independence by Israel. The awful story of genocide against Jewish people finds its ending in the establishment of their own homeland, but there is silence on the cost of Israeli independence for Palestinian people. Palestinian villages were razed and hundreds of thousands fled into exile or into refugee camps. Massacres took place to create the "empty" land into which Jewish settlers could move.

None of this is mentioned at Yad Vashem. For many people it seems the power of the Holocaust memory drives the Israeli occupation of the West Bank and Gaza, an occupation that continues to see Palestinians driven from their land, imprisoned without charge, tortured, and killed, an occupation that still covers the majority of Palestinian territory. Yad Vashem speaks eloquently of the horrors inflicted upon Jewish people in Europe, but for Zionists seeking to expand Israeli territory the memorial feeds the current horror inflicted upon Palestinians. There is a shadow over this Holy Ground.

Holy Ground. The Lorraine Motel. Since 1968 the Lorraine Motel fell on hard times. It became a seedy home for those one razor-thin step up from homelessness. Jackie Smith lived there. She lived there until the day all the residents were forced to leave because construction on the new civil rights museum was going to start. She refused to leave, so the police carried her out and dumped her on the street. Jackie set up a pup tent on the sidewalk, refusing to budge. Friends and supporters brought her food. After a year of housekeeping on the sidewalk, the city of Memphis passed an ordinance banning tents on the sidewalk. Jackie set up a chair with an umbrella to keep off the hot sun and the rain.

I met her and talked with her. She spoke movingly of Dr. King's love for the poor, for people like her. "Dr. King would never throw me out of my home," she protested. Last I heard Jackie was still camped there, only she had been forcibly removed to a spot across the street from the new museum. Right there she continues her nonviolent action, her solitary witness for justice for the poor. At the Lorraine Motel where we honor that great martyr for the poor and oppressed, a poor woman lost her shelter. A shadow over this Holy Ground.

What do these shadows over Holy Ground say to us? What do these places in their complexity tell us about the roots of violence? We want the roots of violence to be like a dandelion root, one big long taproot that may be deep and tough, but you can dig it out, yank it out with one big pull. We want to identify the evil ones, whether great historical figures like Hitler, Stalin, Pol Pot, and Idi Amin, or our local figures of evil, the gang-bangers, muggers, wife-beaters, rapists, and killers in our schools.

Newsweek had a recent cover with a picture of Slobodan Milosevic with the title, "The Face of Evil" (19 April, 1999). Don't we wish it was as simple as that? As we look at the shadows over Holy Ground, I see a far more complex picture. Rather than a simple taproot for violence, I see a massive tangle of roots reaching in many directions, into our souls and our society. The roots of violence are entwined around so much, not just what is blatantly evil, but also around much that we hold in high esteem.

Let's look again at this cover from *Newsweek*. It's true that Milosevic is *the face of evil*. But it's also true that Milosevic is *the image of God*. We could write that right across this photo and be theologically correct. Are we not all made in the image of God? You can take my photo and write across it with equal truth: *the image of God* and *the face of evil*. Our fallen humanness is the mix of both, the glorious image of God stamped upon our very being, but it is cracked, marred, and distorted by the evil of sin. This is true of Slobodan Milosevic and Daniel Buttry and each of us.

The root of violence grows, though, when these two labels are ripped apart. Milosevic is only *the face of evil*. The forces of NATO, the United States, are the divine agents of God's justice, *the image of God* on earth. That is the violence of denying the image of God in another human being. It is the first act of violence. We create the enemy, and the enemy is not fully human. The enemy has lost the stamp of God, leaving them subhuman or demonic. We can give them names: *the face of evil*—how can we allow such evil to continue? Call someone different a name. It's much easier to "grease a gook" than kill a human being. If you call a woman a bitch, what's so bad about slapping her around as if she's a dog? We create names, stereotypes, and distorted images that erode or even expunge the image of God in the other, at least within our own minds. That's where our violence begins.

Once we have separated the *image of God* and *the face of evil*, and we have slapped that label of evil upon our enemy, what are we left with? Why, we are left with the image of God. We are righteous in what we do. Because of the evil of the other and the rightness of ourselves, we are justified in the violence we do against the enemy. I have removed the humility that comes with seeing my own propensity to evil, and what I'm left with is the arrogance of playing God.

The role of divine judge is one I am justified to take up. We can nuke the Japs because they bombed Pearl Harbor. We can gas the Jews because they are vermin controlling our money. We can gun down King because he's a commie-agitating nigger. We can bulldoze Palestinian homes because they're terrorists. We can throw the poor on the street because they are crack heads and welfare cheats. We can kill gays because they're perverts. We can slam kids into lockers because they are geeks or goths. We can shoot classmates because they are dumb jocks. We can execute criminals because they are cold-blooded killers. We can do whatever we damn well please because we are justified by our own righteousness in the face of the evil of our enemies.

Do you see the root of violence? Some violence is sporadic and personal. One husband beats one wife. One kid mugs one pedestrian. One person with a gun kills one, two, five people. Some violence is organized and political. Serbs drive Kosovar Albanians from their homes and massacre people indiscriminately. Americans bomb Serbs, apologizing for the collateral damage of daily civilian casualties. Bombs level embassies in Kenya and Tanzania for causes in the Middle East.

Here the roots of violence show their extensive and tangled nature, for much violence is structural and endemic. The violence of racism is seen in hate-crimes, but is hidden in the hopeless eyes of those who have been locked out for so long. We may see the violence of despair in criminal violence and gang violence, but what about the violence that creates that despair, the violence of racism, poverty, joblessness, and illiteracy? What about the violence of a system that spends more for prisons for the poor than for schools for the poor? Outside the Lorraine Motel, Jackie Smith raised a solitary voice against the violence of an economic system that marginalizes the poor and leaves people with no place to call home. She raised her voice at the site where Dr. King gave his life while serving garbage collectors seeking a livable wage.

Speaking of garbage collectors...I spent a day working on a garbage truck here in the Boston area. I was taking the "urban plunge" for an urban ministry course in seminary. We had to survive on the streets for three days—in January—with only fifty cents. I got a job at the day labor pool working on the garbage truck. After sleeping in a shelter I found myself picking up suburban trash in the snow. What struck me was the system; the trash haulers, reputedly tied to organized crime, hired only the drivers. The two guys on the back were hired only on a day-by-day basis. There was a whole fleet of trucks, all needing three men every day, but only one was hired with benefits. The rest were picked up from the hoards of desperate, hungry people who wouldn't complain about low wages or take sick days or vacations, and they would always be there. There might be a different face tomorrow, but *somebody* would always be there, willing to work for dirt-bottom wages. Real jobs weren't created; the system depended on there being a pool of the unemployed, allowing someone else to get rich and to keep taxes down in the suburbs. Is that structural violence? I felt it when I was cold, wet, and on the streets again that night.

Archbishop Dom Helder Camera of Brazil speaks of the spiral of violence. Violence Number One (Camera's phrase, appears in Beldon C. Lane, "Spirituality and Political Commitment: Notes on a Liberation Theology of Nonviolence" in *The Universe Bends Toward Justice*, ed. Angie O'Gorman [New Society Publishers, 1990]) is the institutionalized violence in society, which is wielded by those in power. Structures are set up to maintain unjust conditions that grind many down while others prosper. Violence Number Two is the violence of the oppressed, responding in anger to the violence of the institutionalized injustice. This can be revolutionary violence or it can be the despairing criminal violence that just lashes out at any victim. Violence Number Three completes the circle as the violence of repression in the name of law and order is utilized by the state. Police violence, prisons, judicial executions are the weapons of Violence Number Three.

In analyzing the roots of violence, it is easy to see only criminal violence and rail at the dynamics that would cause a person to do such a thing. We can see Violence Number Three and justify it because we fear violence sweeping our communities, our schools, our streets. Violence Number One is much harder to see. We all benefit from this violence, at least each of us here in this room. We haven't all benefited from it equally, but we all have access to resources and education and opportunities that identify us among the more affluent in the world. Maybe you never thought of it this way, but attending a PMT consultation is a luxury beyond imagining for most of the people on this planet! Some of our prosperity comes from the hideous conditions in which others live, so no matter how righteous we may feel, there is a shadow over this Holy Ground, too. We are all entwined in the roots of violence. None of us is pure. None of us is without sin.

So where do we turn?

Holy Ground. A hill called Calvary, Golgotha, Place of the Skull. Holy Ground. At the foot of a cross, the soil soaked with the precious blood of Jesus. He is the sinless one, the spotless Lamb of God. He is the Son of God, God in human flesh, the Word come among us. He is dying, a victim of violence, but not a victim. Yes, Romans might have driven those nails in his hands and feet, but Jesus said his life would not be taken from him. He laid it down of his own accord. This was a sacrifice of redeeming love, willing love, love that poured itself out.

255

Holy Ground is at the foot of the cross where we all have knelt. That Holy Ground is shadowed, too, for that cross has been the excuse for unfathomable slaughter. The cross was the emblem on the shields of Crusaders who massacred Muslims and Jews and countless other Christians. It was the rallying symbol for holy wars across Europe and Inquisitions and the genocidal conquest of the Americas. To this day the cross is a symbol for people who attack gays and lesbians or Jews or Arabs or people of color. It's not a shadow from Jesus but a shadow from those who lift up the cross to assault others in his name.

No matter how much that Jesus' nonviolent act of self-sacrifice is blasphemed by those who may raise the cross in violence, there is a redemptive power that comes from that Holy Ground at the cross. Paul, who as Saul was a wielder of violence in the name of God and God's righteousness, was disarmed by the grace of the one he persecuted. Paul wrote, "For I am not ashamed of the gospel; it is the power of God for salvation to everyone who has faith" (Rom 1:16 NRSV). In Jesus at the cross, the cycles of violence are broken. In his broken body peace is made between my enemy and me. The walls of hostility are dismantled. The way is cleared for repentance and reconciliation.

How do we find the way through all the violence and shadows to the Holy Ground where repentance and reconciliation and healing and justice and peace can grow? I find the answers along the way of our journey.

Holy Ground. The Maruki Gallery. The Maruki Gallery is a small art gallery outside of Tokyo. Iri and Toshi Maruki are a couple, both artists. The grounds of the gallery include both their home and an exhibition of their work. The major exhibit is a collection of fifteen wall-sized paintings on folding screens of the experiences of those in Hiroshima on 6 August 1945. The Marukis traveled to the smoldering city a few days after the bombing to search for missing relatives. Their paintings capture the horror, the disorientation, the anguish of the people of Hiroshima.

Two paintings brought in a theme absent from the peace park. One depicted the crows feasting on the piles of Korean dead left unburied. The other portrayed the fate of American POWs who survived the bombing only to be torn limb from limb by their enraged captors. The Marukis' poetic comment next to the painting said, "Our hands tremble as we paint." In an adjacent room was yet another large painting, *The Rape of Nanjing*, which recalls the terrible three-day orgy of violence where more than 300,000 Chinese people were slaughtered by Japanese soldiers. The Marukis vividly presented the suffering caused by the bomb, but they also could recognize with profound grief the violence in which their own society had played the leading role. Their sorrow did not blot out the sorrow of other victims, including those labeled as "enemies."

Here is the beginning of the path to hope and redemption. We can begin to pull out the tangled roots of violence only when we all recognize the other side's suffering and our own complicity in evil. When we have learned the humility to bring together those two labels, image of God and the face of evil, both for ourselves and for our enemies, then we restore our full humanity.

For us as Christians we can only find the grace and strength for this redemptive step through the mercy and grace we receive from the crucified Jesus. This is part of the Holy Ground Christians find at the foot of the cross. There the face of evil in us is seen, is known, and is forgiven. It is covered with grace. There the image of God is restored, purified, and refined by love. Every time we create an opportunity for people to understand the suffering and pain on the other side we help this redemption to unfold. Every time we create a safe place for people to begin to unwrap and grieve over their own complicity in violence we help this redemption to unfold.

Holy Ground. A modest apartment of a rabbi in Jerusalem was Holy Ground to me. The apartment is home to Rabbi Isaac Newman and his wife. Rabbi Newman is the chair of Rabbis for Human Rights in Israel. Out of the fundamental values of the Jewish faith, the Rabbis for Human Rights have resisted the abuses of Israeli authorities against Palestinian people. They speak of God's sovereignty over all humankind, of Abraham's legacy of compassion and generosity, of the Levitical concern to show love and respect to "the stranger," and of the infinite worth of every human life. These tenets of faith are fleshed out in acts for justice and human rights for all people, but in their particular situation most especially toward Palestinians. During the Intifada, when the Israeli government in 1989 deported over four hundred Palestinians accused of being Muslim extremists, Rabbi Newman and other Jewish Israelis joined Palestinian people in an act of prophetic solidarity by living in tents pitched in front of the Knesset building for a couple months.

Yad Vashem honors those few Gentiles who sacrificed to save Jews during the Holocaust by planting trees along "The Avenue of the Righteous among the Nations" in Yad Vashem, a walkway with trees and plaques. Rabbi Newman is one of the righteous among the Israelis who is sacrificing to save Palestinians facing their own historical travail.

Rabbi Newman is exhibiting the kind of "greater love" Christians honor in Jesus. To take the road of redemption we must move to action. The love of God took shape in the incarnational solidarity of Jesus, leading to his self-sacrifice for our salvation on the cross. We need to flesh out the tenants of our faith in acts for justice and human rights. We need to stand in solidarity at the places where violence is taking place around us. We can't do everything, but we can do something. There are stories that can be shared in our own communities and models from the experiences of others that can spur our own creativity in shaping plans for action. Jesus said, "Just as I have loved you, you also should love one another" (John 13:34) and "the one who believes in me will also do the works that I do and, in fact, will do greater works than these, because I am going to the Father" (John 14:12). Our love needs to take shape in actions of self-sacrificing love that break cycles of violence and open the ways to genuine reconciliation. The Holy Ground of the cross extends in the Holy Ground of our action to redeem people and communities from the grip of violence.

Holy Ground. The Freedom Monument in Riga, Latvia, commemorates Lenin's setting the Baltics free. Lenin had said the Baltic Republics would be free forever, cutting them loose from former Czarist Russia. Then in 1940 Stalin conquered them and brought them into the Soviet Union. Winds of change were blowing, and tens of thousands of mostly young people gathered around the Freedom Monument to demonstrate for independence. I spoke with Baptists in their twenties who were dreaming of freedom and wondering how to engage in the struggle of the Latvian people. I passed out booklets of the speeches of Martin Luther King Jr. to teach these Latvians the principles of nonviolent struggle.

An assassin in Memphis thought he could silence the visionary prophet with a bullet. But King's holy incendiary dreams continue to ignite fires of freedom, including helping that growing freedom struggle on the other side of the globe. This nation keeps trying to domesticate Dr. King, giving him a holiday to talk about a dream of all getting along, but his voice keeps breaking free. The National Civil Rights Museum in Memphis teaches us the story and the sacrifice. Jackie Smith reminds us, she demands that we hear afresh his cries for justice. King's teachings have spread to distant peoples and inspired their struggles for freedom, dignity, and justice. As King said, "Returning violence for violence multiplies violence, adding deeper darkness in a night already devoid of stars. Darkness cannot drive out darkness; only light can do that" (*Where Do We Go From Here: Chaos or Community* p.62 Beacon Press, 1968).

Jesus is the light of the world, but Jesus also said we are that light. Martin Luther King Jr.'s light is still driving out the darkness of hatred and violence as his teachings and story are spread around the world. We have a ministry of teaching to undo the forces of violence by giving substantive instruction on the ways of love: how to resolve our conflicts peacefully, how to engage in struggle nonviolently, and how to make loving our enemies a practical agenda.

Holy Ground. There are many places of Holy Ground hallowed by the suffering of the victims of violence. They are places hallowed because Jesus suffered on the cross with those victims and for them. We too can hallow that ground by how we journey with our Lord through this suffering around us. If we recall our own complicity in evil so that all we do comes from a humble spirit that recognizes our common bond with all human beings, even with our enemies, then we will hallow this ground. If we live in solidarity with those who are oppressed by violence, joining in their struggle, doing the things we can do, then we will hallow this ground. If we lift up the vision of nonviolence, light the ways of justice and peace through ministries of education, education in our streets, our battlegrounds, and our communities, then we will hallow this ground.

Let it be so, Lord, let it be so.

APPENDIX 2:

TIMELINE

1952—born September 26 in Oak Park, Illinois, to Harriet and Lucas Buttry

1957–1960—lived in Bedfordshire, England, where I started school

1960–1965—lived in Sunset, Utah

1965–1967—lived at Wakkanai Air Station on Hokkaido, Japan

1965–1970—lived in the Columbus, Ohio, area; met and began dating
    Sharon Crader at Reynoldsburg High School in 1969.

1970–1974—attended Wheaton College in Illinois

1970–1971—enrolled in ROTC at Wheaton

1970—accepted Christ and baptized at Wheaton College

1971—registered with the Selective Service as a conscientious objector

1973—married Sharon on August 4

1974–1978—attended Gordon-Conwell Theological Seminary north of
    Boston, Massachusetts

1975—conducted hunger workshops in Ipswich, Massachusetts

1978–1987—pastored the Dorchester Temple Baptist Church in Boston

1978—ordained at Dorchester Temple Baptist Church in December

1981—active in the campaign to halt deployment of the "Euro-missiles,"
    medium-range nuclear missiles to be based by the U.S. in Europe

1982—

June—participated with about a million people in the demonstration in
    New York City calling for a nuclear freeze

October—Christopher adopted

1983—

November 30—Jonathan born

1985—

May—arrested at a Pledge of Resistance action in Boston

July 20—Janelle born

1987–1996—directed the Peace Program for National Ministries of the American Baptist Churches and was ABC non-governmental organizational representative at the United Nations

1987—

February—my first Baptist Peace Fellowship of North America board meeting, held at Koinonia Farm, Americus, Georgia

"Bible Study Guide on War and Peace" published by National Ministries

1988—

—*Bringing Your Church Back to Life: Beyond Survival Mentality* published by Judson Press

June—organized the religious vigils in support of the U.N.'s Third Special Session on Disarmament

August—participated in International Baptist Peace Conference in Sweden and was part of Baptist Peace Fellowship friendship tour to the Soviet Union

1989—

January—meeting with Saboi Jum to plan for a new Burma peace initiative

February—trip to the Carter Center in Atlanta with Saboi Jum

March–April—trip to Japan for conference on rising militarism in the northern Pacific

1990—

February—trip to Hong Kong for Burma negotiations

August—David Crader killed during build-up for war with Iraq

September—trip to Bangkok, Thailand, and Hong Kong for Burma negotiations

—"A Peacemaker's Journal" published by National Ministries

1991—

January—National Peace Prayer service in Washington DC on eve of launching of the Gulf War

May–June—trip to Chiang Mai, Thailand, for meeting with Democratic Alliance of Burma leaders

November—trip to Nicaragua to plan International Baptist Peace Conference

1992—

June–July—Carl Upchurch's trip to Los Angeles to talk about peace with gangs

July—participated in International Baptist Peace Conference in Nicaragua
  where the idea for the Gavel Fund was conceived

1993—

April—teaching trip to Cyprus, visit to Palestine and Israel.

April–May—National Gang Summit in Kansas City, Missouri

May—Thirtieth anniversary demonstration for the March on Washington
  with vigil at the headquarters of the National Rifle Association

October—Gang summit in Minneapolis/St. Paul

—Spanish translation of "Bible Study Guide on War and Peace" published
  by National Ministries ("Guía de Estudio Bíblico: Guerra y Paz")

1994—

—*Christian Peacemaking: From Heritage to Hope* published by Judson Press

—Gavel Memorial Peace Fund established by the Baptist Peace Fellowship
  of North America

—Gang consultation in Pittsburgh

1995—

January—Baptist Peace Fellowship friendship trip to Thailand and
  Myanmar; first Gavel Fund grant given to Saboi Jum for mediation
  efforts in Burma

May—Planted a Peace Pole at the Mission Headquarters for the American
  Baptist Churches in Valley Forge, Pennsylvania

—*Peace Ministry: A Handbook for Local Churches* published by Judson Press

1996–2003—pastored the First Baptist Church of Dearborn, Michigan, and
  served on the staff of BPFNA as part-time director of the Gavel
  Memorial Peace Fund

1996—

January—Solidarity visit to Myanmar

February—Pastors for Peace action at the U.S./Mexico border south of San
  Diego, first visit to Mexico

May—Baptist Peace Fellowship board meeting in Mexico

June—moved to Detroit

November–December—Intensive Training Conference on Conflict
  Resolution with the Asian Baptist Federation in Chiang Mai,
  Thailand; training trip to Delhi, India, for Chin refugees from
  Myanmar.

1997—

May–June—training and friendship trip to Liberia with BPFNA and
   National Ministries delegation
July–August—Naga peace talks in Atlanta
November—125th anniversary of Christianity coming to the Nagas
1998—
January—training trip to Nagaland, India, and Naga negotiations in
   Bangkok, Thailand
February–March—training trip to Nagaland, India
—*First-Person Preaching: Bringing New Life to Biblical Stories* published by
   Judson Press
—First shipments sent for the library project.
1999—
February—Naga training and consultation in Calcutta, India
November—Naga training and consultation in Calcutta, India
—Second shipments sent for the library project
2000—
March–April—trip to northeast India, Naga negotiations in Thailand
June—Ethiopian/Eritrean Peace Conference in Detroit
—Third shipments sent for the library project
2001—
January—training trip with Daniel Hunter to Myanmar and Indonesia and
   Naga negotiations in Thailand
May—training trip to Cameroon for All-Africa Baptist Fellowship
—Fourth and final shipments sent for the library project
November—Ethiopian/Eritrean Training and Vigils in Washington D.C.
2002—
April—Joint BPFNA/Muslim Peace Fellowship conflict transformation
   training in Detroit
November–December—training trip with Daniel Hunter to Assam and
   Nagaland in northeast India
April—Trip to Manila, Philippines, for mediation among Telegu Baptists
   from India at Asian Baptist Federation Congress
— *Come Stand with Us* (video about the Naga peace process) produced by
   the Baptist Peace Fellowship of North America
2003–Present—Global Consultant for Peace and Justice for International
   Ministries of the American Baptist Churches

2003—

March—training trip to the Philippines with Lee McKenna

August—commissioned as a missionary with International Ministries at
    the World Mission Conference in Green Lake, Wisconsin

September—training trip to Myanmar

December—training trip to Italy with Sharon, Marinetta Cannito-Hjort,
    and Ellen Shippert

2004—

February—training trip to Republic of Georgia with International
    Ministries global consultants and solo to Croatia

March—leading conference on social ministry in Poland with Sharon

May—training trip to Thailand and Myanmar

July–November—the "Call to Prayer" controversy in Hamtramck

September–October—training trip with Daniel Hunter to Ghana and Sierra
    Leone and solo trip to Liberia

December—training trip to Congo

2005—

January–February—training trip to Manipur and Nagaland in northeast
    India with Sharon and a team from Detroit; training trips to Nepal
    and Russia

March—visit to China with Ben Chan, training trip to Hong Kong with Ben
    Chan

April–May—planning and training trip to the Republic of Georgia
    (planning for Xtreme Team with Mike Buckles)

May—training trip to Myanmar

July—leading Xtreme Team to Republic of Georgia

October—training trip to Thailand and Myanmar

—Revision of *A Peacemaker's Journal* with Evelyn Hanneman published by
    the Baptist Peace Fellowship of North America

2006—

January—training trip to Ethiopia

February–March—solo training trip to Bosnia and with International
    Ministries global consultants to Italy

March—training trip to Costa Rica

April—training trip to refugee camp in Thailand

April–May—training trip to Bolivia

October—training trip to Ethiopia with Sharon

November–December—training trip to Hong Kong and Philippines; trip to Israel with Protestant and Jewish dialog group

2007—

January—training trip to Lebanon

January–February—training trip to Ethiopia with International Ministries global consultants; planning meeting for Global Baptist Peace Conference in Rome, Italy

March—training trip to Bosnia

April–May—training trip to Manipur, India, with Sharon and team from Detroit, followed by training trip to Nagaland with Sharon

May—training trip to Jamaica

September—training trip to Republic of Georgia

October—training trip to Indonesia, including West Papua

2008—

January—*Interfaith Heroes* published by Read the Spirit Books

January—training trip to Myanmar and Orissa, India

February—training trip to Bulgaria; planning meeting for Global Baptist Peace Conference in Rome, Italy

March—training trip to Brazil

April–May—visit to North Korea and China, training trips to Orissa, India, and Nepal

June—training trip to Lebanon and Naga reconciliation talks in Chiang Mai, Thailand

August—Naga reconciliation talks in Chiang Mai, Thailand

December—Naga reconciliation talks in Chiang Mai, Thailand, and training at a refugee camp at the Thai/Burma border

2009—

—*Interfaith Heroes 2* published by Read the Spirit Books

January—training trip to Jamaica with International Ministries global consultants

February—Global Baptist Peace Conference in Rome, Italy; attended with Sharon

May—received an honorary doctorate from Central Baptist Theological Seminary in Shawnee Mission, Kansas

June—Had surgery for prostate cancer

September–October—training trip to Myanmar

November—training trip to Republic of Georgia and Ukraine

December—training trip to Manipur, India, with Wungreiso Valui and
    Neil Sowards

2010—

March—training trip to Liberia

May—training trip to Cuba

May–June—training trip to the Philippines with Sharon

June—Naga reconciliation talks in Chiang Mai, Thailand, and training in
    Chiang Rai, Thailand, with Ken Sehested

September—training trip to Zimbabwe

October–November—training trip to Meghalaya and Manipur, India

2011—

February—training trip to Kyrgyzstan

April—*Blessed Are the Peacemakers* published by Read the Spirit Books

June—training trip to Kenya with Sharon and a team from Central Baptist
    Theological Seminary in Kansas City

July—Baptist World Alliance Peace Commission meetings in Malaysia and
    training trips Orissa and Manipur, India

September—training trip to the Philippines

November—training trip to the Republic of Georgia and Ukraine

2012—

January—training trip to Manipur and Assam, India

February—training trip to Thailand and Myanmar with Sharon and a class
    from Central Baptist Theological Seminary in Kansas City

March—training trip to Kyrgyzstan

June—training trip to Kenya

INDEX